MAKING INTANGIBLE HERITAGE

MAKING INTANGIBLE HERITAGE

El Condor Pasa and Other Stories from UNESCO

Valdimar Tr. Hafstein

INDIANA UNIVERSITY PRESS

This book is a publication of

Indiana University Press
Office of Scholarly Publishing
Herman B Wells Library 350
1320 East 10th Street
Bloomington, Indiana 47405 USA

iupress.indiana.edu

© 2018 by Valdimar Tr. Hafstein

Manufactured in the United States of
America

Cataloging information is available from
the Library of Congress.

ISBN 978-0-253-03792-3 (hardback)
ISBN 978-0-253-03793-0 (paperback)
ISBN 978-0-253-03794-7 (ebook)

1 2 3 4 5 23 22 21 20 19 18

Contents

Prelude

Confessions of a Folklorist

FOR ME, IT didn't start with heritage. I came to the study of folklore through mythology. At the age of nineteen, I signed up for a class in Norse myths at the University of Iceland. It was one of the courses taught toward the major in folklore; in the following semester, I took three more. The die was cast. In the following semesters, I studied customs and rites, tales and legends, material culture: the bread and butter of folklore programs in the twentieth century. My interest in myths soon subsided for more pedestrian subjects, like everyday life and the way people give it meaning. Interpretation of texts made way for fieldwork. My parents shrugged, patiently waiting for me to get serious. My father only brought it up once, gently suggesting that whatever I chose to do, I should make sure I could provide for a family. My father had gone to law school, but during finals in his last year he was offered a job at the Ministry of Foreign Affairs. He had his doubts, but my mother wanted to see the world. Within a month of his last exam, they moved with their firstborn to Stockholm. At twenty-six, my father was abroad for the first time—an accidental diplomat.

Growing up, I moved with my family to Brussels and Geneva, Europe's diplomatic capitals, EU and NATO headquarters in the former, the UN office, ILO, WHO, WIPO, and a host of other acronyms in the latter. My father moved up through the ranks. He became ambassador and Iceland's chief negotiator in a number of intergovernmental agreements, treaties, and conventions. My mother raised four children in various cities and took on the many diplomatic tasks that came with my father's position. They were both great at what they did.

It never occurred to me that I had followed in their footsteps. Honestly. Nor to them, I think. It only dawned on me in 2005. I was thirty-two. Thirteen years had passed since I took my first folklore course. This was shortly before my father's death in August that year, a few months after I finished my PhD at Berkeley. By then I had already been going to UNESCO and WIPO meetings for three years as a participant observer. At UNESCO, I was part of the Icelandic delegation, sitting in alphabetical order among other state delegates, most of them lawyers. At WIPO, I sat on the back benches as an observer representing either SIEF (International Society for Ethnology and Folklore) or AFS (American Folklore Society) or both. I was on my way out of WIPO's headquarters, a thirteen-story tower encased in sapphire blue glass by Geneva's Place des Nations. I had spent the week in the conference rooms and foyers following diplomatic debates on copyright and folklore. Crossing the marble floors of the lobby in my blue suit, briefcase in hand, it struck me: I had turned into my father. I was an accidental diplomat.

MAKING INTANGIBLE HERITAGE

CHAPTER 1

Making Heritage

Introduction

WHAT UNITES BEER culture in Belgium with Chinese shadow puppetry? What do Estonian smoke saunas have in common with kimchi making in the two Koreas or with summer solstice fire festivals in the Pyrenees? How about the Capoeira circle in Brazil and the gastronomic meal of the French? How is tightrope walking in Korea like violin craftsmanship in Cremona, Italy, and how are both of these like Indonesian batik, Croatian lacemaking, Arabic coffee, and Argentinian tango? What might connect yoga in India with the ritual dance of the royal drum in Burundi, carpet weaving in Iran, or Vanuatu sand drawings?

The answer: these cultural practices and expressions are all on the Representative List of the Intangible Cultural Heritage of Humanity of UNESCO (United Nations Educational, Scientific, and Cultural Organization). That means they have been selected to represent the diversity of human creative powers. Chosen because they give aesthetic form to deeply held values, they speak of skill and competence, of bonds that tie, and of different relationships to history, society, and nature. They testify to various ways people tend to previous generations, to other people, and to the universe. UNESCO's Representative List displays humanity at its best, showcasing its capacity to create beauty, form, and meaning out of its various particular circumstances. Sharing what they enjoy or endure, people give form to value in their cultural practices and performances (see Hymes 1975). New generations recreate these forms according to their own conditions, cultivating the talent, the knowledge, and the necessary appreciation. It is this creative dynamic that member states of UNESCO have set out to safeguard. The Convention for the Safeguarding of the Intangible Cultural Heritage makes us all responsible for the continued viability of these cultural practices and expressions—for making sure that their practitioners can keep practicing them and that future generations can continue to be inspired by them.

The convention frames them in terms of cultural heritage, a concept into which UNESCO itself has breathed life over the past half century. This concept defines a particular relationship to the objects and expressions it describes, one that is of recent vintage. We tend to assume "cultural heritage" has been around forever; in fact, it is a modern coinage and its current ubiquity is limited to the last few decades (Klein 2006; Bendix 2000; Kirshenblatt-Gimblett 1998; Lowenthal 1998; Hafstein 2012). Its novelty speaks of contemporary societies and to their own understanding of themselves, their past, present, and future (Holtorf 2012; Eriksen 2014). Valuing a building, a ritual, a monument, or a dance as cultural heritage is to reform how people relate to their practices and their built environment, and to infuse this relationship with sentiments like respect, pride, and responsibility. This reformation takes place through various social institutions that cultural heritage summons into being (centers, councils, associations, clubs, committees, commissions, juries, networks, and so on) and through the forms of display everywhere associated with cultural heritage: from the list to the festival—not to omit the exhibition, the spectacle, the catalog, the website, or the book. Folklorist Barbara Kirshenblatt-Gimblett refers to these as metacultural artifacts (1998, 2006): cultural expressions and practices (e.g., lists and festivals) that refer to other cultural expressions and practices (carpet weaving, ritual dance, tightrope walking) and give the latter new meanings (tied, for example, to community, diversity, humanity) and new functions (e.g., attracting tourists, orchestrating difference). A hallmark of heritage, following Kirshenblatt-Gimblett, is "the problematic relationship of its objects to the instruments of their display" (1998, 156). This book brings those problems into plain view. But of course, this book is itself a metacultural artifact, a critical addition to the profusion of publications, websites, newsletters, press releases, and exhibitions brought forth as a result of UNESCO's global success in promoting intangible heritage. The book goes back to the moments of inception, the making of the concept and of the convention dedicated to its safeguarding, and to its genealogy—events, actors, and circumstances that gave rise to intangible heritage.

The book's ambition is to change how we think about intangible heritage. It asks questions that at times go against the grain, challenging official stories and conventional wisdom. Turning the usual order of things on its head, it asks: If intangible heritage is the solution, what is the problem? What problems do people set out to solve with the concept of intangible heritage and with the convention for its safeguarding? With what effects? I have come at these questions from various directions over the past decade and a half, as a scholar, fieldworker, policy maker, and consultant. In this book, I propose some answers.

My account begins inside UNESCO headquarters in Paris with the negotiation of the Convention for the Safeguarding of the Intangible Cultural Heritage. Then I work my way back in a historical analysis of the present moment to reconstruct the challenges that intangible heritage is designed to meet. But the

Fig. 1.1 UNESCO Headquarters, Place Fontenoy, Paris, France. ©Novikov Aleksey / Shutterstock.

book also moves forward and outward to the convention's implementation in different corners of the world. Citing various expressions and practices recognized as intangible heritage, I unearth the ways in which processes of selection, designation, exclusion, preservation, promotion, and display actually affect these practices and the people who practice them—that is, what difference intangible heritage makes, for better and for worse.

UNESCO's Intangible Heritage Convention signals a reformation of the concept of cultural heritage, extending international heritage policy from monuments and sites to the realm of the "intangible." This elusive notion suggests practices and expressions that do not leave extensive material traces, such as storytelling, craftsmanship, rituals, dramas, and festivals. I observed the meetings of the committee that drafted the convention and later of the convention's executive committee. Based on a critical ethnographic approach, complemented by archival research and case studies from the convention's implementation, this book peers underneath the official story to reveal the importance of context for understanding what is happening.

Intangible heritage—the notion of it and the convention dedicated to its safeguarding—conceals a wide divergence of views on cultural production, conservation, control, and dissent. Some of this divergence crystallizes in the concepts adopted and some in the concepts rejected—the gaps and silences of the convention's final text. Stretching the concept of cultural heritage beyond national delimitations and inflecting it to encompass social practices and expressions, the idea of an intangible heritage of humanity is ripe with possibility and paradox.

Fig. 1.2 UNESCO's logo for Intangible Cultural Heritage. Public domain via Wikimedia Commons.

The terms of the convention already define how officials, bureaucrats, scholars, and community advocates carry out cultural work, and it will continue to do so for decades to come. It also sets a standard to which practitioners of various traditions around the globe now adhere in order to receive national or international recognition. The intent of this book is to bring critical awareness to ideas of intangible heritage and to its safeguarding; to open up widely accepted liberal policies (who could be against helping cultural traditions survive?) to critique by embedding them in the organizational contexts, political conflicts, and negotiations out of which they emerge. The stories I tell show how individual personalities and states can shape texts that become the foundation of global narratives and how propositions made for a particular local reason become global instruments with entirely different effects in other corners of the world.

Heritage conservation has long been a pedagogic project. It employs scholars, experts, and professionals to educate people about their identities, loyalties, and affiliations, and to encourage them to manage this heritage, to identify with it, and to take care of it. The pedagogical instrument best suited to these goals is the narrative. In turn, UNESCO's objectives may be summed up as world-building: summoning into being a new collective subject—humanity—and encouraging people and peoples around the world to identify with it and take responsibility for its welfare. Cultural heritage is a major resource in this endeavor, a material metonym for an imagined community, standing in for a unity-in-diversity vision of humankind and charging "us" with common curatorial responsibility. This charge is sustained by the unique affective and argumentative powers of narrative (Lafranz-Samuels 2015).

As a folklorist, I was trained to make sense of narrative communication, one of the discipline's long-standing critical concerns. It shows through in the following chapters. My orientation is shaped by a discipline that is fieldwork-based and historically informed; focused on everyday life and vernacular practices and expressions; and concerned in particular with cultural forms or genres, their uses and circulation, whether these forms are material (objects, dress, food, or architecture), bodily (gesture, posture, or hairstyle), verbal (narratives or proverbs), visual, musical, or technical.

Intangible heritage is very much concerned with such cultural forms, their performance, their circulation, and their uses. But the people—communities, groups, and individuals—that the Intangible Heritage Convention addresses are not alone. The diplomats and experts who negotiated the convention, and the scholars, administrators, and cultural workers charged with implementing it, also share such forms—material, bodily, and verbal. This book brings these forms into focus: UN storytelling about storytelling, or intangible heritage about intangible heritage: meta-folklore, if you will, or meta-heritage, if you prefer. The book makes plain the performative power of words: when spoken under these particular circumstances they bring into being new realities, new concepts and categories that people then draw on in sundry settings around the world.

Ethnographic Detail

My folk roam the hallways of Place Fontenoy, UNESCO's headquarters in Paris. They ride elevators in the Geneva headquarters of the World Intellectual Property Organization (WIPO). They have their own forms of folk speech (distinguishable, for example, by the use of the third-person national: "Iceland finds that. . . ," "Greece supports. . . ," "the United States believe. . . ," and so on), their folk rituals and customs (for example, "as this is the first time that Iceland takes the floor during this meeting, I'd like to congratulate you, Mr. Chairman, on your reelection"), their foodways (coffee/tea and biscuits, anyone?), and their traditional gestures and postures (shaking hands, waving the country badge, applauding, congratulating, and so on), all very much on display during diplomatic gatherings such as those that gave currency to the concept of intangible heritage. Few communications are as deliberate, thought-out, and pregnant with meaning as diplomatic exchanges. As the saying goes, a diplomat thinks twice before saying nothing. That is because in meetings like the ones I describe here, words and actions are one; the debates and negotiations of diplomats in these settings are clothed with the power to fix rules and to shape practice outside the walls of the conference room.

Their traditional folk costume is the dark suit and tie and the skirt-suit; it is a uniform connoting power at work, authority, and respect while deemphasizing differences of gender, class, race, and ethnicity by adhering (with slight variations and a few exceptions) to an unmarked European norm of bourgeois masculinity (there is also a more marked and colorful, festive garb for times of celebration, worn especially by female delegates in connection with the listing of intangible heritage from their country). By the time I took part in UNESCO's General Conference in 2011, I had been attending UN meetings for a decade as a participant observer, following negotiations on intangible heritage at UNESCO and on intellectual property and traditional knowledge at WIPO; I was already steeped in diplomatic folkways. Representing Iceland, I wore a suit of my own. Call it power dressing, call it camouflage, but being an academic I had only the one suit. On the second day, my fly broke. As luck would have it, there was a tailor next to my hotel, and he was so kind as to fix the zipper right away. I must have

Fig. 1.3 Diplomats in meeting at UNESCO. ©UNESCO/Eric Esquivel.

put on weight since I had bought the suit, for two hours later the fly broke again. So, I danced around Place Fontenoy for two weeks, debating world heritage and the freedom of the press, greeting ambassadors and heads of states, conferring with colleagues and casting votes—always with an open fly. I had my shirt tucked out over my trousers, the best I could do under the circumstances. I don't think many people noticed.

Having a broken fly brought me an awkward moment of clarity. Deeply revealing, it spoke to questions of dress and material culture, to questions of etiquette, propriety, and the body; it opened to scrutiny the cultural norms of everyday life in this particular setting. Not culture in its solemn, monumental, high-brow denotation, as in the concept of world heritage, but the more prosaic and commonplace culture of daily life. But it is within the latter that the former is made. Debates about intangible heritage are framed by the cultural practices of the body that this (slightly embarrassing) anecdote spotlights. Because, if you give it second thought, most things, big or small, take place in everyday life and take shape through everyday practices and expressions. That is where the folklorist comes in, or the ethnologist or anthropologist.

In writing this book, one of my ambitions is to contribute to the critical study of cultural heritage from the specific perspective of folklore studies. Another ambition is to contribute to folklore studies proper by following the discipline's concepts, its outlooks and insights, into international organizations where they, partly rehabilitated, gain force and traction to go back to work in the world, shaping people's understanding of their own practices and therefore the practices themselves. A third ambition is to help build an ethnographic perspective on international organizations and diplomatic meetings: to lay bare in ethnographic detail the way they work, and to give context to the artifacts they shape—artifacts such as the concept of cultural heritage.

Heritage as Social Imagination

Taken over from probate law, the concept of heritage (or, in Romance languages, patrimony) points to one metaphor for the nation: that of the family (Poulot 1997, 2006; Bendix 2009; Swenson 2007, 2013; Ronström 2008). Projecting onto the state intergenerational relations, obligations, and succession, the republican nation-state carried over to the cultural sphere a dynastic model that it did away with in other areas of government. At the same time as it evokes an earlier model of the body politic, however, the notion of national patrimony democratizes what belonged to elites alone (Bendix 2000). A common cultural heritage transfers "the goods and rights of princes and prelates, magnates and merchants" (Lowenthal 1998, 60) to the public at large; it throws open the doors of the Louvre to the throng in the streets outside (Poulot 1997).

The simultaneous adulation of material signs of privilege and assertion of universal access to them reveals an interesting paradox in the patrimonial imagination. On the one hand, those castles, manors, monuments, crown jewels, and courtly fashions that figure prominently in representations of heritage all belonged to the few in a society where the many were downtrodden and destitute. Now as before, it is the many who pay for the maintenance of these outwards signs of class privilege. The difference, however, lies in the patrimonial valuation of these material signs, their consecration as "our" heritage, which urges the general population to identify with the façade of its own historical subordination. The present accessibility of these signs of privilege, albeit behind rails or in glazed cabinets, underlines and perhaps overstates the difference of contemporary societies from those of previous eras. Through an act of heritage imagination, identification with these symbols of social distinction helps to foster the illusion not so much of classlessness as of universal inclusion in the ruling class—or, to be precise, inclusion for the museum-going, heritage-conscious middle classes who are most invested in the cultural field. This facility for fantasies of social climbing is an innovative feature of the patrimonial regime, for, as Regina Bendix has remarked, what distinguishes heritage from other ways of aligning the past with the present "is its capacity to hide the complexities of history and politics" (2000, 38).

Extending the scope of heritage to popular, vernacular culture, the notion of intangible heritage makes this more inclusive and encompassing heritage a matter of even greater public, national concern (Mugnaini 2016). In that same act, it helps constitute a national public that identifies as such. The national public thus constitutes itself as a collective subject partly through a curious combination of snobbery and slumming—that is to say, it is partly defined through common investment in and common responsibility for "our palace" and "our folk dance" (Thompson 2006). Spectacles of sanitized slumming combine with fantasies of social climbing to create a versatile instrument for social identification, one that claims our allegiance and channels our social imagination both upward and downward while leaving the impression that social hierarchies are a thing of the past, inciting nostalgia rather than resistance.

National Culture and Cultural Heritage

Whereas cultural heritage obscures class difference, it highlights cultural difference. Formed in all essential respects in the second half of the twentieth century, the patrimonial regime succeeds and partially supersedes the earlier regime of "national culture," the heyday of which was in the latter half of the nineteenth and the first half of the twentieth century (though to be sure it is still invoked to various extents in various places, now usually in conjunction with cultural heritage). If national culture was a tool for forging cultural differences along state borders while suppressing difference within the borders, cultural heritage is a more versatile instrument for representing and orchestrating differences within the state as well as between states. The patrimonial regime presents a postmodern strategy for coping with difference as states come to terms with the failure of the modern regime of national culture.

In the last decades, a vast number of social actors have seized upon the concept of cultural heritage in hundreds of thousands of scattered places. The phenomenal success of this idea puts it on a par with powerful concepts such as "culture" itself (Bennett 1998, 2003), "the economy" (Mitchell 1998, 2002), and "the environment," around which entire discourses are organized. In a pathbreaking work titled *The Heritage Crusade and the Spoils of History*, historian and geographer David Lowenthal compares the rise of heritage to a religious movement, proclaiming that "only in our time has heritage become a self-conscious creed, whose shrines and icons daily multiply and whose praise suffuses public discourse" (1998, 1).

If you ask me, the religious analogy is overblown. I find it more helpful to draw a comparison to the environmental movement, organized around another powerful concept. A relatively recent invention, the concept of the environment has a profound (if insufficient) impact on how we conceive of the material world and how we act on it. There have long been rivers and oceans and atmosphere, but envisioning the environment creates a connection between water pollution in a

Mexican village and rising sea levels in Amsterdam; it ties together the depletion of cod stocks around Newfoundland and the increase of smog in Beijing. Most important, the environment makes common cause for the people affected. There is no question as to whether the environment actually exists; it is a category of things, an instrument for classifying the world and therefore also for changing it. Categories of this kind have performative power. They make themselves real. By acting on the world, molding it in their image, they bring themselves into being.

If the environment is one such concept, cultural heritage is another. Much like the environment, cultural heritage is a new category of things, lumped together in novel ways under its rubric; these are things as motley as buildings, monuments, swords, songs, jewelry, visual patterns, religious paraphernalia, literature, healing dances, and woodcarving traditions. Like the environment, heritage does not seek to describe the world; it changes the world. Just like the environment, the major use of heritage is to mobilize people and resources, to reform discourses, and to transform practices. Like the environment, then, heritage is about change. Don't let the talk of preservation fool you: all heritage is change.

The magnetic field of heritage is so strong that we constantly risk being pulled in and to critique on its terms instead of critiquing its terms. To pull out of its orbit, we need to consider heritage as a particular regime of truth: the patrimonial regime, all at once material and ethical, economic and emotional, scientific and sensory (see Poulot 2006, 153–181). It is a regime in rapid expansion, both across and within our societies. Although deeply implicated in industry and government, its rhetoric is primarily moral; speaking within the patrimonial regime, the moral imperative to conserve is self-evident.

While the patrimonial regime is among other things a formation of knowledge, replete with experts and professionals, journals, and conferences, these concern themselves mostly with means rather than ends: with methods and priorities, or, more often, with particular projects of conservation. They respond to a growing sense of urgency in the face of what are believed to be grave threats of destruction. Rarely is conservation itself questioned, however, nor its urgency examined. As French historian Dominique Poulot observes, within the confines of an ethical discourse of heritage, a radical critique is most easily understood as iconoclasm or vandalism (2006, 157). In other words, the alternative to conserving is not *not* to conserve; the alternative to conserving is to destroy (Holtorf 2006; Holtorf and Myrup Kristensen 2015).

Critique of Heritage

The very prevalence of the patrimonial regime demands our critical attention. Folklorist Barbro Klein warns that "a naïve, uncritical, unhistorical, and untheorized understanding of cultural heritage" (2006, 74) poses a danger in an era in which the modern boundaries between the cultural field, the political field, and the market are blurring. "The term heritage is not innocent," Klein continues, and it is easy to agree that "we must ponder its role in the ongoing worldwide remapping of ideological, political, economic, disciplinary, and conceptual landscapes" (74).

Many explanations have been advanced to account for the rising tide of heritage. Some say it bears witness to intensified historical awareness, others associate it with the development of the tourist industry, and others yet see it as part of a nostalgic zeitgeist, associated with the so-called cultural logic of capitalism. Other explanations include the rise of localisms and patriotisms in the face of globalization; longer life spans and changing family relations; the mobility of individuals and the dispersion of peoples in a deterritorialized world; the exoticization of the past in film and television; the gradual commodification of culture; and the list goes on. No doubt, there is something to each of these explanations, though no one of them will account for all the various invocations of cultural heritage around the globe.

The rise of cultural heritage is perhaps the chief example of a newfound valuation of cultural practices and objects in terms of their expediency for economic and political purposes (Yúdice 2004). This is culture as a resource: a novel configuration in which culture is now a central expedient in everything from creating jobs to reducing crime, from increasing voter turnout to treating mental health, from changing the face of cities to managing differences within the population. In this context, heritage provides a strong but flexible language for staking claims to culture and making claims based on culture.

Heritage under UNESCO

In an important book titled *Uses of Heritage*, archaeologist Laurajane Smith argues that it is "no accident that the very discourses of 'heritage' and concerns about its loss arose in a period perceived to mark major social and cultural changes" (2006, 100). Vastly increased public access to media has helped foster a public debate "about environmental, political and social issues" and Smith argues that a major factor in the recent prominence of discourse about and concern for cultural heritage is that it represents "an attempt to deal with, negotiate and regulate change" (100).

According to Smith, such concerns and debates are partly channeled into "a self-referential 'authorized heritage discourse,' whose authority rests in part in its ability to 'speak to' and make sense of the aesthetic experiences of its practitioners and policy makers" and in part on "institutionalization within a range of national and international organizations and codes of practices" (2006, 28). Smith's "authorized heritage discourse" corresponds to what I term the "patrimonial regime." Its strong institutional matrix is a central factor in the rapid expansion of this regime. Indeed, no discussion of the patrimonial regime is complete without reference to UNESCO, which has been enormously successful in shaping national and local discourses and practices of heritage (Di Giovine 2009).

Thirty-seven countries founded the United Nations Educational, Scientific, and Cultural Organization (UNESCO) in the aftermath of World War II; it now counts 195 member states and ten associate members. The UNESCO constitution opens with the famous passage: "Since wars begin in the minds of men, it is in the minds of men that the defenses of peace must be constructed," penned by American poet Archibald MacLeish. The organization's mandate is broad in the global fields of culture, ideas, education, and information. In addition to preserving cultural heritage, its mission extends to literacy programs, access to education, gender equality, scientific advances, safety of journalists, and freedom of expression. In order to "secure the unanimous, lasting and sincere support of the peoples of the world," the constitution explains, peace must be founded "upon the intellectual and moral solidarity of mankind." Unlike some other organizations of the United Nations, however, UNESCO does not define rights but is defined by an ethical framework: UNESCO attempts to mobilize international opinion and to shape state practice in its areas of competence by means of moral and rhetorical pressure. It exerts such pressure in particular through standard-setting instruments: conventions, recommendations, and declarations.

Since its founding, UNESCO has developed a series of these instruments, beginning in 1954 with the Convention for the Protection of Cultural Property in the Event of Armed Conflict, often referred to as the Hague Convention for short. "Recognizing that cultural property has suffered grave damage during recent armed conflicts," the Hague Convention begins, and "being convinced that damage to *cultural property belonging to any people whatsoever* means damage to the *cultural heritage of all mankind*" (my emphasis), the States Parties to the convention agree to take on various obligations to protect cultural property from theft and destruction. As the preamble makes clear, cultural property and cultural heritage both emerged in international law through the Hague Convention, already recognizably distinct: in the sentences quoted above, cultural property belongs to a people, whereas cultural heritage is attributed to humankind. Cultural heritage and cultural property were thus coined as international legal concepts within a decade of the end of World War II as part of a new world order represented by the United Nations (Skrydstrup 2009, 2012).

Until the 1970s, UNESCO focused its efforts in the field of culture on the legal protection of cultural property. Following up on the Hague Convention, member states adopted in 1970 the Convention on the Means of Prohibiting and Preventing the Illicit Import, Export and Transfer of Ownership of Cultural Property (based on UNESCO's Recommendation of the same name from 1964) and founded in 1978 an Intergovernmental Committee for Promoting the Return of Cultural Property to its Countries of Origin or its Restitution in case of Illicit Appropriation. As the titles make clear, cultural property is at its inception a national concept, used in the context of claims for the return of historical artifacts from one state to another.

Starting in the 1970s, UNESCO began developing a parallel regime, with its own legal instruments and bodies, for what it calls the safeguarding of cultural heritage (as opposed to the legal protection of cultural property). Cultural heritage is the preferred term in contexts that stress common responsibility for safeguarding (i.e., ensuring the viability of) artifacts, buildings, sites, and, most recently, cultural practices. UNESCO is today best known in many parts of the world for its Convention Concerning the Protection of the World Cultural and Natural Heritage (also called the World Heritage Convention) from 1972, the associated World Heritage Committee, and especially the World Heritage List. Rather than acknowledge the rights of states, the World Heritage Convention recognizes their responsibilities to current and future generations and to humanity as a whole.

Of course, the terms are not unequivocal and one should be careful not to reify them. Their distinction is often blurred: social actors across the globe participate in new opportunities offered by both concepts—property and heritage—and help to shape new options in markets and politics that have come to be imaginable through instruments such as inscriptions and lists. But even so, in the international regimes the distinction is clear-cut, and one should not underestimate their importance in diffusing a conceptual matrix and shaping local practices. The term "cultural property" gained universal currency following the adoption of the Hague Convention in 1954, not the other way around. Likewise, the proliferation of cultural heritage in recent decades only gained momentum as a result of the adoption of the World Heritage Convention in 1972.

In recent years, "intangible cultural heritage" has come to exemplify how international conventions, when successful, can act as catalysts: this term, concocted in the assembly halls of UNESCO in the 1990s, has rapidly gained acceptance following the adoption in 2003 of the convention dedicated to its safeguarding. In this, it repeats the international success story of "cultural heritage," propounded by the 1972 convention, not only as a term but as a system of values, a set of practices, a formation of knowledge, a structure of feeling, and a moral code. Its widespread use is in some ways confounding, considering its negative semantics and bureaucratic etymology, not to mention that it is something of a mouthful; indeed, in many contexts it has effectively been replaced by the acronym ICH. Yet in tens of thousands of scattered places all over the world, people now refer to their practices as intangible cultural heritage, or as ICH, and in so doing they make claims that are recognizable with reference to an international regime and validated by a proliferating production of expert knowledge.

Origins of Intangible Heritage

There was a time when the study of folklore was characterized by a search for the origins of cultural phenomena: customs, tales, tools, and melodies. Over the past century, scholars have abandoned this quest, turning attention instead to folklore's meaning, structure, performance, use, and affect; they look at its performativity in helping to gather social collectives, bonding together and setting apart, imagining coherence and contrast. But while scholarship largely abandoned questions of origins, the questions themselves have not gone away. Asking them is a sincere form of curiosity and they retain their intellectual appeal in society at large. If so much ink was spent on the scholarly search for origins in the nineteenth and twentieth centuries, it was because scholars imagined that figuring out where stuff comes from is key to understanding its meaning. Finding where customs or tales or tools had originated and how they had come about would somehow tell us what they were all about. In other words, their origins spoke of their essence and purpose. This idea is still very much with us, not in the scholarly realm perhaps, but certainly in the public sphere outside the university. Stories of origins—etiological accounts—loom large in the media. Advertising and marketing make use of them all the time. Corporations employ them to build their brand. Cultural tourism depends on them. Political campaigns deploy them in support of candidates and platforms, and they are at the heart of political projects, different etiologies justifying different political visions. They also figure in the identity of organizations, in the way they justify their work and motivate their employees—in organizational storytelling, that is. UNESCO is no exception.

A number of stories account for the origins of the Intangible Heritage Convention. I heard them during fieldwork, first as a participant observer in the meetings where the convention was drafted and then as an observant participant in meetings after the convention entered into force. The stories came up in formal interviews and informal conversations, in offices and corridors and elevators, and I came across references to them, short and long, in archives and publications. Recounting or referring to such stories, people give meaning to what they are up to or what they propose to do; to account for origins is to explain, to rationalize, to validate.

Stories that recite the origins of intangible heritage are set in the Andes, in Japan, in Morocco, and they take us to New York and Paris, and eventually around the world. Bringing the perspective of a folklorist to these narratives, I recount them in the chapters that follow so as to get at their uses, their structure, their performance, and their affects—to appreciate how they help imagine coherence, conjure up contrast, and provide charters for action. The stories themselves rehearse well-known themes from folk narrative tradition, recycling traditional motifs and well-worn plots.

If these stories are partly populated by larger-than-life characters—artists, industrialists, generals, and politicians—that should not obscure the intimate involvement of scholars in the making of intangible heritage. Whether in leading or supporting roles, we figure in these stories from beginning to end: from Daniel Alomía Robles to José María Arguedas, from Alan Lomax to Richard Kurin, just to throw a few names out there. In the end, the story of intangible heritage is also a story about the discipline of folklore and the "folklorization" of the public sphere—a sedimentation of the field's perspectives and knowledge over time into everyday life, shaping people's attitudes to their own culture and the way they represent it to others.

I have suggested that cultural heritage is a pedagogic project and that narrative is its most important pedagogical device. But narrative is also a critical device. That is how I deploy it in this book. Taking stories from UNESCO— stories that make grand claims, stories of origins and success stories—I recount them in order to complicate them. Adding context and nuance, they gain critical complexity that undermines their moral imperative. Refusing to stop at "happily ever after," the book follows up on what happens after the stories end.

Ethnography in Glass Elevators

When setting out on the research on which this book builds, I really was not sure if it was bona fide fieldwork, bona fide ethnography, bona fide folklore. Sure, the stuff I heard diplomats discuss in Paris and Geneva was the stuff I study as folklore: from oral traditions to traditional medicinal knowledge, from folk music to festivals, from crafts to rituals to cultural spaces. I recall entire days in WIPO meetings given over to the question of how to define folklore, with lawyers from different parts of the world recycling arguments from the last one hundred fifty years of folklore's disciplinary history (a source of no small amusement for a folklorist at the back of the room). UNESCO abandoned the term "folklore" in the 1990s in favor of this term that the organization created itself, "intangible cultural heritage," or ICH. In WIPO, it happened a decade later, when another acronym filled the seat left vacant by folklore's eviction: TCEs, or "traditional cultural expressions." Less elegant, but also less semantically charged, the new terms encompass most of the cultural practices previously known as folklore but make them more easily legible under regimes of heritage and intellectual property.

So, granted, the lawyers spoke about folklore. But was I really doing the work of a folklorist? And is it really fieldwork if the field site has marble floors and glass elevators? If I wear a suit? Several colleagues have posed these questions, some version of them, at academic conferences and in anonymous peer reviews. Some have suggested I ought to study something different, go somewhere else, talk to other people, see how things work "on the ground." I confess I had moments of doubt, but my answer remains the same: yes, we must go elsewhere too, and yes, this is all very meta, but for all that, this is as real a field as any other; a field, moreover, that it is crucial to enter, analyze, understand, and criticize. It neither looks nor feels quite like the fields to which folklorists and anthropologist have traditionally taken their questions, but then again, it is high time to liberate our disciplinary imagination.

It is already half a century since Laura Nader urged anthropologists to "study up" to understand "the processes whereby power and responsibility are exercised" (1969, 284). To "study the colonizers rather than the colonized, the culture of power rather than the culture of the powerless, the culture of affluence rather than the culture of poverty" would "lead us to ask many 'common sense' questions in reverse," Nader suggested (289). Indeed, I think *unmaking* common sense is perhaps the most critical task of critical scholarship. In this, I take inspiration from Antonio Gramsci and his challenge to folklorists, anthropologists, and social philosophers to make "good sense" from "common sense," the *senso comune* that people encounter everywhere as self-evident (Gramsci 1999, 3:626–667; also Crehan 2016; Gencarella 2010; Patterson 2016). The work of politics—including the politics of cultural heritage—is to define common sense, to disseminate it, and to mark its limits (beyond which lies nonsense). The work of criticism is to question that common sense, to examine, to undermine or invert it; to show how things could be otherwise; to bring the taken-for-granted to critical awareness. To make "good sense." But if that is so, then why not begin with processes that explicitly set out to fix norms and define the standards of common sense? Like, say, at UNESCO's Place de Fontenoy headquarters in the middle of negotiations for a standard-setting instrument?[1]

To cite Nader once more, we "are not dealing with an either/or proposition; we need simply to realize when it is useful or crucial in terms of the problem to extend the domain of study up, down, or sideways" (1969, 292). It is imperative to study the various local relationships into which intangible heritage enters when different social actors mobilize this concept in diverse contexts "on the ground" and around the world; fortunately, a number of folklorists, ethnologists, and anthropologists are already there.[2] I refer to such ethnographically grounded, critical analyses in this book; they form a crucial counterpoint to my work in the meeting rooms of UNESCO. Up, down, in, out: let's not lose sight of the fact that these are relational prepositions. "Up" can't be isolated from "down"; as Ellen Hertz emphasizes, the point is "to link ups to downs, to look at the relations between different arenas of social power" (2010, 3). It is incumbent on us to follow the topics we study where they go. It is incumbent on folklorists in particular to follow the concepts we create or have a hand in shaping—folklore, tradition, traditional knowledge, expressive culture, cultural spaces, cultural heritage—not only into the street, the plaza, or the home, but also into the studio and the pharmaceutical industry, into government offices, electoral politics, and, yes, into intergovernmental committees (Mugnaini 2016).

Engaging with Policy

I attended my first diplomatic meeting in 2002. At the time, I did not have much to model my work on. In the years since, many superb ethnographic studies of UN meetings and organizations have seen the light of day.[3] Their authors each bring their own set of questions to the field site, their own research agendas and priorities. As usual with fieldwork, what they discover on site reforms their agendas, reshuffles their priorities, and reframes their questions. That goes for me too.

My analysis embeds the Intangible Heritage Convention and its central concept in the organizational contexts, ideological conflicts, and diplomatic negotiations out of which they both emerge. Wherever else the analysis takes me, I return time and again to Paris and the 2003 Intergovernmental Meeting of Experts at UNESCO's headquarters, where I observed and took part in drafting the Intangible Heritage Convention. At times, I portray the debates and discussions in intimate detail, then take a step back to explore the historical context of the arguments presented or a step forward to observe the convention's present implementation and effects in various sites around the world, only at long last to sit back down in the meeting room to give the present moment and history a chance to meet. To understand the nuts and bolts of intangible heritage, I think it is important not only to know the official accounts of compromise and solidarity but also to witness diplomatic jostling behind the curtains, the making and breaking of alliances, the confrontation and resistance, all of which marked the path toward agreement and shaped the outcome.

Later, after the convention entered into force, I served as Iceland's delegate to the General Assembly of States Parties to the convention (its sovereign body) and to a meeting of the Intergovernmental Committee for the Safeguarding of the Intangible Cultural Heritage (its executive body). On various occasions, I have also acted as consultant on the convention's implementation to both the Swedish and the Icelandic governments.

Then, in 2011–2012, I chaired Iceland's National Commission for UNESCO. The chairmanship of the National Commission was a thought-provoking experience with a steep learning curve. The most memorable moments were at UNESCO's General Conference in 2011, when I voted (along with a vast majority) for the accession of Palestine as a member state.[4] But such highlights cannot overshadow the mundane work done in countless meetings, consultations, and coordinations. From these, I learned much that informs my broader understanding of how UNESCO works, the conflicts and debates, the underhanded maneuvers and open-minded discussions, the divergence of views and the convergence of positions. It was often tedious, technical, and time-consuming; I recall more than once sitting in meetings with no clear agenda and no end in sight, thinking if I swallowed my keys I might get out. But in truth, I remain deeply impressed that delegations from 195 different states are sometimes able to work out their differences and reach consensus, such as the one that produced the Intangible Heritage Convention. No wonder it takes time and patience.

Over the years, I have given numerous public lectures on cultural heritage in general and on intangible heritage in particular. In 2010, the previous National Commission held a symposium in Reykjavík titled "UNESCO and Cultural

Fig. 1.4 Author at UNESCO's General Conference in 2011. Author photo.

Heritage," opened by the minister of education and culture, followed by the commission's current and former chairs and the country's ex-president (and current UNESCO Goodwill Ambassador), all of them well versed in every aspect of the organization. After a coffee break, three of us spoke in turn on World Heritage, the Memory of the World Program, and (yours truly) Intangible Heritage. I stood last and gave my take on the topic, something akin to a fifteen-minute version of this book, with a fair dose of critique and an ironic twist; it struck a different note from the rest of the proceedings.

A couple of days later, the phone rang. The minister was on the line: would I be interested in chairing the National UNESCO Commission when the term of all persons appointed to the committee, including its chair, ran out later that year? I had to think long and hard about that one. Eventually, I came to the conclusion that if I turned her invitation down, I would also forever give up my right to critique anything related to UNESCO. So, I accepted the challenge. Later, I figured out that my appointment followed a larger pattern; the minister of education and culture, Katrín Jakobsdóttir, a radical politician in her mid-thirties at the time, vice-chair of the Left-Green Party (prime minister and party chair at the time of writing), made it her signature move as minister to find people rocking the establishment boat and make them captains of various vessels in the ministry's fleet: to bring the critics on board to feed critical engagement into policy making. The commission was nominally autonomous, but the ministry controlled its budget and human resources. Alas, some ministry officials found our attitude and activities "un-UNESCO-ish." A couple of strategically placed spanners brought our work to a halt; by the middle of 2012, I handed in my resignation.

The Next Best Thing

That does not mean, however, that I have given up on engagement. We must protect the space for academic inquiry, to be sure; theory and critical analysis are crucial for reflective societies. But folklorists (ethnologists, anthropologists) must also be willing to have their skin in the game (Tornatore 2007; Mugnaini 2016). When the committees and cultural workers of UNESCO engage with the expressions and creative capacities that the field of folklore is about, and when they create an international instrument designed to guide national policies and practices, then folklorists, ethnologists, anthropologists should be there, on every side of the game: in the secretariat, on national commissions, on expert committees, as observers, and as external commentators and critics.

"Politics is the art of the possible" ("Die Politik ist die Lehre vom Möglichen") as Otto von Bismarck famously remarked, the Iron Chancellor who united and ruled Germany in the second half of the nineteenth century (1895, 248). According to historian Eric Hobsbawm, Bismarck "remained undisputed world champion at the game of multilateral diplomatic chess for almost twenty years" after 1871, successfully "maintaining peace between the powers" in Europe (1989, 312). The Intangible Heritage Convention represents the art of the possible, in Bismarck's sense—that is to say, the (least bad) outcome attainable through multilateral diplomatic negotiations in UNESCO in 2003. Granted, the convention was negotiated in record time, in the biennium between the organization's General Conferences in 2001 and 2003. Member states could easily have spent another ten years on the negotiations, but I'm not convinced it would have made much difference for the better. More likely, it would have stopped the momentum and thwarted any kind of result. The art of the possible is about the next best thing.

The Convention for the Safeguarding of the Intangible Cultural Heritage is far from ideal, regardless of position or perspective. It is flawed in fundamental ways and at times counterproductive (just read on and you'll see what I mean). But it is the next best. To put my cards on the table, I think the world is better off with the convention than without it. But that does not put it beyond reproach; it is not even to say it is good, only that the alternative is worse. The next best thing leaves a crucial role for criticism. That is the conviction underwriting my approach in this book. The convention will weather the criticism but would wither without it.

A Note on Sources

The research on which this book is based relies on critical analysis of three different varieties of source material. First, the documentary trail produced by UNESCO: reports, recommendations, questionnaires and responses, regional consultations, position papers, and others. UNESCO's archives are a rich mine in which I discovered a great number of documents to help me piece together the history and gain insight into the changing logic of UNESCO's heritage initiatives. In addition to the physical archives in the basement of the building at Place Fontenoy in Paris, UNESCO's archivists have made available an immense number of documents in a searchable online database, which proved to be of enormous value for my research away from Paris. Finally, Rieks Smeets, when he directed the Intangible Heritage Section, kindly gave me access to the section's own institutional memory in folders and envelopes kept in staff offices. These documents have helped me understand how decisions were made and what the major sticking points have been.

Second, I rely on debates and negotiations in UNESCO's Intergovernmental Meeting of Experts that devised the Convention for the Safeguarding of the Intangible Cultural Heritage. As noted, I attended the third session of this Intergovernmental Meeting of Experts in UNESCO headquarters in Paris, June 2–14, 2003. I received permission from the Icelandic National UNESCO Commission—its chair, Sveinn Einarsson, and its secretary, Guðný Helgadóttir—to tag along with the Icelandic delegation. I kept detailed notes of the proceedings, including verbatim quotations of all statements that seemed particularly eloquent, insightful, problematic, absurd, or otherwise ripe for reference. All discussion of this session in the following chapters is based on my personal observation; direct quotations from the session are from my notes. The same may be said of other meetings that I refer to in the book.

The evidence of documents and direct observation is supplemented by consultations with UNESCO staff and national delegates. This is the third variety of sources on which I base this study. Several members of the UNESCO secretariat generously shared their time and firsthand knowledge with an inquisitive outsider; my interlocutors include, but are not limited to, the staff of the Intangible Heritage Section. I cite these as personal communications.

Notes

1. In France, Marc Abélès showed the way in institutional ethnography in the 1990s with his works on everyday life in the European Commission (1992, 1995, 1996) and later his anthropological study of the French Parliament (2000).

2. See critical contributions to edited volumes, such as Foster and Gilman 2015; Adell, Bendix, Bortolotto, and Tauschek 2015; Bendix, Eggert, and Peselmann 2013; Bondaz, Graezer Bideau, Isnart, and Leblon 2017; Bortolotto 2011; Stefano and Davis 2017; Stefano, Davis, and Corsane 2014; Arizpe and Amescua 2013; and Smith and Akagawa 2009. See also case studies by Alivizatou 2016; Aykan 2013, 2015, 2016; Beardslee 2014, 2016; Bille 2012; Bortolotto 2009; Camal 2016; de Jong 2013, 2016; Foster 2011; Fournier 2011, 2012; Graezer Bideau 2012; Kuutma 2009; Kwon 2017; Lowthorp 2013; Margry 2014; Noyes 2006; Rodenberg and Wagenaar 2016; Sánchez Carretero 2015; Schmitt 2005; Tauschek 2009, 2010; Tebbaa and Skounti 2011; Tornatore 2012.

3. For example ethnographic studies by Regina Bendix (2013) and Stefan Groth (2011, 2016) on WIPO's Intergovernmental Committee on Intellectual Property and Genetic Resources, Traditional Knowledge, and Traditional Cultural Expressions; Christoph Brumann (2014, 2016), Aurélie Elisa Gfeller (2015, 2017), Lynn Meskell (2011, 2012, 2013, 2014), Thomas Schmitt (2009), Luke James and Tim Winter (2017), and Jan Turtinen (2006) on the World Heritage Committee; Sally Engle Merry (2006) on the UN Commission on the Status of Women; Ellen Hertz on the International Labour Organization (ILO) (2010, 2014); Lauren E. Eastwood (2013) on the Intergovernmental Forum on Forests; Birgit Müller on the Food and Agriculture Organization (FAO) (2011); Irène Bellier on the Indigenous People's Forum and indigenous representation in other UN organizations (2013, 2015); and Kristin Kuutma (2007, 2012) and Chiara Bortolotto (2008, 2010, 2013, 2015) on UNESCO's Intergovernmental Committee for the Safeguarding of the Intangible Cultural Heritage.

4. As this book went to press, the United States announced its full withdrawal from UNESCO in 2018 in reaction to Palestine's accession, only fifteen years after the United States rejoined the organization, following its earlier withdrawal in 1984 under the Reagan administration.

CHAPTER 2

Making Threats

The Condor's Flight

THIS IS A book about intangible heritage—about how a new concept and category comes into being and goes to work in the world. It is a book about folklore, about cultural practices and expressions, and about what happens to them when they come under the sign of intangible heritage. It is about how intangible heritage was made, and how it makes, forms, and transforms the expressions and practices within its purview. It begins with a story. With a twisting plot, a colorful set of characters, and a red herring, this story recounts the origins of intangible heritage and how it was inscribed on the international agenda.[1]

The story opens with a letter. Before the letter, a song. We will get there soon enough. In the top right-hand corner, a place and a date:

La Paz, April 24, 1973

Addressed to UNESCO's director-general, the letter is sent from the Ministry of Foreign Affairs and Religion of the Republic of Bolivia. Its opening paragraph announces:

> My ministry has made a careful survey of existing documentation on the international protection of the cultural heritage of mankind.

This survey found that all existing instruments

> are aimed at the protection of tangible objects, and not forms of expression such as music and dance, which are at present undergoing the most intensive clandestine commercialization and export, in a process of commercially oriented transculturation destructive of the traditional cultures. (UNESCO 1977)

21

I had heard many people refer to this letter when, with help from UNESCO's archivist, I dug it up from the organization's archives in the basement of its Paris headquarters. It took a bit of searching. The letter is brief, but a detailed memorandum accompanies it. Here, the Bolivian minister impresses upon the international community how urgent it is to take action:

> The current revalorization of folk arts due to their notable invasion of the consumer market is currently giving rise to the *de facto* situation of which the following examples afford a rundown. (UNESCO 1977)

The examples follow, three in number (as in all good stories), testifying to just how bad things were:

> In the musical sphere, there are instances of melodies being wrongfully appropriated by persons unconnected with their creation who register them as their own compositions to secure to themselves the benefits conceded by copyright regulations. This leads, amongst other things, to the debasement of the folkishness of the piece. (UNESCO 1977)

"In the sphere of the dance," the minister continues, folk dances are

> appropriated by other countries wholly unconnected with their genesis to be passed off by them, even in international competitions, as folk dances of their own. In the particular case of Bolivia which, owing to its geographical situation, suffers greatly from depredations of this kind, certain organizations from neighboring countries go so far as to send here [for] complete sets of costumes for the main Bolivian folk dances, and engage "embroiderers," "mask makers" and even choreographers (of peasant "folk" origin) to organize this switching or deliberate non-spontaneous transculturation process which amounts to the filching and clandestine transfer of another people's culture. In this way, the creator peoples gradually lose their folk-art assets, while others, with better financial facilities, present as their own what was never a part of their tradition. The themes may, in some cases, be similar, but the décor and choreography are usurped. (UNESCO 1977)

The third example is crafts. "In the realm of popular art," writes the minister,

> which likewise forms part of national folklore and which has, at present, a large consumer market, there are similar filchings, as in the case of countries which reach the point of industrializing themes and techniques from the traditional patterns of the cultures of particular population groups and offering them at cut prices on the international markets with no statements of origin— a process which, in addition to lowering the quality of the objects, means the "submarginalization" of large population groups who often depend for their livelihood on this paying work. (UNESCO 1977)

Note the plaintive vocabulary of misappropriation in the minister's letter and memorandum. It is there in every other sentence: "export," "invasion," "appropriation," "depredation," "switching," "filching," "clandestine transfer," "loss," "usurpation," and (my personal favorite) "deliberate non-spontaneous transculturation process."

Export is one: the problem is foreigners. This is a national problem, in other words—a challenge to national culture—and therefore also an international problem, because borders are permeable and no one patrols the circulation of culture across them. The term *invasion* suggests acts of aggression, even if they are commercial in their motives and means.

Filching, usurpation, depredation: so many ways to name a thief. The colorful lexicon of theft in the minister's letter emphasizes ownership. It goes to support the minister's main point, namely, that folklore should be considered cultural property controlled by states, on the model of UNESCO's Convention on the Means of Prohibiting and Preventing the Illicit Import, Export and Transfer of Ownership of Cultural Property, adopted two and a half years before the letter was drawn up:

> The international conventions drawn up by UNESCO now provide protection for anonymous works in the domains alike of archeology and of the plastic arts, but it has only been thought fit to do this in respect of tangible objects, and not of forms of artistic expression transitory in time and space, such as music and dance, but none the less, works of art which are, today, subject to the most intense clandestine commercialization and export, despite the fact that they form part of States' cultural heritage. (UNESCO 1977)

Consider the actors and owners here: the states. According to the Bolivian letter, these artistic expressions form part of "States' cultural heritage." This is no slip of the pen:

> The Bolivian Government, by Supreme Decree No 08396 of 19 June 1968, has proclaimed State ownership of the folk music (anonymous, popular and traditional) of its territory, of the music currently being produced by unidentified composers in peasant and general folk groups and of the music of Bolivian composers deceased 30 or more years ago.
>
> Legislation extending the application of these measures to folk dance, popular art and traditional literature is in process of enactment.
>
> The Government of Bolivia, in informing the Director-General of UNESCO of these decisions taken in the exercise of its legitimate authority and of its ownership of expressions of folk art, ancient or modern, which have grown up or become traditional on its territory, of anonymous works at present performed by ethnic or folk groups, and of works by composers deceased 30 or more years ago, would indicate that the national registers of these forms of cultural property are scientifically checked by specialist researchers. (UNESCO 1977)

Enter the folklorists, ethnologists, anthropologists, historians, and heritage workers: "specialist researchers" corroborating national registers of cultural property.[2] Nearly half a century later, UNESCO's Convention for the Safeguarding of the Intangible Cultural Heritage still envisions a similar role for us in what are now called national inventories of intangible heritage.

The Bolivian letter serves as the opening salvo in UNESCO's own account of the origins of the Convention for the Safeguarding of the Intangible Cultural Heritage, also known as the Intangible Heritage Convention. In spring and summer 2003, in a meeting room in UNESCO's headquarters in Paris, I listened to a Bolivian rapporteur in an intergovernmental meeting stress the importance of finishing the convention, "preferably this year," then pause for dramatic effect before adding: "There is thirty-years' worth of work behind this, at the international level as well as at the regional and national levels. This process has been brought to maturity." His "thirty-years' worth of work" refers back to La Paz, April 24, 1973, when another Bolivian statesman signed the letter to UNESCO's director-general. When finally I unearthed this letter from the archives, I was blown away by just how closely the work still being done follows the formulations of the Bolivian minister, for better and for worse. I will have cause to refer to it elsewhere in this book.

The third session of the Intergovernmental Meeting of Experts on the Preliminary Draft Convention for the Safeguarding of the Intangible Cultural Heritage took place over two weeks in June 2003. It met in a large conference room in the basement of UNESCO headquarters at Place Fontenoy in Paris. I attended the meeting in the capacity of an "expert" on the Icelandic delegation. As such, I was alphabetized by state ("Islande") and sat to the right of the Indian delegates (the Iranians were absent, as were the Iraqis, who did not command a sovereign state at the time). On my right-hand side sat Guðný Helgadóttir, head of the delegation and the only other delegate in attendance from Iceland. I had a headset on one ear and turned the other toward Guðný. Next to the headset plug-in was a knob where I could switch back and forth between simultaneous translations in French and English. A microphone stood on the desk in front of us. Behind us, the Doric columns of the Parthenon commanded the room in a giant rendition of the UNESCO logo, reminding delegates of the gravity of their mission, no more and no less than to uphold civilization. In front of us, the chair, secretary, and rapporteur faced us from an elevated stage, flanked by two giant screens with the draft text of the convention in English and French.

At one point, I had drinks with the Swedish delegate, Peder Bjursten, after a long day of drafting and diplomacy at Place Fontenoy. Neither of us had much experience with meetings like these and we agreed that participating in this one was at once fascinating and tedious, like being an extra on the set of a James Bond film. Bjursten reminded me of the opening scene of the 1973 film *Live and Let Die*, in a meeting room much like the one in Paris, where a Hungarian delegate is addressing the United Nations General Assembly. The camera pans past

Fig. 2.1 Death of a diplomat. Film still from *Live and Let Die* 1973. ©MGM Studios.

a number of national delegations, each with a sign on the desk in front of them and headsets on their ears, just like us. The camera then pans up to the translators' booth where a black hand emerges from off screen. It switches plugs in the unit connected to the headset of a drowsy British diplomat, replacing the soothing hum of simultaneous translation with a deadly, pulsating noise that swiftly bleeps him to death. The hand belongs to Dr. Kananga, a dictator from the fictitious Caribbean island of "San Monique." Bjursten and I both reached up instinctively and touched an ear.

According to the Secretariat Report, 249 participants representing 103 member states took part in this third session, in addition to ten delegates from UNESCO's three permanent observation missions, and representatives from two intergovernmental organizations (IGOs) and five nongovernmental organizations (NGOs). In fact, no more than half that number of people took part. I only noted one NGO in the room. It is fascinating how wide the gap is between official reports and what one actually observes at these meetings; I mention the number of participants only by way of illustration. The reports tend to gloss over conflicts, omit confrontations, and downplay disagreements all the while emphasizing points of convergence and insisting on consensus, even in its absence (see James and Winter 2017, 11). In fact, they are instrumental in creating the convergence

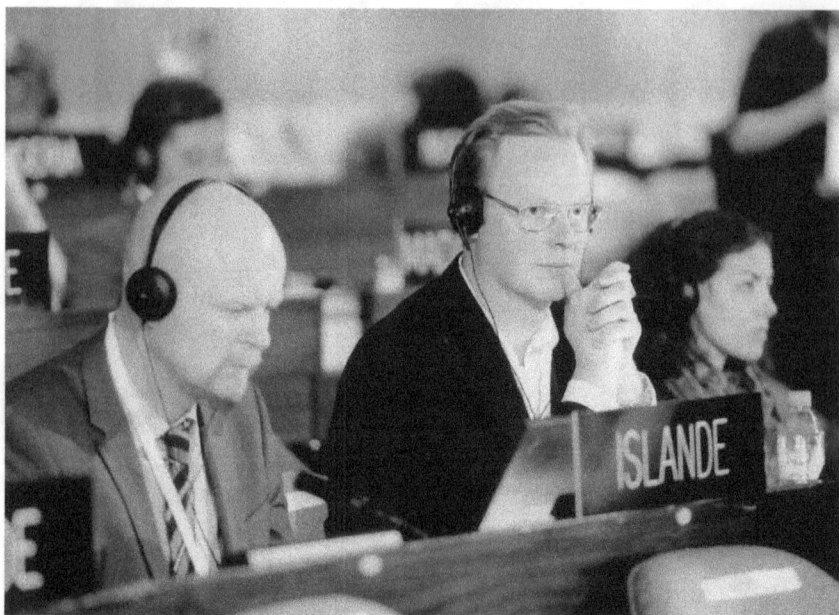

Fig. 2.2 Author at UNESCO's General Conference in 2011 with Einar Hreinsson, Secretary-General of Iceland's National Commission for UNESCO. Author photo.

they portray. Observing such discrepancies, one soon learns not to take the official presentation at face value but to read against the grain of these documents. In fact, nothing ought to be taken at face value. Behind the scenes, there are always other negotiations, ulterior motives, strategic alliances, and historical logics. To understand the process and the outcome, it is crucial at every stage to put it into larger context. All that I gathered from participant observation and personal communications is fundamental to my understanding of the process, supplemented by archival sources and, well, experience. As noted in the previous chapter, since the Intangible Heritage Convention entered into force in 2006 (once thirty states, including Iceland, had ratified it) I have served as an Icelandic delegate to the General Assembly of the States Parties to the convention and as official observer of a meeting of the Intergovernmental Committee in charge of executing the convention, as expert consultant to the Swedish government on its ratification and implementation, and, in 2011–2012, as the chair of the Icelandic National Commission for UNESCO.

In the course of my research, before and after the adoption of the convention, I often heard references to the Bolivian letter. Some were brief and condensed, such as the "thirty-years' worth of work," while others developed into full-blown narrative form. I think very few people had actually read the letter—they would have had to dig deep in the archives to do so—but that did not stop anybody from making it a cardinal reference in their story of how UNESCO came to concern itself with intangible heritage: The Bolivian minister had inscribed it on the international agenda.

When UNESCO personnel, delegates, diplomats, and experts refer to the letter from Bolivia to explain why we are here (at work, in the office or meeting room or café or conference call) or to stress how long we have been here, they are engaged in what students of business administration call "organizational storytelling." The genre in which they speak is what folklorists call an "etiological narrative," that is, an account of how something came to be.

Within UNESCO, like other organizations, storytelling is rife. Moving in diplomatic circles or reading how the organization presents itself and its work in its own publications, one comes across other official stories of origins, recounting, explaining, and justifying some of its other endeavors. Stories told about the World Heritage Convention from 1972 recount how international cooperation in UNESCO's Nubia Campaign rescued the Abu Simbel temples and other monuments from the Nubian Valley in the 1960s before the Aswan High Dam submerged the valley in water—"a defining example of international solidarity when countries understood the universal nature of heritage and the universal importance of its conservation" (UNESCO World Heritage Centre 2009). The monuments were relocated beyond the reach of the flood, to the shores of the reservoir, Lake Nasser, and to the Sudan National Museum in Khartoum, and the success of these salvage operations demonstrated the necessity of international cooperation to protect cultural heritage. So the story goes (UNESCO 1982). There is more to it, of course. The forced displacement of the inhabitants and the destruction of their villages remains untold. So too does the disappearance of mud-brick building, a vernacular form of architecture that relied on alluvial mud no longer deposited by the Nile but trapped behind the dam (Mitchell 2002). And the larger political context is also crucial to understanding the "heritage diplomacy" of the Nubia campaign. As Tim Winter remarks, "With the Soviet Union providing financial assistance for constructing the dam that would lead to the flooding of the valley further south, Abu Simbel presented a number of Western allies the opportunity to assemble for a diplomatically expedient initiative, a project UNESCO has subsequently described as a 'triumph of international solidarity'" (2016, 19; see also Carruthers 2016; Betts 2015; Allias 2012).

The international community came together once more in 1966 to save the built heritage of Venice from sinking into the Mediterranean in the wake of disastrous floods, rallying experts and resources in an effort orchestrated by UNESCO (Di Giovine 2015). These campaigns are cited time and again in storytelling about the origins of the World Heritage Convention: the way the story goes, member states of UNESCO created the convention to confirm their

Fig. 2.3 René Maheu, UNESCO's Director-General, at the inauguration ceremony of the Abu Simbel Temples in 1968. ©UNESCO.

commitment to the cooperation fostered by the "Save Nubia" and "Save Venice" campaigns. By becoming parties to the convention, they pledged to go on working together to save heritage of outstanding universal value.

Remind you of anything? The flood is coming, build an ark! From the Sumerian flood myth in the tale of Ziusudra (seventeenth century BCE) to the Mesopotamian epic of Gilgamesh (thirteenth to tenth century BCE) to the Abrahamic story of the Flood and Noah's Ark in the Book of Genesis (tenth to fifth century BCE), the flood is a frequent motif in myths of creation, recounting how the world and mankind came to their present circumstances. Outside of Western Asian traditions, floods are or were a feature in traditional stories of origins among peoples as widely dispersed as the Maasai and Yoruba on the east and west coasts of Africa; Hopis and Inuits in North America; Incas and Tupis in South America;

among the peoples of Hawai'i, Malaysia, Korea, and China; and in Hindu, Norse, and Greek mythologies. Indeed, as folklorist Alan Dundes noted, "The flood myth is one of the most widely diffused narratives known" (1988, 2). Storytelling in the United Nations is not so different from storytelling elsewhere. The invocation of the flood motif gives UNESCO a protagonist role equivalent to that of Noah in the Book of Genesis, charged with the survival of creation as a whole. It frames the World Heritage Convention as its Ark.

As stories of origins, these narratives set the tone, the register in which UNESCO likes to describe its efforts in this arena. Like other stories of origins—like, say, the story of Adam and Eve, the apple and the snake, and the fall of man—the story about the letter from Bolivia tells us something important about its subject—about the human condition in the case of the one, about intangible heritage in the case of the other. We know that intuitively; it is a generic expectation that stories of origins evoke (much like the oral formulas "Once upon a time" or "A duck walks into a bar" evoke their own generic expectations). That something important is not always explicit, but it is brought into bold relief in those versions of UNESCO's etiological narrative that explain the motivation for the Bolivian minister's letter (e.g., Albro 2005, 4; Honko 2001; Sherkin 2001, 54, note 13).

Returning now to our story of origins for the Intangible Heritage Convention, this is where the plot thickens. We left off at the letter from Bolivia and various references made to it, but the story as told in the UN goes on to set the letter in context. Stepping back three years before the diplomatic courier delivered the letter to Paris, the story breaks into song.

In 1970, Paul Simon and Art Garfunkel released the album *Bridge over Troubled Water*. It was their last studio album and marked the end of a successful collaboration that had begun thirteen years earlier. On one track, Simon and Garfunkel perform "El Condor Pasa," which they credit as "an 18th century Peruvian folk melody." *Bridge over Troubled Water* won the Grammy award for the record of the year and instantly reached the number one spot on Billboard's pop albums chart, where it sat for six weeks. It also topped the albums charts in Australia, Canada, France, Germany, Japan, the Netherlands, Norway, Spain, Sweden, and the United Kingdom. *Bridge over Troubled Water* was Simon and Garfunkel's highest-selling album, and it is still among the best sellers of all time, with over eight million copies sold in the United States alone.

"El Condor Pasa" was its best-selling single and worldwide hit. Later that same year Perry Como covered the song on his own album, called *It's Impossible*. In the United Kingdom, Julie Felix had a top 20 hit that year with the same song. Gigliola Cinquetti in Italy; Fausto Papetti, Gianni Morandi, and Mimma Gaspari, also in Italy; Jurgen Marcus, Antonio Conde, Hugo Strasser, Marianne Rosenberg, Mary Roos, and Monika Hauff with Klaus Dieter Henkler, all of

Fig. 2.4 Simon & Garfunkel: "El Condor Pasa," Single sleeve. ©CBS/Columbia Records.

these in Germany; Caravelli, the Paul Mauriat Orchestra, Franck Pourcel and his Grand Orchestra, and Los Chacos, all in France; Karel Gott in Czechoslovakia (the "Golden Voice of Prague"); Andy Williams, Anita Kerr, Chet Atkins, Dick Hyman, Nokie Edwards, and Henry Mancini in the United States; the Cables in Jamaica; Laurie Bower in Canada; Jørgen Ingmann in Denmark; Svante Thuresson, Mia Adolphson, and Jan Lindblad (a whistling artist) in Sweden; Claudius Alzner in Austria; Esther Ofarim, Daliah Lavi, and the Parvarim, all three (separately) in Israel; Kai Hyttinen and Markus in Finland; Teresa Tang in China, Taiwan, and Indonesia; Minoru Muraoka together with Tadao Sawai in Japan; Ryoko Moriyama, also in Japan; Takeshi Onodera and Los Onoderas, in Japan as well—all these recorded their own covers, and that's just scratching the surface. In 1970, '71, '72, and '73, hundreds of artists from every continent except Antarctica released their own cover of the song. In the decades since, artists across the world have produced their own versions of "El Condor Pasa" in various musical genres. By the count of Raúl R. Romero, director of the Institute of Ethnomusicology of the Pontifical Catholic University of Peru in Lima, more than four thousand versions have been recorded worldwide, set to over three hundred different lyrics (*Redacción La Industria* 2013). That is surely a conservative estimate.

The story as told in UNESCO circles does not go quite into that level of detail, but Simon and Garfunkel's release of "El Condor Pasa" is front and center. Perhaps they meant to show solidarity with poor, oppressed, native peoples in South America by recording the song; perhaps the intent was to support the revolutionary ethos that Andean music had come to be associated with in cosmopolitan circles in this age of Latin American dictators, revolution, and the international cult of Che Guevara. If so, that was not explicit; in any case there was no jubilation in the Andes. As seen from the Andes, this looked less like a celebration of indigenous music and more like exploitation. Rich Americans had ransacked the musical tradition of poor people in the Andes and they had made a lot of money. None of it went to those who considered themselves the rightful "owners."

The pattern was not unfamiliar—it was not that different from the colonial expropriation that shipped gold and silver from the Andes to Europe and (later) copper to North America. This time around, though, even the condor was siphoned off, bird of the Incas and symbol of native pride. As our story has it, the way it is often recounted, the whole affair made for troubled waters indeed and left a bad taste in many mouths.

By this account, the Bolivian letter to UNESCO's director general in 1973 is a political expression of that bad taste (see, e.g., Sherkin 2001, 54, note 13; Canclini 2001, 15). This is the "wrongful appropriation" that the Bolivian minister wrote about. This is what he called "the most intensive clandestine commercialization and export," the "transculturation" that he warned would destroy traditional cultures.

That is how the story is told in UNESCO circles. Its appeal is not hard to recognize, the way it sets international diplomacy to a tune many can whistle and pegs the birthday of UNESCO's endeavors to the calendar of pop music history. The story purports to tell us something interesting and important about intangible heritage and it justifies particular courses of action in the present.[3] But stories we tell about ourselves sometimes reveal more than we know, more even than we would like. Reading against the grain, this story too is more intricate: the song's provenance is more complicated, questions of ownership and appropriation are more nuanced, and the ethics of protection are not as straightforward as the story makes them out to be.

Begin with the provenance. The first to challenge Simon and Garfunkel's use of the song was a Peruvian film director, Armando Robles Godoy. His father, Daniel Alomía Robles, registered the song as his own composition in the US

Fig. 2.5 "El Condor Pasa" (Inca Dance). Original sheet music for piano from 1928. Public domain.

Copyright Registry in 1933, in a piano arrangement with the title "Condor Pasa: Inca Dance" (Library of Congress Copyright Office 1933, 410). His son filed a lawsuit against Paul Simon in a New York court in 1970. It was an open and shut case; recognizing the legitimacy of the claim, Simon settled the suit out of court (Bondy 2008).

CATALOGUE OF COPYRIGHT ENTRIES

9636   pt. III, n. s., v. 28

Come to Chicago; waltz song. © May 15, 1933; E pub. 36287; George Thompson. 9636

Come to the fair; song, w Camille Callaway. © 1 c. May 6, 1933; E unp. 71100; Leonard P. Smith. 9637

Comme la neige; tango, de La joie de Paris, 1933, paroles Robert Marino, d'après l'original de P. Mendes, m Vittorio Mascheroni. © Mar. 25, 1933; E for. 29996; Editions Joséphine Baker. 9638

Company (The) of heaven; poem J. G. Whittier, m Marion Besly. © Apr. 11, 1933; E for. 29633; Boosey & co., ltd. 9639

Complément (Le); 200 leçons de solfège pratique, L. J. Rousseau, Marguerite Rousseau, Cécile Rousseau et François Rousseau. Cours élémentaire, nos. 1-3. © Mar. 1, 1933; E for. 29677; L. Julien Rousseau. 9640

Concert a-moll für violine; mit begl. des orchs., Willi Czernik, op. 86; klavier-auszug mit solo-violine. © Oct. 11, 1932; E for. 29570; Henry Litolff's verlag. 9641

Concerto grosso; von Rudolf Moser, op. 32; streichorch. u. cembalo o. klavier. Partitur u. stimmen. © Mar. 20, 1933; E for. 29615; Steingräber verlag. 9642

Condor (El) pasa; Inca dance, Daniel A. Robles; pf. © May 3, 1933; E pub. 36127; Edward B. Marks music corp. 9643

Connecticut waltz; w and melody. © 1 c. May 15, 1933; E unp. 71449; Rodley Delmus Stoutenburg. 9644

Contest (The) winners; march, J. S. Taylor; band pts. © May 25, 1933; E pub. 36476; C. L. Barnhouse, inc. 9645

Coon (The) among the chickens; novelty pf. or xylophone solo, Malcolm Ives; orch. pts. © Apr. 21, 1933; E for. 29594; Hawkes & son (London) ltd. 9646

Corcovado; par Darius Milhaud, transcription Maurice Maréchal; violoncelle et pf. © Mar. 15, 1933; E for. 29324; Editions Max Eschig. 9647

Cornish sea pictures; w F. Keeling Scott and Lawrence Taylor, m L, Taylor; mixed cho. © Apr. 12, 1933; E for. 29514; Charles Laraude & co. 9648

Coro (Il) dei cori; versi Domenico Tumiati, m Vittore Veneziani; coro a 4 voci maschili. Partitura. pte. 1, no. 1-5.—pte. 2, no. 6. © May 17, 1933; E for. 29957; G. Ricordi & co. 9649

Coronado; tango serenade, Ellis Levy; violin and pf. © Apr. 11, 1933; E pub. 36345; Carl Fischer, inc. 9650

Cottage episode attacca; by Herbert Stothart, orch. arr. by Paul Marquardt; [pf.-conductor.] © 1 c. May 3, 1933; E unp. 70939; Metro-Goldwyn-Mayer corp. 9651

Covadonga; paso-doble sinfónico; orch. pts. © May 2, 1933; E for. 29869; Juan Duran Alemany. 9652

Covenant concert band march; conductor. © 1 c. May 3, 1933; E unp. 70923; Alfred Strobeck. 9653

Cowboy's heaven; w Frank Marvin, melody G. Autry and Frank Marvin. © 1 c. May 6, 1933; E unp. 71111; Gene Autry. 9654

Cradle song; w Charlotte H. Coursen, m F. Ries, arr. Cyr de Brant. 1. Mixed voices.—2. Sop. 1, 2 and alto. © Mar. 21, 1933; E pub. 36325, 36326; Carl Fischer, inc. 9655, 9656

Cradle song of the Ozarks; w and m C. Dadswell. © 1 c. May 4, 1933; E unp. 70991; Cyril Dadswell and Margaret Lord. 9657

Crescent moon; w N. Freilich, m L. Pittler. © 1 c. May 20, 1933; E unp. 71714; Lila Pittler and Norman Freilich. 9658

Croix de guerre; march, Ralph Hueston Woods, op. 21; band pts. © May 12, 1933; E pub. 36270; Carl Dillon music co. 9659

Crossing the bar; w Alfred Tennyson, with melody. © 1 c. May 27, 1933; E unp. 71996; Steve Lovas. 9660

Cruel; pf. with w. © 1 c. May 27, 1933; E unp. 71997; Felix Joseph Bongiorno. 9661

Cryin'; w Bert Thistle, melody Maurice Merl. © 1 c. May 17, 1933; E unp. 71568; Albert Thistle. 9662

Cummings (Florence Amelia) Rondeau; w Thomas Moore; mixed voices. © Apr. 28, 1933; E pub. 36200; White-Smith music pub. co. 9663

Czecho-Slovakian dance song; partsong, w C. F. M., popular melody arr. Charles F. Manney; male voices.

410

Fig. 2.6 Copyright notice for "El Condor Pasa. Inca Dance" from US Copyright Registry, 1933. Public domain.

Daniel Alomía Robles—the man in whose name "El Condor Pasa" is registered—was a Peruvian composer, folklorist, and collector. At the turn of the twentieth century, he traveled all over Peru, through the Amazon rainforest, and to remote villages in the Andes mountains to collect myths and legends and music. His collecting journeys even took him across the borders into Bolivia and Ecuador. His collection includes more than six hundred songs he recorded and transcribed and many others he collected with the help of correspondents around the country (Varallanos 1988, 31). He was also a published scholar of traditional music. Daniel Alomía Robles is most famous, however, neither as a collector nor as a scholar, but as a composer—one who frequently found inspiration in, cited, arranged, and recycled traditional melodies. In this, he resembles another accomplished folklore scholar and collector, better known in Europe and North America: his Hungarian contemporary, Béla Bartók.

Fig. 2.7 Daniel Alomía Robles (1871–1942). Public domain.

El Cóndor Pasa is originally the name of a zarzuela—a dramatic work of musical theater—that premiered in the Teatro Mazzi in Lima, Peru, in December 1913; with music by Daniel Alomía Robles and a libretto by Julio Badouin y Paz. The zarzuela is set in Cerro de Pasco, a mining town built in Quechua territory by the conquistadores in the sixteenth century around one of the richest silver deposits in the world. Its silver veins were largely exhausted by the end of the nineteenth century, first by the Spanish administration, then, after Peru's independence in 1821, by local patrónes and foreign interests, all making use of indigenous labor, sometimes coerced, at other times heavily exploited, in all cases with unspeakable toll in terms of human life and health, social fabric, and environment (Deustua 2000; Abeyta 2005; Bedoya Garland 1997; Dewind 1975). In 1902, a syndicate organized by US mining magnate James B. Haggin with J. P. Morgan, William Randolph Hearst, and the Vanderbilt heirs, among others, bought up local titles to the mines and consolidated them in the Cerro de Pasco Copper Company with headquarters in New York, near Washington Square Park, less than a mile from the studio in Greenwich Village where Simon and Garfunkel would later record *Bridge over Troubled Water* (Abeyta 2005, 139–140). After building a smelter and a railroad, the company began large-scale industrial copper mining operations in 1906 (McLaughlin 1945). In 1911–13, Haggin expanded his operations to Morococha, halfway between Lima and Cerro de Pasco, under what the vice president of the company later called the "skillful and forceful" direction of Harold Kingsmill (McLaughlin 1945, 510). Locally, the Cerro de Pasco Copper Company "came to be known simply (and disparagingly) as 'la compañía'" (Abeyta 2005, 192).

This is the background of the zarzuela. It dramatizes a conflict between indigenous miners in Cerro de Pasco (the "Indios") and the American bosses (the "Sajones"), following a labor dispute. The sympathy is with the miner Higinio when he kills the mean and exploitative company boss, Mr. King. The old boss, however, is soon replaced by the new boss, Mr. Cup, and the fight continues. The condor soaring above stands for the freedom the miners fight for and for Incan pride in the face of foreign exploitation.

The zarzuela nourished anti-imperial sentiments and cultivated a leftist brand of Peruvian nationalism on the eve of the centennial celebrations of the country's independence. The Cerro de Pasco Copper Company was by far the largest US corporation exploiting the mineral wealth of Peru. In fact, its investment in Cerro de Pasco and Morococha was the largest investment made in copper mining in the world up till then (Clayton 1999, 87). One historian remarks that the company "functioned as a virtual autonomous economic and political entity within the Peruvian nation" (McArver 1977, quoted in Clayton 1999, 112).

In 1916, an American commentator wrote, "It would be hard to find a dirtier town than Cerro de Pasco," adding that indigenous homes were "indescribably filthy." The gringo managers, on the other hand, had "a well-kept bowling alley, swimming pool, gymnasium, billiard room, reading room, library, dance hall, card room, bar, and barber shop, plus tennis court outside" (Clayton 1999, 117).

The audience at the Teatro Mazzi was invited to identify with defiant indigenous miners who rose against the gringo neo-imperialists. It is not likely, however, that many in the audience were indigenous. Most will have been blue-collar laborers or middle class, politically liberal or radical, and ethnically mestizo, that is of mixed ancestry. The zarzuela *El Cóndor Pasa* celebrated mestizo identity; its main protagonist, Frank, is born of a white father and an indigenous mother, and he is identified with the condor, who embodies all good hopes for the future. The Teatro Mazzi in the Plaza Italia in Lima was the venue for other radical social dramas in this period; associated with the nascent labor unions, it was attended by working-class audiences (as opposed to the more prestigious and conservative Teatro Principal, which catered to the upper crust) (Toledo Brückmann 2011).

El Cóndor Pasa inscribed itself into a cultural-political movement in Peru and neighboring countries known as *Indigenismo*, which made a strong mark in the early decades of the twentieth century. Indigenismo might be described as the cultural logic of a postcolonial nationalism that swept through Latin America in the first half of the century under conditions of an emerging capitalism and class-based politics (Abercrombie 2001). Indigenismo was an attempt to forge an autonomous and inclusive national identity against the "utopian horizon" of the Inca and an imagined indigeneity (Flores Galindo 2010, 152–196). This was an enormous challenge in Peru, with its multiple ethnic groups and languages; with mountains, rainforests, and coast; with vast economic disparities and a colonial legacy still very much in evidence. Many scholars have emphasized that the

Fig. 2.8 Advertisement for the premiere of *El Condor Pasa* in Teatro Mazzi, Lima, 19 December 1913, from Peruvian Newspaper, *La Nacion*. Public domain.

cultural project of Indigenismo is intimately allied with the ideology of cultural and racial mixing known as *mestizaje*, designed to "shape homogeneous citizens for the nation-state" (Bigenho 2006, 268). As anthropologist Michelle Bigenho and ethnomusicologist Henry Stobart note, "In the first half of the twentieth century, Andean indigenous cultural expressions . . . went from being disdained by mestizos to being the core of a national project . . . *Indigenismo* nationalized and celebrated these indigenous expressions, but without challenging the structures that continued to marginalize the country's indigenous peoples" (2016, 144; see also Mendoza 1998).

The zarzuela that premiered in Lima in 1913 was on the cusp of this movement. In the second and third decades of the twentieth century, there was an "explosion of voices on indigenous matters" (Coronado 2009, 14) as intellectuals, artists, and politicians in Lima and the provinces began to recuperate and disseminate "the figure of the indigenous—of Indian popular tradition, dress, and folklore—as a means of redefining national cultural paradigms" (Williams 2002, 43). In the libretto for *El Cóndor Pasa*, it is the mestizo who emerges as a symbol of Peru's future, a dialectical solution to the contradictions of the ruling *criollo* class, and the conquered indigenous population. The mestizo is both and neither: Frank is a new man for a new century. The music that Daniel Alomía Robles wrote to the zarzuela follows a parallel logic. It is a showcase of musical Indigenismo, a musical experiment in national unification. The score to *El Cóndor Pasa* follows a tripartite structure, beginning in the *yaraví* genre, moving into a *pasacalle*, and culminating in the *huayno* genre. Each of these genres is associated with a distinct geographic area, social class, and ethnic identity, but in Robles's music they compose a whole, bigger than the parts. Likewise, the instrumentation of the score fuses Peru's social and musical divisions, with the European guitar and mandolin strumming together with the colonial-era *charango* while precolonial wind instruments like the *quena* flute and *siku* panpipe play the melody. In brief, Spanish, indigenous, and mestizo musical traditions come together in the music and instrumentation of *El Cóndor Pasa* to create something new: modern Peruvian music, anchored in the past but appealing to a national constituency in the present, above and beyond the divisions of language, geography, race, and class (Dorr 2007; Turino 1988, 131–132; Varallanos 1988).

The final part of the score caught on: the melody played at the end of the zarzuela, as its climax. When passing through Lima, the French folklorists Raoul and Marguerite d'Harcourt saw *El Cóndor Pasa* in the Teatro Mazzi in 1913 or 1914. The couple noted that afterward they heard street musicians playing the tune (1925, 542–544; Rios 2008, 160). In other words, it was an instant hit.

But whose hit? Whose is this tune? Is it an original composition by Daniel Alomía Robles? Or did he "merely" arrange music that he collected in the Andes? In a sense, we know what he did; the question is what to call it. The answer depends on what we mean by original and what we mean by arrangement. If Robles registered the tune as his own, that is no more than most collector-composers of his generation did—it was common practice, not only in South America but also in North America, Europe, and Asia.

Regardless of the degree of Robles's original contribution to the tune, we may say for sure that in the Teatro Mazzi, oral musical tradition passed into written musical tradition. The beauty of it is that the tune, thus modified, then passed right back into the oral musical tradition of street musicians in Lima.

The d'Harcourts published the melody as the last piece (no. 204) in their book, *Inca Music and Its Survivals* from 1925, under the title "Wayno" (i.e., huayno) and with the notation "heard in the street" ("entendu dans la rue"). Their commentary follows the music:

> This piece offers an interesting example of how, in all countries, folk melodies are fixed, or rather of how they are transformed and modeled. The melody of this fragment came originally from the folk; it is an indigenous theme that Mr. A. Robles, whom we have previously mentioned, used in a small lyrical story, *El Cóndor Pasa* . . . , staged with success in Lima. From this work, the folk has retained the fragments that were already familiar to it, and it is one of these fragments that street musicians tried to reproduce from memory; we have in turn tried to transcribe it as we heard them play it. (d'Harcourt and d'Harcourt 1925, 544; my translation)

Indeed, according to his biographer, historian José Varallanos, Daniel Alomía Robles himself acknowledged that the huayno movement—the hit, that is—was based on a traditional melody, "Soy la paloma que el nido perdió" (I am the Dove Lost from the Nest) (1988, 62, also 20, 29, 56, 61–62, 70; see also Llórens Amico

1983, 100–105, and Tucker 2013, 45; cf. Salazar Mejía 2014). The genre was certainly common in the Cerro de Pasco mining district where the zarzuela is set as well as in the Peruvian Andes and across the borders in parts of Bolivia, Ecuador, and the north of Argentina.

Actually, the French folklorist couple, Raoul and Marguerite d'Harcourt, also recorded a variant in the Jauja province of Peru. It appears in their book as melody no.47, complete with lyrics in Quechua and French: "I raised a dove / And loved her with all my heart. / Is that why she leaves me, / When I have done nothing to hurt her?" (d'Harcourt and d'Harcourt 1925, 303–304; my translation).[4] Thus both our song (as performed by street musicians in Lima) and the song from which it was adapted, about the dove lost from the nest (as performed by musicians in Jauja), may be found within the covers of La musique des Incas et ses survivances, separated by some 240 pages.

In March 1917, two sound technicians from the Victor Talking Machine Corporation (later acquired by RCA, which in turn was acquired by Sony Music Entertainment, which also acquired Columbus, Simon and Garfunkel's label) set out on a recording trip from the company headquarters in Camden, New Jersey, to Argentina, Chile, Bolivia, Peru, and Ecuador. They arrived by boat in Lima in August, and over the next three weeks they recorded a number of Peruvian artists. On August 27, they recorded Lima's zoo café orchestra, la Orquesta del Zoològico, performing the hit huayno from the zarzuela El Cóndor Pasa. Two days later, the technicians recorded another version of "El Condor Pasa," performed by the Banda del Batallón Gendarmes No. 1, the band of the military police's first battalion. The Victor Talking Machine Corporation released both recordings on 10-inch discs.

In 1919, Daniel Alomía Robles moved to New York. His solo piano version of the last movement of El Cóndor Pasa was published in the United States in 1923 and 1928 as sheet music with the title "Inca Dance." His music was performed in concerts in Central Park, on university campuses, and at gatherings of the Pan American Union in Washington, DC, by, among others, Edwin Franko Goldman's Goldman Band and the United States Marine Band. In 1930, the Marine Band recorded the song for a Columbia Records album. Then, in 1933, Robles transferred his rights in the song to the Edward B. Marks Music Company, which registered it in his name in the US copyright registry. That same year Robles moved back to Peru, but five years later Edward B. Marks released its own recording of the song on The Other Americas: Album of Typical Central and South American Songs and Dances (Rios 2008, 160; Varallanos 1988, 23–24).

As an attentive reader will have noticed, this story moves back and forth between Cerro de Pasco, Lima, and New York. That is equally true of the story the zarzuela tells and the story of the subsequent circulation of its score. But the latter also takes us across the Atlantic, to Paris. Starting in the 1950s, a growing number of Latin American musicians moved to Paris, and more than one club opened dedicated to Latin American music. Music from the Andes, in particular, was in high vogue, though most of the musicians actually came from cosmopolitan lowland Buenos Aires and not from the Andes at all (Rios 2006).

It is here, in Paris, in the 1960s, that *El Cóndor Pasa* is a hit, once again—not the whole zarzuela, but the closing melody; the huayno that caught the ear of street musicians in Lima. The Ensemble Achalay was probably the first to record it, an ad hoc group of Argentinian and Italian musicians living in Paris, including Ricardo Galeazzi and Jorge Milchberg: it is the last track on their album from 1958, *Musiques Indiennes des Andes*. According to ethnomusicologist Fernando Rios, they picked the song up from a Peruvian recording (2008, 161; 2005, 440).[5] In 1963, Los Incas, the first and best-known Andean music ensemble in France, released another version of "El Condor Pasa," with a considerably different arrangement, on their album *Amérique du Sud*. Rios has noted that Los Incas were already a musical sensation: a fixture at Paris's Latin American clubs, sometimes with Brigitte Bardot on vocals, performing at the Olympia concert hall with French singer Marie Laføret, having even played at Grace Kelly's wedding to Prince Rainier in Monaco in 1956. Both Galeazzi and Milchberg were members of Los Incas; both performed "El Condor Pasa" on the 1958 Achalay as well as the 1963 Incas albums (2008, 148–162).

Those who know Simon and Garfunkel's version have listened to Los Incas: they play the song on *Bridge over Troubled Water*. Paul Simon visited Paris in 1965, while he lived in England, shortly before he hit the big time. Backstage at a concert in the Théâtre de l'Est parisien, he was introduced to Jorge Milchberg, who gave Simon a copy of *Amérique du Sud*. Later, Simon got Milchberg's permission to use the 1963 recording of "El Condor Pasa" on *Bridge over Troubled Water* (Rios 2008, 161; Kingston 1997, 107). Paul Simon dubbed the track with his own voice, singing his own, original lyrics: "I said, 'I love this melody. I'm going to write lyrics to it. I just love it, and we'll just sing it right over the track'" (Luftig 1997, 86–87).

On the album sleeve, the producer lists the song as "an 18th century Peruvian folk melody" but also credits Jorge Milchberg as composer, under the pseudonym "El Inca," and Paul Simon for lyrics. Most artists who covered the song in the following years did the same. When the royalties poured in, Milchberg's bandmates in Los Incas were none too happy; it seemed to some of them that Milchberg had taken the credit while they didn't see a cent. The band broke up (Rios 2005, 635). Some of its musicians, however, led by Jorge Milchberg, joined Simon and Garfunkel on a world tour under the new band name of Urubamba. Legal proceedings made it unfeasible to use the previous band name for a while, as Milchberg's attribution "pitted him in a protracted legal battle with the family of Daniel Alomía Robles" (Rios 2005, 635n388; 2008, 172, 181n78).

In the lawsuit he filed with a New York City magistrate, Armando Robles Godoy claimed the song was neither an eighteenth-century folk melody nor

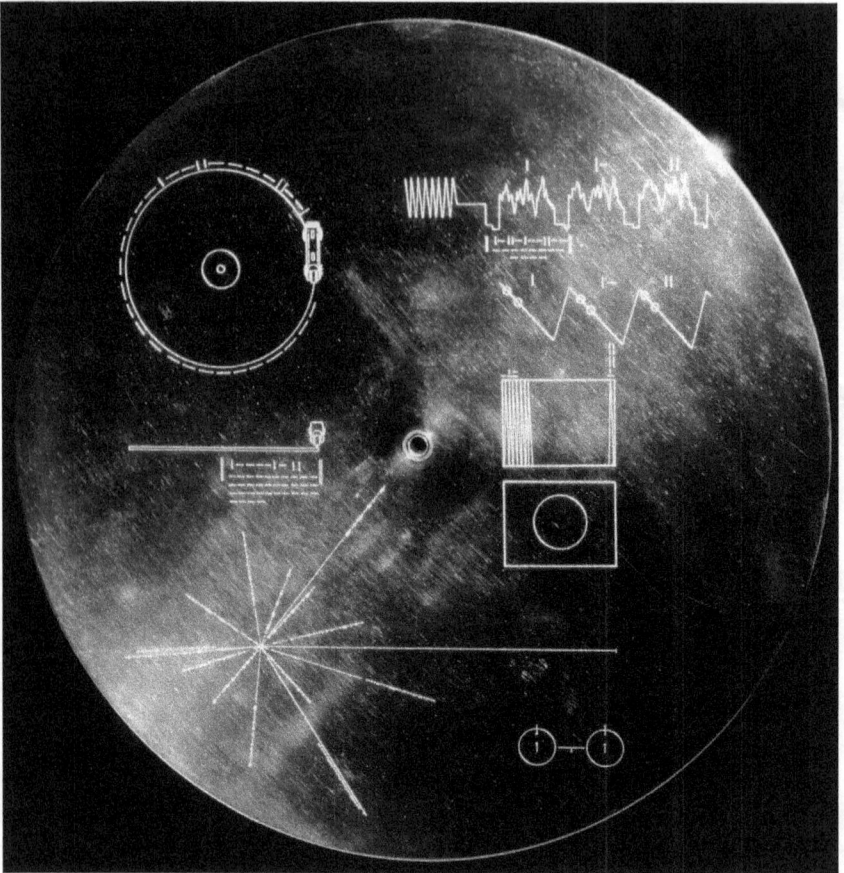

Fig. 2.9 Sounds of Earth. Cover for the Golden Record on the Voyager spacecrafts. NASA/ Public domain.

the work of Milchberg, but a composition by his father, copyrighted in 1933 and registered in the US Copyright Registry. Unlike Milchberg, Paul Simon soon settled: "It was almost a friendly case," the plaintiff said in an interview three and a half decades later: "Not only is Paul Simon a genius, he is also someone who loves culture. It wasn't a case of neglect on his part. . . . They told him it was a folk melody from the eighteenth century, and not that it was a composition by my father" (Bondy 2008, 4–5; my translation). Two years later, in 1972, Simon and Garfunkel's *Greatest Hits* album gave triple author credits for "El Condor Pasa": Robles/Simon/Milchberg.

The rest, as they say, is history. In the next few years, the song traveled the world a thousand times over, appearing on albums and cassettes in dozens of different places, and street performers carried it to town squares across the world. They are playing it still, in a street near you. I'm willing to wager you've heard them perform it.

The condor's farthest journey is still ongoing with no end in sight. In 1977, NASA sent two Voyager spacecraft to study the boundaries of the solar system. Moving at nearly 50,000 km/hour, at the time of writing, Voyager 1, traveling north, has entered interstellar space, while Voyager 2 is southward bound and soon out of the solar system. No man-made object has ever traveled farther. Forty years after their launch these probes still have another forty thousand years to go before either may come remotely close to another star. To put that span of time into perspective, the last of the Neanderthals roamed the earth forty thousand years ago. Both Voyagers carry a special message for intelligent extraterrestrials who might find them in a remote future when humanity may long have ceased to exist: a golden record, with greetings from the people of earth, images, natural sounds, poetry, an address from Jimmy Carter and good wishes from Kurt Waldheim, and—here's the kicker—a selection representing the music of humankind. It includes Mozart's "The Queen of the Night's Aria," Javanese gamelan music, Mexican mariachi, a *Brandenburg Concerto* by Bach, Beethoven's fifth symphony, an Australian horn and totem song, "Johnny B. Goode" with Chuck Berry, and— guess what—a panpipes and drum Song (or fifty-five seconds of it) recorded in Peru (archived at the Casa de la Cultura in Lima), a version of "El Condor Pasa," or of the traditional melody on which it is based—"Soy la paloma que el nido perdió"—"I am the Dove Lost from the Nest." And lost it is (Sagan et al. 1978; Brown, Cantillo, Landau, and Cook 2017).[6]

In 2004, Peru's National Institute of Culture (an institute of the Cultural Ministry) officially declared "El Condor Pasa" a national cultural heritage of Peru—a formal recognition of great distinction (Trujillo 2012). This recognition is also part of a continuing national campaign to make it known that this is a Peruvian song—not a Simon and Garfunkel song; not some generic Andean song; not a Bolivian folk tune; but a Peruvian masterpiece by one of Peru's maestros: Robles. "From now on," the director of the National Institute of Culture argued in an interview with *La República*, "no modification of the original version can be accepted" (Escribano 2004).

Meanwhile there is still grumbling across the Bolivian border, and voices may still be heard saying, as they have been saying since at least the 1960s, that "El Condor Pasa" is actually a Bolivian song. Thus, there was no less outrage in Bolivia than in Peru over Simon and Garfunkel's release in 1970. Fernando Rios cites a La Paz gossip columnist, Lolita, who chastised the Bolivian Ministry of Culture that year for "failing to charge the duo for the appropriation of this 'national tune'" (2014, 217), and he adds that Bolivian musicians "have often asserted to me that El Condor Pasa is Bolivian" (2005, 636n391).

Conversely, there was a media furor in Peru in September 2009 when the vice president of the Peruvian parliament, Wilbert Bendezú, publicly railed against the usurpation of "El Condor Pasa" by several official Bolivian websites associated with the state, promoting Bolivia in part with a performance of this song without due acknowledgment of its authorship or national origins. The story made television and radio news and headlines in the papers for three days in a row and was the subject of excited discussions and colorful accusations (Correo 2009a, 2009b; EcoDiario 2009; Los Andes 2009; RPP Notícias 2009d, 2009e).

On the third day, Pablo Groux, Bolivian minister of cultures, finally issued an announcement declaring that "the composer of this song is Peruvian and although many groups from Peru, Ecuador, and Chile perform it, its authorship is not in doubt" (RPP Notícias 2009e my translation). He contrasted this case with that of "La Diablada" (The Dance of the Devil), a traditional dance in masks and costumes, which was at the center of another dispute between Bolivia and Peru over cultural appropriation one month earlier.

"La Diablada" is a highlight of Bolivia's Oruro Carnival and it figures on UNESCO's Representative List of the Intangible Cultural Heritage of Humanity. Characterized by "grotesque masks with terrifying teeth and huge horns covered with serpents and lizards and bulging eyes," the devil dancers are dressed in "shimmering capes studded with colored stones and sequins, the breastplates with their golden dragons, and the heavy aprons with hundreds of antique coins sewn on" (Guss 2006, 312–313).

In August 2009, Miss Peru, Karen Schwarz, represented her country in a stylized costume inspired by "La Diablada" in the Miss Universe beauty pageant, claiming it as typical Peruvian heritage. This set into motion street protests in the Bolivian capital, with Diablada dancers sending a message to their government, to the beauty queen, and to the world that they would not tolerate the filching of what was rightfully theirs. The Bolivian ambassador to UNESCO demanded "that urgent, adequate, opportune and pertinent measures be taken to protect Bolivian cultural patrimony and the respect of the origin of our customs and ancient traditions" (CNN 2009). At the same time, the minister of cultures, Pablo Groux, sent a letter to the pageant's organizers and its owner, the real estate tycoon and reality television star Donald Trump, threatening a lawsuit and citing evidence that "La Diablada" is from Bolivia and belongs to its people (Emol. Mundo 2009a). "La Diablada is as Bolivian as Pisco is Peruvian" (Clarin Notícias 2009; my translation), he asserted, referring to the fiery grape brandy that Peru and Chile each claim as their own. Groux even threatened Peruvian authorities that he would refer this grievous appropriation of Bolivian national culture to the International Court of Justice in The Hague and to the World Intellectual Property Organization in Geneva (Clarin Notícias 2009; Emol.Mundo 2009b).

Peru's foreign minister, José Antonio García Belaúnde, dared Groux to make good on his threat, adding that he was sure it would be clear to the court that "La

Diablada" is an Aymara tradition and that it could therefore not be the exclusive property of any of the three Andean countries where the Aymara are indigenous, Peru, Bolivia, and Chile (*Emol.Mundo* 2009b). Cecilia Bakula also dismissed the claim as director of Peru's National Institute of Culture (the following year she became Peru's ambassador to UNESCO). She argued that Bolivia has no grounds to claim the dance, adding "We have not 'appropriated' anyone's cultural patrimony. It is ours" (*Latino Perspectives Magazine* 2009). She cited documentary evidence of "La Diablada" from the city of Puno in Peru, dating back to 1892, while the best-known Diablada in Bolivia, in the Carnival of Oruro, only dated back to 1904. It must be added that Bakula is cherry picking her evidence, as 1904 is the year that a long-standing tradition was institutionalized with the formation of an organized dance troupe, la Gran Tradicional Auténtica Diablada Oruro (the Great Traditional Authentic Diablada of Oruro)—the name says it all (*Andina* 2009; *Emol.Mundo* 2009b; *RPP Noticias* 2009c; see also Abercrombie 1992; Cordova 2012).

Indeed, "La Diablada" is emblematic of the Bolivian carnival, with the devils standing in for the underworld of the Oruro mines, dancing in honor of the Virgin of the Mineshaft (la Virgen del Sovacón). Thus, Bolivian folklorist, Jorge Enrique Vargas Luza, author of a monograph on the masking traditions of "La Diablada" in Oruro (Vargas Luza 1998), made known to the international press his indignation that Miss Peru could claim that the Diablada costume she wore in the contest was from her country (*RPP Noticias* 2009a). The Oruro Carnival was among the first cultural practices proclaimed as a UNESCO Masterpiece of the Oral and Intangible Heritage of Humanity in 2001, as part of its Proclamation program that preceded the Intangible Heritage Convention (see more on that in chapter 3). This recognition bolstered Bolivian confidence in the ownership of "La Diablada" in this polemic and in the popular indignation and political upheaval that ensued from Miss Peru's costume in the Miss Universe contest (Bigenho and Stobart 2016).

Meanwhile, Karen Schwarz, the pageant contestant, took the moral high ground as she patiently explained to the Bolivian media that "we have a dance that unites us because the Diablada is danced in Bolivia and Peru," adding that "we can't lose tolerance or respect between both countries" over petty grievances like this one (CNN 2009). "We are siblings, we are nearly one, we have practically the same costumes, the same culture, and we have bigger problems to solve or to fight over" (*RPP Noticias* 2009b; my translation). However, when Bolivia's president, Evo Morales, invited Ms. Schwarz to join him in dancing "La Diablada" in the Oruro Carnival, she declined, saying she would love to but alas she would be busy dancing "La Diablada" in Puno, Peru (*El Comercio* 2009; *Telemetro* 2009).[7]

Two weeks later, President Morales and his minister of cultures sent out a diplomatic invitation to the governments of Peru, Colombia, and Ecuador—their partners in the Andean Community trading bloc—to a meeting in La Paz to discuss the creation of a map of intangible heritage in the Andes, which would make clear once and for all what belongs to each country and what they share across national borders (*Emol.Mundo* 2009c). That seems not to have obviated the need for unilateral action, however. In 2011, Evo Morales signed a bill passed by the Bolivian parliament, declaring the Diablada dance to be the cultural and intangible heritage of the Plurinational State of Bolivia. Morales explained to those gathered that they needed law no. 149 of July 11, 2011, so "some neighboring countries do not take over our dances and our traditions, like the Diablada" (*La Razón* 2011). Copies were promptly dispatched to UNESCO in Paris and to the World Intellectual Property Organization (WIPO) in Geneva (WIPO, 2011).

In 2014, however, as Bigenho and Stobart describe, the Diablada dance in Puno, Peru, once again roused the Bolivian government, stirring up national indignation, "when several dances they considered to be their own appeared in a video that Peru had presented to UNESCO" (2016, 142) as part of the candidature of the Festival of Virgen de Candelaria of Puno for the Representative List of Intangible Cultural Heritage of Humanity. The Bolivian Organization for the Defense and Dissemination of Folklore organized a protest in front of UNESCO offices in La Paz, Bolivians in and outside of Bolivia mobilized online, and the Bolivian minister of cultures lodged a formal objection to Peru's nomination, accompanied by an eighteen-minute statement circulated on YouTube (156). He was not successful in preventing the festival's inscription on the Representative List, but in response to Bolivia's forceful protests, and following extended discussions, the Intergovernmental Committee in charge included two unusual articles in its decision to add the festival to the List, one "taking note" that "cultural expressions associated with the Festivity of Virgen de la Candelaria of Puno are shared by Andean communities from the region" and the other "recalling that inscription on the Representative List does not imply exclusivity" (UNESCO Intangible Cultural Heritage 2014). Following this fiasco, Evo Morales requested the minister's resignation.

Various scholars have noted the "ubiquitous nationalist discourse regarding transnational musical appropriation" in Bolivia, where outrage regularly flares up, usually directed at Argentines, Peruvians, or Chileans (Rios 2014, 198; Bigenho and Stobart 2016). Thus, already in 1965, a contributor to the Bolivian newspaper *El Diario*, outraged by what the writer saw as Chilean cultural appropriation, denounced the "exact imitation of the Diablada of Oruro," a "faithful copy of the Bolivian huayno," and the use of the *charango* and the *kena* among Chile's Nueva Canción musicians: "I do not know to whom one could denounce these actions. . . . I wish there was some international organization that one could approach like a Police Station when one denounces the theft of a wallet" (translated in Rios 2005, 542–543). In 1973, the year the Bolivian minister wrote the letter to UNESCO's director-general, such outrage was widespread. At the First Charango Congress in June, the director of the Ministry of Education and Culture charged that "foreign assailants" coveted the charango and promised "'radical measures' to protect 'ownership rights' over all local folklore," pledging that "the charango will be decreed a 'traditional Bolivian instrument'" (quoted in Rios 2014, 208). And in November that year, the Ministry of Education passed Resolution 823, "'Rules for the Protection of Folkloric Music, Declared the Property of the State,' whose ostensible aim was to curtail the 'continuous appropriation . . . inside and outside of the nation's territory' of Bolivia's 'folkloric expressions'" (209; see also Bigenho and Stobart 2016, 153).[8]

Recall the Bolivian minister's complaint to UNESCO in 1973 that Bolivia was especially susceptible to cultural appropriation because it is surrounded by foreign countries only too willing to steal its traditions? Well, "El Condor Pasa" and "La Diablada" are two cases in point, from the Bolivian perspective. Thirty-six years separate the Bolivian government's official complaints to UNESCO in these two cases, with an important distinction: in 1973, the minister bemoaned the lack of an international instrument to protect "forms of expression such as music and dance, which are at present undergoing the most intensive clandestine commercialization and export"; in 2009 such an instrument existed and "La Diablada" was already on its Representative List, as part of the Oruro Carnival in Bolivia. However, as gleaned from this episode, all it is good for is to allow Bolivians to cite international authority in their diplomatic hand-wringing over the Miss Universe act.

Of course, all that is from the Bolivian perspective. Peru offers an alternative view. As Karen Schwarz noted during the uproar around her costume in the Miss Universe contest, these cultural expressions are common across the political border. "La Diablada" is an Aymara dance and costume tradition, and exists on either side of various political borders that the Aymara have not taken part in drawing. Likewise, the musical genre to which "El Condor Pasa" belongs is common in Quechua musical tradition in Bolivia as well as in Peru.

We also know that Robles crossed the border on his collecting journeys. The Peruvian insistence on Robles's authorship must be understood, at least in part, as a cultural politics of ownership: if Daniel Alomía Robles is the composer, then the song is from Peru—none of this vagueness of oral and instrumental circulation that knows no border. An author is a citizen. Unlike oral tradition, the author carries a passport. And the Republic of Peru issued Robles's passport.

Let's return now to that Bolivian letter to UNESCO's director-general. Consider the political backdrop: the letter bears the signature of the minister of foreign affairs and religion of the Republic of Bolivia, Mario Gutiérrez, leader of the Falangist socialist party—a fascist. The government he represented was a military

Fig. 2.10 La Diablada Ferroviaria at the Carnival of Oruro, Bolivia, 2009. Creative Commons via Wikimedia Commons.

Fig. 2.11 La Diablada at the Fiesta de la Candelaria in Puno, Peru, 2013. Creative Commons via Wikimedia Commons.

Fig. 2.12 General Hugo Banzer Suárez, Bolivian dictator. Keystone Pictures USA/Alamy.

dictatorship, led by General Hugo Banzer Suárez who came to power by coup in 1971. Before it got around to sending the letter, this government had suspended the trade unions and shut down the universities; it tortured dissidents, interned some in concentration camps or prisons, and others disappeared without a trace.

Banzer's regime also had strained relations with indigenous groups. The Aymara and the Quechua lived in abject poverty in the highlands and towns of Bolivia, their lands confiscated and their identities suppressed in a "transcultura-tion" rather different in kind from the one that Banzer's minister complained about (Ströbele-Gregor 1996; Hylton and Thomson 2007). Already in 1953, the ruling Revolutionary Nationalist Movement (MRN) decreed that "Indios" no longer existed in Bolivia; from now on, they would be referred to as "campesi-nos," peasants. Meanwhile, the military regime celebrated indigenous expressive culture and appropriated it as the national-popular culture of the new mestizo Bolivia (Abercrombie 2001, 96–97; Rios 2010, 283–284).

General Banzer was in power during the golden age of the folkloric spec-tacle, which celebrates traditional costume and music and dance in colorful performances of national pride and harmony; indeed, the folkloric spectacle was a favorite form of entertainment under dictators, from Franco's Spain and Salazar's Portugal to Pinochet's Chile and Banzer's Bolivia (see DaCosta Holton

2005; Ortiz 1999; Guss 2000, 13). Thus the Bolivian ruler patronized folkloric festivals, hosted traditional music performances at the presidential palace, posed with indigenous music ensembles for newspaper photographers, and even led the dancers in the Gran Poder festival "all the way down the Prado, La Paz's most elegant commercial avenue" (Guss 2006, 315; Rios 2005, 481–485).

It is important to understand, then, that the Bolivian government's efforts to protect an indigenous Andean folksong, "El Condor Pasa"—and by extension, its efforts to protect other folk music, dance, and crafts—hide the real oppression of indigenous peoples within Bolivia in this period. In fact, the government's efforts to safeguard this expressive culture were part of its oppressive regime: a tool for cultural disenfranchisement. This is especially insidious because "El Condor Pasa" is a song of resistance, but through Supreme Decree no. 08396 it was nationalized, as the Bolivian government proclaimed state ownership of the folk music of its territory, and subsequently of "folk dance, popular art and traditional literature." Incidentally, the Supreme Decree was issued in 1968 by President René Barrientos, another military dictator much enamored of folklore. Banzer completed the work of expropriation through a resolution he issued in 1973 declaring traditional, anonymous, and popular music not only state property but also part of the national cultural heritage ("Patrimonio Cultural de la Nación"; Resolución Ministerial No 823 del 19.XI.1973, cited in Bigenho, Cordero, Mújica, Rozo, and Stobart 2015, 151). To borrow a phrase from Pete Townshend: meet the new boss, same as the old boss.

As a matter of fact, the South American dictators of the 1970s also appropriated the Andean condor, converting a symbol of defiance to a symbol of compliance enforced at gunpoint: along with Pinochet and others, Banzer was one of the ringleaders in "Operazion Condor," essentially an intergovernmental murder ring coordinated by intelligence agencies to quash dissent (McSherry 2005).

The lesson of "El Condor Pasa" thus extends well beyond the transnational flows of culture; beyond even its intergalactic circulation. Usually told as an account of origins, narrating how folklore was inscribed on the international agenda, the story offers an ethical rationale for safeguarding intangible heritage with concerted international efforts. At closer look, however, it complicates that provenance, muddies the ethics, and subverts the rationalization. When we scratch the surface, and persist in scratching, we soon come upon a different set of lessons about intangible heritage and its protection. These concern the uses of heritage in hegemonic strategies within states no less than its transnational circulation between them. What is more, these are difficult to disentangle. Invoking a threat from the outside—invaders, thieving neighbors, foreign corporations, or indeed "the most intensive clandestine commercialization and export"—justifies state intervention. It warrants urgent measures for protection. The threat from the outside is presented as a greater source of danger than the cultural politics of the state. In effect, protection itself becomes the means of dispossession: a cooptive strategy, draining symbols of resistance of their power, or shuffling their semiotics to invoke the state itself as signified, adjusting their emotional register to claim allegiance to the nation.

We speak always of ourselves, and the lexicon of theft in the minister's letter—of appropriation and depredation, of filching and usurpation—reflects critically on his regime and its cultural policy. Beyond Bolivia's borders, however, this story leaves us with a question, both current and critical as we hear stories from various parts of the world about the implementation of UNESCO's intangible heritage programs. The stories come from Marrakech and Catalonia, from Malawi and Korea and Kerala, for example, places where UNESCO has recognized particular practices as the intangible heritage of humanity and where local actors claim they are losing control over their cultural practices. Now that authorities have taken an interest in their traditional practices, they complain, an administrative grid is superimposed on these practices to safeguard them. Once their practices are translated into the language of intangible heritage, local actors no longer have as much of a say in the work of representation.

The question concerns the relationship between communities and states, between empowerment and subjection, between heritage and governmentality. It is a question that is as crucial to theorizing intangible heritage as it is to writing it into policy and putting it into practice. When is protection not a means of dispossession? I'm not presupposing an answer and I'm not assuming there is none; it's not a rhetorical question. When, that is under what conditions and which circumstances, is protection not a means of dispossession?

Notes

1. I tell a condensed version of this story in a 30-minute documentary film released at the same time as this book is published, and freely available online in Open Access. Co-produced with anthropologist and filmmaker Áslaug Einarsdóttir, the film is titled *The Flight of the Condor: A Letter, a Song and the Story of Intangible Cultural Heritage*. Look it up!

2. Actually, we are always already there. The memorandum accompanying the minister's letter was composed by the prolific Bolivian folklorist Julia Elena Fortún (Vargas 2014, 65), who created the Departamento de Folklore of the Bolivian Ministry of Education and Culture in 1954, was founding president of the Sociedad Boliviana de Antropología from 1961, established the Museo Nacional de Arte Popular in 1962 and later became the ministry's director-general of culture, a position from which she founded both the Instituto Nacional de Antropología and the Ballet Folklórico Nacional in 1975 and organized the first Conferencia Nacional de Folklore in 1976. Fortún was also a prolific author and published books on the indigenous music of Bolivia, calendrical customs in Bolivia, the Diablada dance, popular crafts, foodways, festivals, and cultural politics (Vargas 2014, 35–70). Julia Elena Fortún was decorated in 1979 with the highest civilian distinction awarded by the Bolivian state, the Orden del Cóndor de los Andes. Thanks to folklorist Áki G. Karlsson for bringing her authorship of the memorandum to my attention.

3. Thus, in a UNESCO briefing paper from 2001, anthropologist Néstor García Canclini cites "the well-known example of the appropriation of the traditional Bolivian song El condor

Pasa by Simon and Garfunkel" to "illustrate the need for transnational legislation that could regulate the global use and diffusion of ethnic music" (2001, 15).

4. It may be noted in this context that Daniel Alomía Robles served as justice of the peace in Jauja in the last years of the nineteenth century, during the period of his travels and field-work in Peru, and that is where met his future wife, Sebastiana Godoy Agostini.

5. As Rios shows in ethnographic detail, musicians "from the Andean countries played little part at first in bringing the music of the Andes to Europe. Initially, the main protagonists were expatriate Argentines from Buenos Aires who had learned to perform highland Andean instruments and genres while living in Paris" (2008, 171).

6. The music for the Golden Record was chosen by a committee that astrophysicist Carl Sagan chaired, advised by folklorist Alan Lomax, who played a crucial role in proposing and advocating the inclusion of music outside the classical Western canon, including blues, jazz, rock'n'roll, and popular music from around the world. In his book on this project, *Murmurs of Earth: The Voyager Interstellar Record*, Sagan wrote that Lomax "was a persistent and vig-orous advocate for including ethnic music even at the expense of Western classical music. He brought pieces so compelling and beautiful that we gave in to his suggestions more often than I would have thought possible. There was, for example, no room for Debussy among our selections, because Azerbaijanis play bagpipe-sounding instruments [balaban] and Peruvians play panpipes and such exquisite pieces had been recorded by ethnomusicologists known to Lomax" (Sagan et al. 1978, 16). One of these "ethnomusicologists known to Lomax" was Peru-vian novelist, folklorist, and ethnologist José María Arguedas, who collected, studied, and published indigenous music and dance, and was officially appointed as "conservador general de folklore" by the Ministry of Education in 1946 before he became director of the National Museum of History and, later, of La Casa de la Cultura (which later became the National Insti-tute of Culture, or INC) (Cerrón Fetta 2017; Casas Ballón 2017). Arguedas recorded the "Pan-pipes and Drum song" featured on the Golden Record and made the recording available to Alan Lomax. It is credited to La Casa de la Cultura, but comes without further attribution.

In his book on the Golden Record project, *Murmurs of Earth*, Sagan writes of the Peru-vian "Panpipes and Drum Song": "The Voyager selection is played on one of these two-row panpipes. Hollow wood sticks are cut to different lengths, open at the top; sound is produced by blowing across the opening. The ramshackle, irregular tempo of the drum accompani-ment is intentional and evidences no lack of expertise; the player deliberately manipulates the rhythm in favor of the unexpected. It may be played here by a one-man band. Musicians play-ing panpipes and drum simultaneously can be seen on pottery painted in Peru prior to Inca conquest, and on the streets of Peruvian cities today" (Sagan et al. 1978, 190).

7. It is interesting to compare this row with the rather more sober assessment of Bolivian statesman Mariano Baptista Gumucio, who was minister of education and culture in 1969–70, before Hugo Banzer's coup d'état in 1971, and again in the first civilian government after Banzer was toppled in 1979 (and later Bolivian ambassador to the United States). Before he took office in 1979, at the request of the Bolivian National Commission for UNESCO, Baptista Gumucio prepared a study of cultural policy in Bolivia for a UNESCO series called "Studies and Documents on Cultural Policies." In a chapter titled "Looting of Works of Art and Folk Culture," Baptista Gumucio wrote:

> Another aspect of the loss of works of art and of cultural identity is the appro-priation by other South American countries of songs, dances and masques from the native and mestizo folk culture of Bolivia; and it is aggravated by the fact that, in these countries, unscrupulous individuals record and sell them as their own, receiv-ing royalties for them, which is quite dishonest.

The complaints of Bolivian musicians and composers are directed particularly at Argentina, although the matter is not so simple. The point is that Argentina has about 500,000 Bolivian immigrants, many of them labourers working initially on the sugar harvest and who have stayed on to live in the villas miseria or shanty-towns of Buenos Aires and other cities and towns. This enormous body of workers of native origin takes with it its cultural tradition, its music and other forms of folk culture, which come to be considered as products of the north of Argentina. Furthermore, this region was at one time settled by the Aymaras and Quechuas, and there are Quechua-speaking towns in the country whose folk culture is similar to that of Bolivia.

This appropriation of typically Bolivian cultural forms is particularly evident in the imitations which dance troupes from the south of Peru and the Chilean pampas have been making in the last few years, by presenting the traditional Diablada of the miners of Oruro as their own creation.

An agreement between the governments involved could put a stop to the illegal appropriation and dissemination of folk culture and popular songs, through the organization of effective machinery for mutual communication and rapid sanctions. (1979, 78)

8. Fernando Rios suggests that the specific incident prompting the Bolivian letter to UNESCO may have been a controversy surrounding the film *Argentinísima*, which premiered in La Paz four days before the letter is dated. It bears noting, however, that controversy surrounding the film did not flare up in Bolivia until two weeks after its first screening, ten days after the letter is dated. For more detail, see Rios 2014.

CHAPTER 3

Making Lists

The Dance-Band in the Hospital

PERHAPS THE MOST controversial issues in the negotiation of the Convention for the Safeguarding of the Intangible Cultural Heritage concerned the creation, designation, and purpose of its lists. The final text provides for three types: a Representative List of the Intangible Cultural Heritage of Humanity, a List of Intangible Cultural Heritage in Need of Urgent Safeguarding, and national inventories of intangible heritage. The first of these is a compromise solution reached after intense confrontations among national delegates who wanted a merit-based "List of Treasures" or "List of Masterpieces" similar to the World Heritage List, those who preferred an inclusive universal inventory of traditional practices, and those who wanted no list at all. In the final text, the provisions for the Representative List were left vague enough to postpone the debate until after the convention entered into force.

In what follows, I analyze the arguments put forward by delegates in the debate on listing—from incentive and promotion value to divisiveness and hierarchization—and I argue that these go to the heart of heritage practices, which are always and inevitably selective. The system of heritage is structured on exclusion: it gives value to certain things rather than others with reference to an assortment of criteria that can only ever be indeterminate. In this respect, heritage and lists are not unlike one another: both depend on selection, and both decontextualize their objects from their immediate surroundings and recontextualize them with reference to other things designated or listed. It is hardly surprising that listing seems constantly to accompany heritage making. Heritage lists fuse esthetic, ethical, and administrative concerns in a rather unique fashion. They celebrate the virtues of particular populations while fueling a cultural contest among them. Making a people visible to itself and their practices to the world at large, such lists are ultimately designed to channel funds and attention to safeguarding. Once they have been made and are available for circulation, however, lists take on a life of their own; they can be put to uses quite unlike—even diametrically opposed to—those their creators had in mind. The World Heritage List is a case in point, with tourism gradually taking precedence over preservation as its driving concern and principal context of use. The same may be said of the Representative List.

Shooting Diplomats

As a member of the Icelandic delegation to UNESCO, I observed and took part in the third session of the Intergovernmental Meeting of Experts on the Preliminary Draft Convention for the Safeguarding of the Intangible Cultural Heritage that took place in June 2003 (the two previous sessions were held in September 2002 and February 2003). The session was held in a large conference room in the basement of UNESCO headquarters at Place Fontenoy in Paris and the task it set itself was to finish the work on this new convention to propose it to UNESCO's General Conference for adoption (see chapter 1).

Before the June session, the UNESCO secretariat distributed to delegates a draft they had themselves negotiated at the previous session (and a smaller intersessional committee had then refined). In one of its articles, this draft convention proposed to create a "List of Treasures of the World Intangible Cultural Heritage," or alternatively a "List of Masterpieces of Intangible Cultural Heritage." The first paragraph of this article provided that this list should be established, kept up to date, and published to "ensure better visibility of the intangible cultural heritage, to promote awareness of its significance and encourage dialogue" (UNESCO 2003a, Appendix II, 9).

The trajectory of this idea may be traced to a formal proposal from the Korean Republic in 1993 to establish a UNESCO system of Living Cultural Properties. Later that year, the executive board of UNESCO responded with a resolution (UNESCO 1993) in which it invited member states to establish, where appropriate, a system of Living Human Treasures in their respective territories (UNESCO 2002a, 8).[1] The Korean proposal suggested that as part of this new program UNESCO would establish "its own Committee on Living Human Treasures, whose functions are similar to those of the World Heritage Committee"; that the committee, once established, would "institute a World Living Human Treasures List, similar to the World Heritage List"; and added that "to institute this system, a convention on living human treasures may be needed" (UNESCO 1993, 2).

This comparison to the World Heritage Convention is key for understanding developments in this area within UNESCO. The Convention Concerning the Protection of the World Cultural and Natural Heritage (its official title) was adopted by the General Conference in 1972 and has been one of UNESCO's great successes. In terms of the number of states that have ratified it, the World Heritage Convention numbers among the most successful of all international conventions; at the time of writing, 193 states are parties to it, following closely on the Geneva Convention (196), the Convention on the Rights of the Child (196), and the Convention on Biological Diversity (195). That makes it practically universal. The associated World Heritage List has been a great public relations coup for UNESCO and is no doubt what the organization is best known for in many parts of the world. With 178 states ratifying in fifteen years, the Convention for the Safeguarding of the Intangible Cultural Heritage is already a great success by the same measure.[2]

The Korean Republic's proposed world list of living human treasures was, as their proposal made clear, modeled on the World Heritage List and its associated legal instrument and executive committee. Thus, Korea's proposal was to build on UNESCO's experience with world heritage, apparently in hopes of sharing in its success in that domain. UNESCO's executive board welcomed this proposal and expressed its "hope that if the national list proves successful, UNESCO could, as a next step, institute a world list" (quoted in UNESCO 2002a, 51). Four years later, in 1997, the General Conference adopted a resolution creating that list: the Proclamation of Masterpieces of the Oral and Intangible Heritage of Humanity.

Although modeled on the World Heritage List, the Proclamation of Masterpieces paled in comparison: it did not rest on a convention, was not equipped with an intergovernmental executive committee, and had no financial resources committed to it by member states at the General Conference. Instead, the Proclamation relied on an international jury appointed by the director-general and was altogether dependent on voluntary contributions for funding. Richard Kurin, acting provost of the Smithsonian Institution (at that time director of the Smithsonian's Center for Folklife and Cultural Heritage), was one of eighteen members of this jury. In a comment in *Current Anthropology* in 2002, he describes himself as a skeptical participant and readily grants that the jury was challenged: "Diverse colleagues of goodwill engaged in a difficult task about which there were substantial disagreements on terminology, concept, application, and interpretation. . . . We needed more information and better expert advice, more explicit action plans, and a better feel for how practitioners and community members were involved. We sometimes wrestled with the tension between a cultural relativistic view of human expressions and universalistic accords on human rights in deciding whether to deem a tradition treasured" (2002, 145).

Behind the scenes, the situation was no less complex. Filling me in on some of the things that never make the reports or minutes, Kurin told me that when the jury debated the merits of one particular nomination, a member of the jury argued for listing it because "otherwise, I will be shot when I come home" (Kurin, personal communication, August 1, 2017). Brutally honest, that argument betrays the diplomatic stakes in the jury's negotiations. Twenty-eight scholars, artists, princesses, and diplomats served on the eighteen-member jury for UNESCO's Proclamations (2001, 2003, 2005) from twenty-seven states (Japan had two). Twenty-one of these states (more than three-quarters) had at least one cultural element proclaimed as a masterpiece, and some more than one. That is one way to make a list.

Japanese Heritage

In the negotiations that led to the World Heritage Convention in 1972, the question of whether to create lists as instruments of the convention was also hotly debated (Titchen 1995, 147–151). The negotiations focused on the creation of a trust fund for conserving the world's outstanding heritage, an expression of international solidarity in heritage conservation, and not on producing lists. In fact, an intergovernmental meeting of experts in 1969 declared that it would not be useful to establish an "international register" of monuments, groups of buildings, and sites of universal value (though some participants felt that a "limited list" of immovable heritage in danger would be helpful to "alert world opinion") (148). The World Heritage List of cultural and natural heritage of "outstanding universal value" was only added late in the game: in a reversal of its previous opposition and in the face of resistance from some delegations, the United States government threatened to withdraw its support for the convention unless it provided for a World Heritage List (150–151; see also Schuster 2002, 2).

By creating the Proclamation of Masterpieces in 1997, UNESCO's General Conference brought into being the list that the Republic of Korea had proposed in 1993, though it was by no means equivalent yet to the World Heritage List. In his preface to the first Proclamation brochure from 2001, UNESCO director-general Koichiro Matsuura explains that the Proclamation program is the first of "two complementary and parallel lines of action"; it addresses short-term goals. "The second, the preparation of a normative instrument for the safeguarding of intangible heritage, has long-term objectives" (UNESCO 2001a, 2). "In time," the director-general asserts, "these two programmes will inevitably become even more effective by their combination" (UNESCO 2001a, 3). That was the plan all along.[3]

The first Asian director-general in UNESCO's history, Matsuura, a Japanese career diplomat and ambassador to France, directed the organization for a decade from 1999 to 2009. A former chair of the World Heritage Committee, Matsuura concerned himself a great deal with the cultural sector. Any number of witnesses will corroborate the testimony of a UNESCO administrator, who readily acknowledged, "Matsuura really, really pushed this [intangible heritage] convention very much" (personal communication, November 26, 2003). In this, Matsuura enjoyed the full support of the Japanese government, which had "organized fierce campaigns" for his election (Akagawa 2015, 111).

As heritage scholar Natsuko Akagawa has explored, cultural heritage is "a key component in Japan's foreign policy strategy to strengthen its presence on the international stage" (2015, 1) and UNESCO is the most important ground on which that strategy plays out (102–113). Japan became a UNESCO member in 1951, the year it regained sovereignty and rejoined the international community after World War II, five years before it joined the United Nations (Saikawa 2016). In the 1980s, Japan expanded its financial and technical assistance for conservation outside its borders and became a leading player in the international heritage field. When Ronald Reagan and Margaret Thatcher withdrew the United States and the United Kingdom from UNESCO in the mid-1980s (Imber 1989; Nordenstreng 2012), they left Japan as the leading contributor to UNESCO's budget. It took on a leadership role within the organization, setting up new Japan/ UNESCO Funds-in-Trust to sponsor even more of the organization's work with voluntary contributions and to shape its priorities. As a result, more Japanese specialists worked on UNESCO projects; and cultural heritage assumed an ever more central role in UNESCO's remit (Akagawa 2015, 44–46).

Even in light of Japan's extensive involvement in UNESCO affairs, its leadership in the domain of intangible heritage is remarkable. A report for an executive board meeting in May 2002 affirms that "the Japanese contribution has largely contributed to the sustainability of activities related to the Proclamation of Masterpieces, since a number of countries need assistance for compiling inventories of intangible heritage, preparing candidature files and implementing action plans" (UNESCO 2002c, 5). In the year 2000 alone, the Japan/UNESCO Funds-in-Trust supported the creation of candidature files from more than forty countries for the Proclamation program (2) in amounts of up to US$20,000 each. In addition, the Japanese funds supported the organization of the intergovernmental expert meetings necessary for the preparation of the new Intangible Heritage Convention, including costs incurred from subsidizing the attendance of delegates from developing countries—expenses that, according to another member of the secretariat, it is impossible to provide for from the regular budget (personal communication, November 25, 2004). As may be gleaned from this, the Japan/UNESCO Funds-in-Trust is a telling example of the extent to which member countries can influence a multilateral organization like UNESCO (where ambitions always outpace resources) through voluntary contributions to their preferred projects and policy areas, translating economic power into moral leadership.

Addressing the Intergovernmental Meeting of Experts in June 2003 on behalf of the director-general, Mounir Bouchenaki, assistant director-general for culture, thanked the government of Japan for its contribution "which has, once more, made it possible to hold a third session." Japan's contribution was the subject of much scuttlebutt during breaks in the meeting; I was apprised over several cups of coffee and lunch plates that Japan in fact covered the travel and living expenses of a great number of African delegations attending this meeting in Paris.

Japanese leadership in this arena is not limited to financial contributions. Noriko Aikawa, a UNESCO administrator from Japan, served as the chief of the organization's Intangible Heritage Section from 1993 to 2003. Aikawa was in charge of refocusing UNESCO's work in this area, steering it away from the previous archival documentation model of Western origins toward the Japanese/ Korean model of Living Human Treasures. Between the two of them, with political and financial backing from Japan and Korea, Matsuura and Aikawa successfully inscribed intangible heritage at the top of UNESCO's agenda.

In fact, the relationship of South Korea and Japan as collaborators and contenders in UNESCO's intangible heritage initiatives mirrors that of Spain and Italy in the initial phase of the World Heritage Convention (or so I learned from a member of UNESCO's secretariat). Italy eventually got the upper hand in that contest, much as Japan took the lead after Korea's early initiative in proposing Living Human Treasures systems to UNESCO's executive board. This comparison may guide us toward an alternative perspective on the alliance of Japan, Korea, and the African states, viewed with suspicion by many Western delegates. For its full implication to emerge, this perspective calls for a small detour through world heritage history.

World Heritage

The World Heritage Convention of 1972 brought together what up until then had been two distinct historical currents: on the one hand, a movement for the protection of historical monuments, emerging out of Europe where it had gained momentum in the aftermath of two destructive wars; on the other hand, environmentalism, rising in the face of unprecedented degradation of the natural environment and extinction of species (see Pressouyre 1997, 56–57). The idea of combining the conservation of culture and nature in one convention came originally from the United States, which had called, as early as 1965, for a World Heritage Trust that would stimulate international cooperation to protect "the world's superb natural and scenic areas and historic properties for the present and the future of the entire world citizenry" (UNESCO World Heritage Centre, "World Heritage Convention").

As noted in chapter 2, one catalyst for the creation of the World Heritage Convention was an international effort coordinated by UNESCO in the 1960s to save the Nubian temples and fortresses of Egypt and Sudan—including the Abu Simbel Temple—from total submersion following the construction of the Aswan high dam that began in 1960 (Hassan 2007; Berg 1978). This campaign cost US$80 million, half of which some fifty different countries donated. It involved leading archaeologists, engineers, architects, and museum professionals from around the world; they were supported by an honorary committee of patrons chaired by the king of Sweden and including the queens of Belgium and Greece, princesses of Monaco and Denmark, and prince of Japan, as well as Eleanor Roosevelt, Dag Hammarskjöld, André Malraux, and Julian Huxley (Hassan 2007, 82).

The Nubia campaign showed what could be achieved if the world's nations assumed shared responsibility for conserving outstanding historical monuments. Other international campaigns followed in its wake, such as those in Venice, Italy, and Mohenjo-Daro in Pakistan, both threatened by rising waters. The World Heritage Convention gave an institutional framework to the international solidarity displayed in these rescue operations (Gfeller and Eisenberg 2016, 281–285; UNESCO World Heritage Centre, "World Heritage Convention"; see also Schuster 2002, 2; Hassan 2007).

Despite its unquestioned success, the World Heritage Convention has come under criticism for several reasons; taken together, these have contributed to a conspicuous imbalance in the convention's most auspicious instrument, the World Heritage List. States Parties to the convention are invited to nominate heritage sites in their territories to be inscribed on this list, which represents the "world heritage of mankind as a whole." However, judging by the list, humanity's heritage appears to be overwhelmingly European, Christian, and cultural. The natural heritage represents only a small minority of sites listed, while an overwhelming majority is cultural (at the time of writing, 832 out of 1,073 sites). The countries of Europe, particularly those bordering on the Mediterranean, have a vastly disproportionate number of sites inscribed on the list, and churches and cathedrals seem to be favorite objects of inscription. Going by the list, more than half the world's cultural heritage is concentrated in the relatively small continent of Europe, particularly in the south of Europe, while merely 6 percent is in Africa south of the Sahara—the cradle of humankind. Italy alone has fifty-three cultural heritage sites inscribed on the World Heritage List, more than the entire sub-Saharan African continent. Actually, the imbalance is even greater, for as Henry Cleere has noted, "Several of the cultural sites are not indigenous but early European colonial creations, including the infamous Ile de Goree (Senegal), centre of the slave trade" (Cleere 1998).

In response to criticism and dissatisfaction with this imbalance, UNESCO adopted in 1994 a global strategy for a balanced and representative World Heritage List. This strategy calls, on the one hand, for an upsurge in underrepresented varieties of heritage and an increase in the number of submissions from underrepresented regions through awareness raising, capacity building, and cooperation; on the other hand, it deems necessary a thorough revision of the concept of cultural heritage and the criteria of evaluation used by the World Heritage Committee (Gfeller 2015; Di Giovini 2009, 419–429).

The figures cited above show that the global strategy still has a long way to go toward addressing the disproportion. It testifies, however, to a shift in the discourse on world heritage. What was originally conceived as a list representing masterpieces of such outstanding universal value that they are the common heritage of humankind has over time become a list representative of humankind's heritage; in other words, the assumption that certain sites of heritage are so valuable that humanity as a whole must accept responsibility for their conservation has ceded to the assumption that all peoples and communities have a right to heritage and to its international recognition and protection. Universalism has yielded to pluralism.

Besides the global imbalance in representation on its list, the World Heritage Convention has met with other serious criticism in the years since its adoption. These may be summed up under the headings of "monumentalism," "materialism," "ecological apartheid," and the "doctrine of authenticity."

Monumentalism

In the first place, the convention's definition of cultural heritage has been characterized as monumentalist and far too firmly rooted in a European, classical conception of historical structures: castles, palaces, cathedrals, abbeys, temples, pyramids, mausoleums, and megaliths.[4] The conception of what makes up the cultural heritage of humankind is thus informed by quaint ideas of excellence, best expressed through such (frequently invoked) notions as treasures, masterpieces, and wonders. This monumentalism is infatuated with size and privileges those large-scale and highly charged material traces of the civilizations that spawned it to the detriment of vernacular architecture and the material traces of nonmonumentalist civilizations.

Materialism

Closely related to the charge of monumentalism is the critique of materialism. At an expert meeting on world heritage in the African context, Dawson Munjeri, regional director of the Great Zimbabwe monuments administration, argued that in contrast, notions of heritage in "traditional African societies [are] not based on the cult of physical objects, the tangible, and certainly not on condition and aesthetic values" (2001, 18). The category of intangible heritage is the obverse of this materialist concept of heritage. The negative modifier of intangibility in the 2003 convention may be read as a negation of the materialist value system of the 1972 convention. It cuts the old convention down to size, qualifying it and limiting its scope to "tangible" heritage. At the same time, however, it confirms this dichotomous conception of heritage and underscores the central importance of materiality. The concept of tangibility stands here for Western discourses and practices that appear almost self-evident to those who are positioned within them. Within this dominant discourse, heritage conservation represents mind acting on matter, a Eurocentric dichotomy if ever there was one.

Ecological Apartheid

Third in this series of exclusions is what Munjeri characterizes as "ecological apartheid" (Munjeri 2001, 19). While the World Heritage Convention brings together in one legal instrument concerns about natural and cultural conservation, it thoroughly distinguishes between them and separates the one from the other. To be inscribed on the World Heritage List, the two are measured against different criteria; cultural heritage must meet the "test of authenticity" (on which more below) while natural heritage has to meet "conditions of integrity." As Munjeri notes, "The concept of integrity emphasizes 'wholeness,' 'virtuosity,' unfettered by organic and inorganic human and non-human intrusions," and finds its principal expression in natural reserves and national parks. The motivation behind the conditions of integrity and the conservation of natural heritage more generally in the World Heritage Convention was "to transmit to future generations a number of 'virgin' natural sites, unspoilt by mankind" (Pressouyre 1997, 57), on the model of the national park.

This practice depends on a nature-culture dichotomy that does not see human populations and activities as a natural element of the habitat. Instead, human exploitation of nature is thought to "spoil" it; human penetration of "virgin" land violates its purity and value (one might ask, following Sherry Ortner 1974, is female to male as natural heritage is to cultural heritage?). As Melissa Baird notes, such conservation practices have "displaced communities worldwide as a way to 'protect nature'" (2015, 211). It would not be inappropriate, I think, to label such conceptions and practices Edenic. They create sanctuaries for nature from which human populations are deliberately excluded. Through such practices, indigenous communities have been marginalized within the great tracts of land they inhabit and alienated from their management (Munjeri 2001, 19). In effect, this amounts to a rehearsal of the Fall, with these populations cast out of reconstituted Gardens of Eden.

Doctrine of Authenticity

Moving from nature to culture, the doctrine of authenticity—the final in the series of four exclusions and dichotomies identified above—has been the topic of a great deal of reflection and reevaluation in recent years. It is now generally recognized that the concept of authenticity, as it was practiced (and this is an important qualification), is exceedingly Eurocentric and detrimental to the global reach and credibility of the World Heritage List. This topic will take us back—via a Parisian restaurant—to Japan and the East-Asian rehabilitation of Western precepts of heritage conservation.

Temples of Horyu-ji

One night during the first week of the expert meeting in Paris in June 2003, Guðný Helgadóttir (head of the Icelandic delegation) and I had dinner with the other Nordic delegates at a small restaurant a short walk away from UNESCO headquarters. We arrived fashionably late and sat down in the two seats still available at the table. I sat across from the head of the Norwegian delegation with whom I had not yet spoken. We introduced ourselves and it came out we are both folklorists; his name, Magne Velure, rang a bell. As a student, I had read articles by him on folklorism (Velure 1972). We began talking about my research and I wondered out loud about Japan's role in pushing the Intangible Heritage Convention forward. In response, Velure explained that Japan has an age-old architectural heritage but few authentic old buildings to show for it—"authentic," that is, by Western standards. It is not the buildings as such, in their materiality, that are valued but rather the underlying know-how and tradition. As long as these are not lost, he continued, people can reconstruct the buildings. Though intangible, this is the heritage toward which Japanese safeguarding practices are geared. Velure's insight—though it is by no means his alone—helped me to understand Japan's commitment. Some further notes on the recent history of world heritage will develop this insight.

The imbalance of the World Heritage List and its problematic definition of heritage had stirred debates before, but the accession of Japan to the World Heritage Convention in 1992 launched a process of reflection within UNESCO and in the conservation profession at large. It brought in its wake a reconsideration of basic approaches and concepts (Lévi-Strauss 2001, 72; Luxen 1995, 373). Herb Stovel was secretary-general from 1990 to 1993 of ICOMOS (International Council on Monuments and Sites, an organization that is one of two principal advisors to the World Heritage Committee); he recalls that "following Japan's decision to sign the Convention, conservation authorities within the country expressed to ICOMOS apprehensions concerning global acceptance of Japanese approaches to conservation and to authenticity. The Japanese feared that their practice of periodically dismantling significant wooden structures would possibly be seen as inauthentic if judged from within a Western framework. In fact, their fears were legitimate: levels of understanding of Japanese heritage and its conservation outside Japan are relatively low" (1995, xxxv).

Two Japanese heritage sites were at the center of attention in debates launched by Japan's accession and its subsequent nomination of properties for inscription on the World Heritage List. Both are the subjects of stories rehearsed in various forms and at varying length in meetings, coffee breaks, reports, and publications (this one included). Recall the reference to organizational storytelling in chapter

2 and the story that traces the Intangible Heritage Convention to a letter from La Paz and a song of uncertain origin. That is one story of origins. This is another one, which also explicitly locates the convention's origins and implicitly defines its purpose. If the first story makes Bolivia a main protagonist and identifies the impetus for creating a convention in foreign acts of appropriation of native culture, this second story is set in Japan and the impetus is a bias in the World Heritage List, which speaks to a bias in the concept of heritage, which in turn reflects a bias in the international order, one that Japan sets out to correct. There are other stories still; chapter 4 opens with an etiological account set in Morocco. There seems to be one for every continent. Each story lays out a different logic for safeguarding intangible heritage.

The Nordic dinner party in June 2003 provided the setting for one of these storytelling sessions, one of very many like it in UNESCO circles in the past decades of negotiation and implementation of the Intangible Heritage Convention; the stories are also carried far from UNESCO headquarters into the field worldwide in any number of seminars, meetings, and training sessions for safeguarding intangible heritage. Folklorists are no less involved than anyone else; as folklorist Alan Dundes noted in answer to his own question, "Who are the folk?": "Among others, we are" (1977, 35). The story that concerns us here features two Japanese heritage sites, sometimes one and sometimes both: the Horyu-ji temple and the Ise shrine.

The Horyu-ji area in Nara Prefecture (at the center of the Japanese archipelago) counts around forty-eight Buddhist monuments, some of which date from the late seventh or early eighth century. They are among the oldest surviving wooden buildings in the world and their construction coincided with the introduction of Buddhism to Japan from China by way of the Korean Peninsula. As heritage sites, they commemorate an important turning point in the history of religion, art, and architecture. However, the methods by which they have been conserved did not sit well with many heritage professionals in the West. Some believed the authenticity of the buildings had been compromised beyond repair. They would never meet the convention's "test of authenticity." Maintenance works have been carried out continuously for 1,300 years. Some buildings have periodically been dismantled and reassembled, either partially or completely. The last major reconstruction of the buildings of Horyu-ji took place as recently as 1934 to 1955 (Inaba 2001; Droste and Bertilsson 1995, 11–12).

The "test of authenticity," as laid out in the Operational Guidelines, takes into account the materials, design, craftsmanship, and setting of cultural heritage. However, as applied, the test was first and foremost based on the "authenticity of materials," judging the authenticity of heritage by the presence of original materials and the absence of new ones. Where the introduction of new materials had been unavoidable, they had at least to be clearly set off from the original material

Fig. 3.1 Temples of Horyu-Ji, Ikaruga, Japan. ©Prakich Treetasayuth/Shutterstock.

structure. Critics were right that the temple and buildings of Horyu-ji would not have met this test if applied with the conventional emphasis on materials.

As Japanese conservation specialists pointed out, however, there were sound reasons for conserving the buildings by these methods. In a climate characterized by high temperatures and humidity, wood rots easily and suffers frequent damage from insects, mold, and fungi (Ito 1995, 39). In time, buildings twist and lean to one side, timbers rot, and joints are crushed. Simply put, the buildings require periodic repair in which damaged parts are patched or replaced. The Japanese specialists stressed, however, that where possible the parts were replaced "by new wood of the same species and quality as the original ones" and always "the same carpentry techniques are applied" (Ito 1995, 43; see also Inaba 1995, 331).[5]

Evidently, the World Heritage Convention and its Operational Guidelines were not designed with perishable, vegetal material in mind. Most historical buildings in Japan are constructed from such materials, and even more so their counterparts in Africa and Oceania. Naturally enough, these require constant renovation and regular replacement of some of their structural elements. The convention, as noted, emerged out of a discourse defined by monumental stone architecture of which the Acropolis, the Palace of Versailles, and the Cologne Cathedral provide prime examples. Clearly, there were good grounds for renewed reflection in the conservation profession (Gfeller 2017).

Despite this predicament, the World Heritage Committee inscribed the Horyu-ji area on the World Heritage List in 1993. In response to the difficulties raised by its nomination and what seemed to be incommensurate outlooks on historical conservation, the Japanese government proposed an expert meeting in cooperation with UNESCO's World Heritage Centre, ICOMOS, and ICCROM (International Centre for the Study of the Preservation and Restoration of Cultural Property, an intergovernmental organization affiliated with UNESCO). Japan hosted the meeting in the Nara Prefecture in November 1994, gathering leading professionals and scholars of heritage, conservation, and history from around the world (Larsen 1995a). Their views diverged widely, ranging from the position that without authenticity "a monument became a replica or a reconstruction" and that things were either "authentic or non-authentic: there was no possibility of qualification of authenticity" (Cleere 1995, 253) to the suggestion that "in practice the concept of authenticity is so vague that it permits of any manipulation" (Choay 1995, 106). The great majority of participants agreed, however, that the conceptual framework needed adjustment if it was to apply to the world's heritage. As one participant put it, the "conference is symptomatic of a reflective cultural heritage profession that is concerned about the relevance of its endeavours in post-colonial societies" (Galla 1995, 318).

Halfway through, the meeting adjourned for an excursion to the Horyu-ji temple, located in Nara Prefecture (Akagawa 2015, 70). The assembled experts then drafted, as an outcome of their deliberations, a recommendation to the World Heritage Committee, entitled the Nara Document on Authenticity (see Larsen 1995b, xxi–xxiii; ICOMOS 1994). They affirm the continuing central importance of authenticity to the evaluation of cultural heritage, conditioned, however, on a doctrine of cultural relativity. Authenticity, they pronounced, varies from one cultural context to another. The "test" should therefore not be applied indiscriminately. This means its assessment will not be the same in Japan or Benin as in France or Italy. The idea is that "each culture"—and this assumes discrete units—has its own conception of authenticity. The value of its heritage ought therefore to be assessed with reference to that conception. Knut Einar Larsen, editor of the conference proceedings, sums this up in his preface: "The *Nara Document* reflects the fact that international preservation doctrine has moved from a Eurocentric approach to a post-modern position characterized by recognition of cultural relativism. . . . [As a result,] preservation experts are forced to clarify the use of the concept of authenticity within their own countries and cultural spheres. Only then can they encounter their colleagues from other parts of the world in an open dialogue in the understanding that the search for authenticity is universal, but recognizing that the ways and means to preserve the authenticity of cultural heritage are culturally dependent" (1995b, xiii).

Doubts were expressed, however, within the international heritage profession about whether the "search for authenticity" truly is or ought to be universal (Ito

1995, 35–36; Jokilehto 1995a, 73–74). The move that Knut Einar Larsen character-izes as postmodern amounts, in effect, to a nationalization of the test of authen-ticity; the administrators to whom it leaves the elaboration of emic criteria of authenticity are civil servants or contractors to national governments. The move thus does not mark incredulity toward metanarratives as much as it marks their national administration and subservience to state interests. Diversity is distrib-uted among "cultures," not within culture; cultures are reified as administrative and moral units, each with its own native concept of authenticity. In fact, Larsen himself believes the test of authenticity is rendered superfluous by its relativiza-tion, since states are not likely in the first place to nominate to the World Heri-tage List any sites, buildings, or monuments that would be deemed inauthentic at home (1995c, 363). Others, however, including archaeologist Henry Cleere (at the time World Heritage Coordinator for ICOMOS, the International Council on Monuments and Sites), speak out in favor of "national codes of authenticity, analogous to and linked with heritage protection legislation" (1995, 254).

Of course, authenticity is socially constructed (Muños-Vinas 2005, 91–114; see also Jones 2010; Jones and Yarrow 2013). That much goes nearly without say-ing, now that social constructivism has been a dominant paradigm in cultural theory for half a century. The Nara Document recognizes this. What its formula-tion deliberately ignores, however, is that each community does not construct it autochthonously. Rather, it is a historically overdetermined concept (on its his-tory, see Bendix 1997; Choay 1995, 101–104). Constructed in Europe, it was sub-sequently exported and imposed through a professional terminology, a set of conservation practices, and a moral imperative. Taken together, these define the parameters of heritage discourse and their reach and authority extend around the globe through the World Heritage Convention itself.

In fact, the demand that each "culture" define authenticity for itself as an operational principle of conservation insists that the relation of the present to vestiges of the past continues to be defined in terms of authenticity. It reinforces the concern for originality (Jokilehto 1995a, 18; Droste and Bertilsson 1995, 4) and upholds "the search for truth in the field of culture" (Jokilehto and King 2001, 33; see also David Lowenthal in Jokilehto 1995b, 72). When it comes right down to it, the so-called postmodern move of the Nara Document moves above all toward efficient dossier review. The resulting mono-mentalist rendition of relativity (one state: one heritage: one authenticity) is grounded in bureaucratic expediency (Gfeller 2017; Winter 2014).

Ise Shrine

The Horyu-ji temple is one site, I noted. The other Japanese heritage site that fea-tures in this story of origins is the Ise shrine. It is even better suited to the task, more dramatic in the narrative work it does and the contrast it draws between

Western conservation dogma and its alternative. In Mie Prefecture in central Japan, next to the Nara Prefecture that is home to the Buddhist Horyu-ji temple, the Ise Jingu or Ise shrine consists in fact of two Shinto shrines in the city of Ise, known as Naiku (the "inner shrine") and Geku (the "outer shrine"). According to local etiological accounts, the inner shrine was first raised 2,000 years ago as a shrine to Amaterasu Omikami, the sun goddess, from whom the imperial family claimed descent. The outer shrine is dedicated to Toyouke Omikami, goddess of agriculture and industry, and was, according to the same etiology, founded some 1,500 years ago (Ise Jingu 2015a). One hundred twenty-five subsidiary Shinto sanctuaries are in the surrounding area. Together, Naiku and Geku are Shinto's most sacred shrines. In the present context, the most remarkable thing about the Ise shrine is that every twenty years its wooden sanctuaries are completely razed and rebuilt on a contiguous lot from new materials. According to official accounts, this ceremonial system, known as Shikinen Sengu, has been in place for over 1,300 years; the first Shikinen Sengu was performed in the period of the forty-first emperor Jito, ca. 690 CE (Ise Jingu 2015b). Though this system of rebuilding was practiced at other Shinto shrines in earlier times, the Ise shrine is now the only one where this practice is upheld. The reconstruction of the Ise shrine takes place over eight years, beginning with chopping the cypress wood to build it and ending with the shrine's consecration and the leveling of its predecessor. The last one (the sixty-second Shikinen Sengu at Ise) was completed in 2013; the next one begins in 2025 (Bernard 2000).

The Ise shrine has been cited a great deal in discussions on heritage in the past quarter century, as received notions have been challenged and the World Heritage Convention criticized for its parochial underpinnings (Luxen 1995, 373). Japanese heritage professionals are quick to point out, however, that "this tradition has no relation with conservation practice—it is a part of the ritual practice of the Shinto religion" (Inaba 1995, 331; Akagawa 2015, 8–9). That is true; it is not a model of material conservation, unlike the case of Horyu-ji. Nevertheless, the Ise shrine has great value as a tool for reflecting on conservation. It is good for more than worship; it is good to think with, to adopt a phrase from Claude Lévi-Strauss. The Ise shrine helps one to think through issues of authenticity and materiality with respect to how the past is articulated to the present. More so than the Buddhist tradition of partial or complete dismantlement and reassembly, the Shinto conservation philosophy strikes one as completely alien to dominant paradigms in conservation. Even if it is exceptional, it presents a challenge to conventional practices; through contrast, it helps bring out the materialist basis not only of the test of authenticity but of the conservation profession in general, the subservience of its approaches, theories, and practices to a fetishism of the past.

Shikinen Sengu could represent an alternative vision of heritage, one founded not on permanence and substance but on transience and the insubstantiality of

Fig. 3.2 Ise Grand Shrine (Naiku), Mie, Japan, 1953. Nyotarou/Creative Commons via Wikimedia Commons.

things. In this regard, the Ise shrine is a mise-en-abyme for Japanese culture, to which the notion of impermanence is central; according to ancient beliefs and rituals, not only shrines but also castle towns and even the capital were periodically dismantled, moved, and rebuilt at new locations in past centuries (Bognar 1997, 3). The Buddhist consciousness of evanescence and ephemerality plays a part here, and architectural historians have pointed out that this traditional outlook is palpable in modern-day Tokyo and other Japanese metropoles: constantly under construction and demolition, they are characterized by an "architecture of the ephemeral, a radically volatile world with a 'ruined map'—a place where one's sense of reality is profoundly challenged by the scenography of rapidly changing architecture" (3; see also Bharne and Shimomura 2003).

In terms of dominant heritage discourse, developed with reference to stone monuments, the practice of Shikinen Sengu can only be conceived of as reproduction and the Ise shrine as a replica to the sixty-second degree. Yet there is more to them. For one thing, the practice assures the transmission of traditional knowledge from master carpenters to apprentices as well as observance of ceremonial customs, establishing firm links between past, present, and future. Moreover, there is a sense in which the sanctuaries of Naiku and Geku *are* ancient, even if the cypress in the buildings was cut only in 2005 and the structures' assembly completed in 2013. The design, craftsmanship, and setting are ancient, though the materials are not. The example of the Ise shrine thus underlines the pivotal importance of materiality in European-inspired conservation practices, which emerge, in comparison, as techniques of embalming (Choay 1995, 112). They curate what historian Pierre Nora terms *les lieux de mémoire*, "no longer quite life, not yet death, like shells on the shore when the sea of living memory has receded" (Nora 1989, 12).

At the Nara Conference on Authenticity in 1994, Nobuo Ito, professor at Kobe Design University, drew an interesting comparison, suggesting that the "principle in the reconstruction system found in [the] Ise shrine," unique as it may seem, is in fact similar to Japan's system for the protection of intangible cultural property, where transmission from "senior well-experienced experts to the younger generation" preserves techniques and skills in performing and applied arts (1995, 44). There are important parallels between these two systems of cultural reproduction. The easy acceptance of replication as a means of transmission is remarkable for its contrast with the anxiety of Western conservation philosophy in the presence of the replica.

As Bernd von Droste (of UNESCO's World Heritage Centre) and Ulf Bertilsson (of Sweden's National Heritage Board) explained at the Nara Conference in 1994, the original intention behind the requirement that "'each property should meet the test of authenticity' was to exclude copies, or fully reconstructed monuments—'modern fakes'—from entering the World Heritage List" (Droste and Bertilsson 1995, 4).[6] In that spirit, Finnish architectural historian Jukka Jokilehto, chief of ICCROM's architectural conservation program, contributed a long and learned "general framework for the concept" of authenticity to the Nara Conference, in which he expounds on its etymology and semantics. Jokilehto asserts that the authentic "can refer to the original as opposed to the copy, or to real as opposed to pretended; it can refer to the reputed source or author, or to being genuine as opposed to counterfeit." Moreover, "being authentic describes . . . being original, creative, unrepeated, unique, sincere, true, exceptional or genuine" (1995a, 18).

The particular relationship to the past that these terms circumscribe is founded on linear temporality and an ideal of permanence set in stone, developed in civilizations with stone monuments and historical stone buildings. The Ise shrine, in contrast, represents a relationship to the past constructed in organic materials, embodying transience and ephemerality, its regular deconstruction and reconstruction a commemoration of cyclical temporality.

The discursive construction of authenticity in the heritage profession, stressing as it did material items of heritage, systematically excluded modes of historical continuity and ways of relating the past to the present not rooted in the European outlook and emphasis on the material. Although Japan's heritage figures prominently in debates on this issue and its government and delegation have in fact played the lead role in challenging the hegemony of European heritage materialism, Japan is only one among numerous non-Western states adversely affected by the hegemony of this mode of relating to the past, as indicated by the poor representation of African heritage on the World Heritage List. As noted above, European-inspired definitions of heritage do not map easily onto traces of the past valued in Africa, especially below the Sahara Desert; perishable, organic materials are prominent in buildings, the natural not readily distinguishable from the cultural, and no sharp distinction between the monumental and the vernacular; in many cases, Cartesian distinctions between tangible and intangible make little sense (Saouma-Forero 2001).

Universal Categories

Returning once more to Paris, it seems not far-fetched to speculate that this analysis sheds light on the alliance of Japanese delegates and delegates from various African countries in the deliberations of UNESCO's Intergovernmental Meeting of Experts—the alliance interpreted by many European delegates rather in conformity with the rumor that Japan pays the expenses of the African delegates and gets in return their compliance with the Japanese agenda. The two explanations are not necessarily mutually exclusive, but if the rumor motivates resistance or cynicism, the story of Japan's accession to the World Heritage Convention and the incommensurability of its conservation practice with the monumentalist and materialist ethos of world heritage motivates a more sympathetic response. Narrative and counternarrative, these stories rationalize the order of things and legitimate different positions.

Ideals of authenticity were thus an essential background to the main points of contention in creating the Convention for the Safeguarding of Intangible Cultural Heritage in 2003. Ironically, this convention is itself a copy. Delegates who took part in its drafting from day one told me that to create a first working document, Mohammed Bedjaoui, the meeting's chair, had taken the 1972 Convention concerning the Protection of the World Cultural and Natural Heritage and inserted the qualifier "intangible" in front of every occurrence of the term "cultural heritage." A study of the various drafts of the convention more or less confirms this (Blake 2006, 6–7, 129–141). On the first day of the June 2003 meeting in Paris, Bedjaoui reminded delegates, "We have been paying tribute to the 1972 convention and following it both as regards content and form. We've taken up a number of formulas from the 1972 convention and I've taken inspiration in it myself" (author's ethnographic notes; see also Bedjaoui 2004, 152–153). Later that same day, he added in a more critical tone: "I have followed these discussions from the outset and I find that many states feel they can be reassured if we copy the 1972 convention. So, this chapeau is almost word-for-word from the 1972 convention. All very reassuring, of course, we were moving into well-charted territory and we were making headway. But now that we have a draft convention and can stand on our own two feet, maybe we can revise the wording."

Some delegates were concerned that the new convention was a carbon copy of the old one. Discussing finances at the Meeting of Experts in June 2003, a French delegate remarked, "As it is this convention looks very much like the 1972 convention, which is very costly," and asked, "How can we avoid that kind of squandering here?" A year earlier, a meeting of national UNESCO commissions from the European Union protested the "attempt to 'copy' the structure of the convention from 1972" (EU National Commissions for UNESCO 2002). Others, however, rejoiced in the likeness of the two instruments. It was clear as day that the east Asian architects of intangible cultural heritage strove for maximum correspondence between the conventions.

From the Nara Conference (1994) to UNESCO's intangible heritage section, led by Noriko Aikawa (1993–2003), and from Matsuura's Proclamation of Masterpieces (1999–2006) to the Intergovernmental Meeting of Experts that negotiated the Intangible Heritage Convention (2001–2003), Japan has created forums for reconsideration, built alliances, rallied support for its cause, and led a coalition of states to revise concepts and categories, to reengineer existing instruments, and to create new ones. This effort has realigned the parameters of professional and political discourse on heritage. It is through such parameters, concepts, and categories that states build hegemony on the global stage. Hegemony is not won through dominance or imposition but rather by rehabilitating existing universal categories and presenting new ones by which all heritage can be defined. When universal categories by which heritage was classified and assessed were in harmony with categories and values of monumentalist civilizations in Europe, the heritage of these states provided prime examples of the treasures of humanity; their conservation practices were textbook examples of best practices in the field. Insofar as Japan and the coalition it leads has been successful in realigning the parameters of heritage discourse, the heritage of these states is emerging through the Representative List of Intangible Cultural Heritage as prime examples of humanity's heritage; their methods of intervention stand out as best practices; and their expertise in these methods is sought after by other states in programs of international cooperation (often funded by Japan). In collaboration with its allies, Japan is thus competing for global authority in the cultural sector.

Proclaiming Irony

The first Proclamation of the Oral and Intangible Heritage of Humanity was launched with great ceremony on May 18, 2001. Much like the subsequent ones, it received a mixed response. Local media in countries whose cultural traditions were recognized as masterpieces of humanity's heritage ran congratulatory stories. The Proclamation met with less enthusiasm, however, not to say indifference, in other contexts. Thus, it is safe to assume that Cullen Murphy's ironic tour de force in the *Atlantic Monthly* ruffled feathers among the Proclamation's proponents. Expressing his initial delight with the initiative and his sense of anticipation while waiting for the first announcement of what, after all, would surely be "the intangible equivalent of Angkor Wat or the Acropolis, of Tikal or the Taj Mahal," Murphy had found that, "alas, the list, promulgated at UNESCO's Paris headquarters, proved to be a little underwhelming." "The overall impression," he explains, "is of a program listing for public television at 3:00 AM." Happily, however, all was not lost, for UNESCO still had an opportunity to "inject vitality and ambition into the enterprise" in the second Proclamation of Masterpieces in 2003. Cullen Murphy suggests "some candidates of real distinction" to add to the list, including the white lie ("its social utility is hard to overestimate"), the passive voice ("a conceptual space that at some point shelters everyone"), the space between things ("a crucial but intangible component of all relationships"), self-fulfilling prophecies, silence, and irony (2001, 20–22).

Murphy's candidates highlight some peculiarities of the Proclamation of Masterpieces and the Representative List. It would be a prejudiced jury that did not concede that irony is a masterpiece of the human spirit. What might disqualify its candidature is that its continued practice is hardly under threat. It fails to constitute heritage for it does not justify intervention. The other factor that stands in the way of irony's proclamation as the intangible heritage of humanity is that no community or state can claim irony as its own—it is not territorial, and there is no delimited population that identifies with it (Fernandez and Taylor Huber 2001).[7] Paradoxically, irony (and the rest of Murphy's candidates) is too common to be proclaimed the common heritage of humanity.

Discussing the merits of this program, a UNESCO administrator explained to me that for a country like Zambia,[8] which is not good at sports nor distinguished in "high art," the importance of the recognition that the Proclamation of Masterpieces affords should not be underestimated. The Proclamation gives pride to communities, he emphasized, but it also measures out responsibilities to governments. The Proclamation is not only a list, he stressed, it is also a program: behind the list is a plan of action for safeguarding the proposed items.

As a mechanism of display, the list of proclaimed heritage parallels other public spectacles of international scale. It is a recent arrival among a range of instruments by which "a people is made visible to itself and its virtues celebrated in a way which puts them in competition with other nations" (Bennett 2001a, 16), much like world exhibitions, the World Cup, and Miss World. It can be characterized as a cultural Olympics (see Turtinen 2000, 20–21). In this, it follows the example of the World Heritage List, and like world heritage it is designed to harness national pride in the service of safeguarding (see Turtinen 2006).

In spite of the director-general's forceful encouragement, the Intergovernmental Meeting of Experts was torn over the question of lists. In this, it resembled its precursor that drafted the World Heritage Convention. Resistance was apparent from the outset and had been voiced in no uncertain terms at the meeting's previous sessions. In fact, a reunion of national UNESCO commissions from the European Union had previously found that "the Proclamation of Masterpieces . . . which relies on the establishment of a list, is not a convincing precedent" for a list-based approach to safeguarding intangible heritage (EU National Commissions for UNESCO 2002).

By the time the third session of the expert meeting rolled around in June 2003, it had become clear, however, that there was no avoiding the list: a considerable majority of member states seemed to back the creation of lists, in the plural, as central instruments of the convention. The previous session in February had reached consensus to provide for national inventories of intangible heritage and an international Register of Intangible Cultural Heritage in Need of Urgent Safeguarding, both modeled on the World Heritage Convention. The precise nature and content of a second international list of a more general nature was, however, still up for debate. Many delegations previously opposed to such a list had now shifted their position to regain diplomatic footing. Some abandoned their resistance altogether, picking instead battles where they stood a fighting chance, while others set out to create a list that would at least be as unobjectionable as possible.

Registers, Lists, Inventories

On Monday morning, June 2, 2003, as we waited for other delegations to sit down and for the third session of this Meeting of Experts to begin, the head of the Icelandic delegation, Guðný Helgadóttir, filled me in on the background to the meeting. She explained that the committee was divided between states that wanted a list of masterpieces (based on the World Heritage List and the Proclamation of Masterpieces modeled on that list) and other states that preferred to see an inclusive "register" without reference to esthetic criteria. Japan spearheaded the former group. I later heard through the grapevine that the Japanese delegation was busy taking other delegates to lunch. All kinds of lobbying and negotiations were taking place behind the well-lit scenes of the meeting room at Place Fontenoy, out of earshot from microphones and multilingual headsets.

Two large stacks of paper lay on top of a small desk in the foyer, through which delegates passed on their way to the meeting room. One contained a proposal submitted by Grenada, Saint Lucia, Barbados, and Saint-Vincent and the Grenadines, for a new article creating an International Register of the Intangible Cultural Heritage, in place of the List of Treasures/Masterpieces foreseen in the draft convention. The other stack was taller and contained, on four stapled pages, an explanatory note in fifty paragraphs, laying out objections to the List of Treasures/Masterpieces and outlining the advantages of an International Register.

The Caribbean proposal distinguished itself from the List of Treasures/Masterpieces chiefly in that it proposed to do away with the mechanism of selection. Inscription on the International Register of the Intangible Cultural Heritage would, according to this proposal, "be made at the request of the State Party concerned." The only conditions for inscription would be technical requirements for "complete documentation" of the heritage, including a description of any "national legislation which concerns it," a "plan of action for its safeguarding," and "identification of the custodian(s) of this heritage."

The explanatory note that accompanied the proposal identifies at least three major interrelated problems with the List of Treasures. First, the note argued that the list "bears such a close resemblance to the World Heritage List that it is difficult to tell them apart."[9] Second, it claimed that a selective list based on criteria of excellence would divert the aim of the new convention, "its underlying objective becoming inscription on the list rather than safeguarding." And third, such a list would be "subjective and elitist" like the Proclamation of Masterpieces from which it is adopted; "replacing the term 'Masterpiece' with that of 'Treasure' does not make it any less so," it asserted, adding that "selection will always be based on criteria of 'exceptional value,' regardless of the terms used." In contrast, the Caribbean alternative—the International Register—would "not eliminate any form of ICH [intangible cultural heritage] under the criteria of excellence or aestheticism." In hindsight, the Caribbean delegates were right in every respect. All their warnings, unheeded, have been borne out by the facts. Then again, I think that was already clear to most everyone in the meeting room in 2003. The Caribbean Cassandra complex was not because other delegates did not believe them but because they did not care.

During a coffee break, a Nordic colleague remarked that the UNESCO secretariat was in favor of a list based on excellence. In his opinion, however, such a list was absurd. "It is impossible," he explained, "to take folkdances from Finland, Turkey, and Japan, and say one is better than the others." Another delegate from northern Europe made no secret of his intense dislike for the List of Treasures. He would prefer to have no list at all, "but that is not going to happen." Over coffee, they grudgingly agreed that, as things stood, the best course of action was to lend support to the Caribbean proposal, the lesser of two evils; it was, at any rate, preferable by far to a merit-based roster of treasures or masterpieces.

There was a great deal of informal diplomatic maneuvering during coffee and lunch breaks, and no doubt also over white-clothed Parisian dinner tables such as the one the Nordic delegations shared on a Wednesday night. Alliances formed and broke around lists and other controversial issues, such as questions of national sovereignty and the role of communities in the convention (see chapter 4), but also around the proposed Intangible Cultural Heritage Fund, the amount of national contributions to the Fund, and the compulsory or voluntary character of these contributions. As Luke James and Tim Winter note with reference to meetings of UNESCO's World Heritage Committee: "Public displays of support in the main auditorium might well have been months in the making, and sewn up in the corridors and lunch rooms that day" (2017, 4). Behind the curtains, the stage was set for an elaborately scripted no-holds-barred confrontation.

On Thursday afternoon, having plowed through preceding articles, we reached the lists. An article establishing national inventories was adopted in plenary at the previous session as was the principle of an international Register of Intangible Cultural Heritage in Need of Urgent Safeguarding. The controversy concerned the List of Treasures (or Masterpieces).

The committee's chairman, Algerian ambassador Mohammed Bedjaoui, signaled that it was time to move on to this article and to draft it in such a way that it would at least be acceptable to a majority of delegations. Several states had asked for the floor when Grenada called a point of order, thus halting the proceedings. The Grenadian delegate asked for the Caribbean proposal to be discussed before the articles in the draft convention; once the committee had revamped the text of the draft convention and reached a consensus, she explained, the Caribbean proposal would be superfluous.

This intervention brought on another point of order from Japan. The Japanese delegate insisted that the committee confine itself to discussing the draft convention, otherwise all its work until this point would have been in vain and no progress would be made. Further points of order followed. There was clamor in the meeting room as the tension grew palpable. A Senegalese delegate spoke out to support Japan and accused Grenada of obstructing the work of the committee.

The Grenadian delegate expressed her resentment at the accusations made by the delegations of Japan and Senegal: of course the draft convention was under discussion at this meeting, she conceded, but it was not sacrosanct and surely the delegates were entitled to propose amendments. The Venezuelan delegation followed suit with another point of order, protesting the allegations against Grenada and the other Caribbean states behind the proposal. The Venezuelan delegate raised his voice in a rare display of emotion, exclaiming that the delegates who made these unfair accusations were compromising the cordial atmosphere of the negotiations. I must have looked puzzled; Guðný Helgadóttir, head of the Icelandic delegation, turned to me with a smile and told me not to take this too seriously. Expressions of anger and indignation, she explained, are tools of diplomacy to which delegates occasionally resort. Defusing the tension, chairman Bedjaoui promised the Grenadian delegate she would, in due course, be given the floor to present the Caribbean proposal. But for now, he declared, "let us move on for the sake of giving us all the feeling we are getting something done."

A debate ensued on the list articles, which degenerated alarmingly quickly into a squabble over vocabulary. In an insightful essay on "Making a List," J. Mark Schuster notes that "if one wishes to consider listing as a tool in historic preservation . . . one immediately confronts a rather contorted and confusing set of vocabulary: schedules, inventories, lists, classifications, surveys, registers, [and] records." Each of these terms is polysemic and signifies "different processes with different implications in the countries in which they are used simultaneously" (2002, 3).

Schuster's warning was borne out by the debate at Place Fontenoy. For the better part of the afternoon, one after another, different national delegations spoke out in favor of one: register, list, or inventory, with yet other terms thrown in, such as registry and "relaçion." One delegate claimed that "register is the technically appropriate word here," without further explanation, while another complained that "'register' is too formal and implies formalities of registration." An African delegate spoke out in support of the term "register," because it "gives importance to the item inscribed on it," while a South American delegate advocated the use of "inventory" instead, as the term "register" carries formal implications in copyright law. Just when I thought diplomacy could not get any sillier than this, the South African delegation brought the discussion to a new level of absurdity, stating a preference for the term register, which should be defined thus: "a register is a listing of intangible cultural heritage in need of safeguarding and forms part of an inventory."

In a point of order, the Netherlands called for an immediate vote to save time: "We spent a long time on the relative merits of the terms 'register' and 'list' in February. We've already spent two hours on this today and it is a simple choice: either we use 'register' or we use 'list.'" Japan spoke out in support of the Netherlands. Others objected that before proceeding to a vote, they needed to understand what the different terms meant, and asked for the indulgence of the Dutch and Japanese delegates. In response, the Netherlands asked a legal advisor from UNESCO who was present to define the difference between a register and a list. The legal advisor made the rather obvious point that "it really doesn't matter which word you use in this convention; what is important is what you put in that list or register, how it is to be treated, etc." His answer left the issue unresolved, however, and the delegate from Saint Lucia asked whether questions of terminology could not be deferred until the committee had reached a decision on the content of the article. "We're repeating the debate from the previous session," she complained in exasperation; "absolutely everything said now has already been said." Seizing this as his cue, Bedjaoui closed the session for the day. He announced that the following day we would begin with a presentation of the Caribbean proposal; thus, he called a halt to terminological wrangling for the time being.

Inviting a Noisy Dance-Band into a Hospital

Concealed beneath the astonishing sterility of this debate is a political dispute of some importance, though losing sight of it amid the diplomatic charade is easy. At stake is the relationship between the convention under negotiation and the existing World Heritage Convention. The Argentinean delegate summed it up when he expressed support for the term "register" rather than "list," so as, in his words, "to avoid confusion with the World Heritage List." Though not all delegates were consistent in their terminology, overall the preference for "list" was aligned with support for the List of Treasures/Masterpieces on the model of the World Heritage List. Conversely, those who preferred the term "register" were likely to be skeptical of that List and favorably disposed toward the International Register proposed by the four Caribbean island states.

The following day Grenada presented this alternative proposal. In her speech, the Grenadian delegate stressed the inappropriateness of designating certain practices and expressions as treasures or masterpieces of humanity while excluding others: "The intangible cultural heritage of any group is valuable and precious to them, if only to them. The convention, therefore, should not just recognize intangible cultural heritage of 'exceptional' value." She emphasized also that this convention should not be used to compensate for imbalance in the World Heritage Convention and warned that, if that were the idea, the results would surely come as a disappointment: "Safeguarding should not be a competition. Rich countries have already put money into safeguarding, so what will happen is that their intangible heritage will go on the international list, while developing countries will once again be the losers."

A lively debate ensued and delegations presented arguments for and against the Caribbean proposal. It soon became clear, however, that this was a losing battle; a much greater proportion of those who took the floor spoke out against the proposal than in its favor.[10] Still, several delegates argued for the proposal while others expressed sympathy for the general idea but stopped short of supporting it because they worried that a universal register would be unwieldy.

A Uruguayan diplomat declared that "the fundamental objective of this convention is safeguarding cultural heritage as a whole and not registering masterpieces," and the Danish delegate agreed that "this proposal really captures the true meaning of safeguarding." Argentina, likewise, warned against "focusing on safeguarding a few objects, whether we call them masterpieces or treasures," and proposed to add to the convention "programs, projects, and activities for the safeguarding of intangible cultural heritage" (this latter proposal was accepted and adopted as article 18).

Saint Lucia and Barbados rejected treasures and masterpieces because the terms suggest a hierarchy among heritage. The Spanish delegation had previously argued that "intangible heritage is not a beauty contest," and it now reiterated its objections: "The experience with the World Heritage List," said the Spanish delegate, "is that through it hierarchies are established that are hard to justify and it creates tensions in countries whose submissions to the list are not accepted"— this from a delegate whose state (along with Italy and, as rapidly rising latecomer, China) ranks at the top of the world heritage hierarchy, with a greater number of inscriptions on the list than any other country.

Another delegate (whose nationality escaped me but whose English sounded sub-Saharan African) took a similar position, and expressed his concern with great eloquence: "How will we determine 'outstanding quality'? This will generate competition where we should have cooperation. The search for masterpieces will draw attention away from endangered intangible cultural heritage, which most requires our attention. *It would be like inviting a noisy dance-band into a hospital!*" The point is, he concluded, that "masterpieces do not need help." Comparing the convention to a hospital, this delegate invoked the moral imperative of conservation in the eleventh hour. Lest the committee lose sight of this imperative in a celebration of heritage highlights, the hospital metaphor is a reminder that safeguarding is a matter of life and death—as is implicit in the concepts of survival and revitalization.

This metaphor is regularly invoked also in connection with the World Heritage Convention, for as art historian Dario Gamboni states, "In a sense, 'world heritage' is an ambulance that follows an army and tries to precede it" (2001, 8). More delegates, however, spoke out against the Caribbean proposal and rose to defend the List of Treasures/Masterpieces—the "noisy dance-band." Many among them referred to the success of the World Heritage List and the Proclamation of Masterpieces. The Chinese delegate, for instance, noted that the Proclamation had been very successful in China and added, "The World Heritage List has been a tremendous source of publicity for UNESCO—I don't see why we would want to move away from that." A Japanese delegate cautioned that "the registry will be nothing but a huge database and will show no visibility," pointing out that "in my country alone it is said there are more than sixty-thousand items of intangible cultural heritage; this register would include not only all those but all intangible cultural heritage from all parts of the world!" Skirting past the absurdity of this quantification of heritage, a delegate from Chile concurred, saying that "the register is about to become a phonebook." And speaking on behalf of the African group, the delegate from Benin added, "To refuse to proclaim masterpieces of the intangible cultural heritage of mankind would give a dangerous message: that this convention is second rate, that it is not as good as the 1972 convention, and that this is because certain states forced us to do so."

What Is Beautiful Is Beautiful. Full Stop.

The majority of delegates at the meeting dismissed charges of elitism and hierarchization. Thus, the delegate from Cape Verde was "not really bothered by this business of masterpieces or treasures because what is beautiful is beautiful. Full stop." The head of delegation from the Democratic Republic of Congo likewise said she could not "see anything wrong with masterpieces and treasures; it's a bit romantic, which is exactly what we want in this convention." In a confusing intervention, the Dominican Republic's delegate expressed support for "the brilliant initiative from the delegates from the Caribbean" which she found particularly appealing because "it is not elitist," but then she went on to argue against it based on the claim that "there are works of human genius that are masterpieces; we must be careful not to trivialize culture by denying this." "Unfortunately," the Dominican delegate added, "the human race has not produced these everywhere, but it is nonetheless very important to recognize them where they have been produced."

The delegate from Benin protested that the anti-elitist argument did not hold water and made the important observation that "hierarchy is a fact of history." "Every culture always considers some items of heritage above others," he stressed. A Brazilian delegate noted, to much the same effect, that "there is a difference between the anthropological view of heritage and the political view of heritage." In contrast to the descriptive perspective of anthropology, the political view of heritage is premised on the fact that resources are never limitless; or as the Brazilian delegate spelled out, "We cannot safeguard everything, and this means we cannot value everything equally."

These astute remarks underline how central questions and mechanisms of selection are to heritage practices. As folklorist Barbro Klein maintains, "It is hardly possible to speak of cultural heritage without using the word politics," for cultural heritage comes into existence through a political operation when "individuals or groups nominate or designate it as such" (1997, 19; my translation). Through the same operation, a far greater number of traces of the past are bulldozed, or left to rot, or put to new uses. Heritage making inevitably creates casualties; in the words of Dario Gamboni, "Preservation and destruction are two sides of the same coin." Heritage, Gamboni explains, "results from a continuous process of interpretation and selection that attributes to certain objects (rather than others) resources that postpone their degradation" (2001, 9).

The politics of selection thus extend well beyond the composition of the list. Heritage making is itself not unlike list making. In his classic analysis of lists as social and cognitive instruments, anthropologist Jack Goody has noted that lists rely on discontinuity and boundaries, giving whatever is abstracted from ordinary speech and placed on a list a generality it would not otherwise have, especially if the list is sanctioned by official institutions (1977, 80–81, 105–106). Much the same applies to heritage, for whatever is so designated is abstracted from its previous context and placed in relation to other things, sites, practices, or expressions also selected into the category of heritage. Individuals and institutions that sanction the selection imbue this category with authority, and objects inducted into the category are accorded a value of a different and more general kind than any value they previously had. It should come as no surprise, then, that listing shadows heritage making.

A Mexican delegate to the meeting made an important remark about this selectivity. Discussing the obligations of states at the national level, he protested: "There is a lack of assessment of importance in the text at present. As the text stands now, any communities can demand that their traditions be recognized as intangible cultural heritage. They are both judges and parties. This can cause all kinds of problems, with all communities demanding financial support for their culture and with no way of adjudicating among them, no instrument to assess the importance of the proposed intangible cultural heritage."

What is remarkable here is the acknowledgment that traditions have to be *recognized* as intangible cultural heritage, that they are *proposed* but that to be recognized authorities must *assess* their importance and *adjudicate* among them. Intangible cultural heritage is, in other words, an official seal of approval. It is a filing cabinet in the ministry of culture, and whatever is not recognized and filed there ends instead in the dustbin of history. That is why, as many delegates objected, an international register of heritage without a mechanism of selection is "not practical" (Vietnam), "not convenient" (Colombia), and "too huge for any-one's administration" (Uganda). In fact, the dustbin ("the round file") is perhaps the instrument that effective administration can least do without. A boundless list of everything is not administrable. It is not even a list: lists are distinguished by their boundaries and the discontinuity of their contents from all they exclude.

Uses of Lists

Lists itemize culture. They cannot avoid doing so: enumeration and itemization is their very essence. Such itemization is at the heart of the Intangible Heritage Convention. Not only are lists the central instruments for safeguarding and promoting intangible heritage at the international level, but the primary obliga-tion that the convention imposes on states is to draw up comprehensive national inventories of intangible heritage in their territories (see Kurin 2004, 71–72).

These lists of intangible heritage artifactualize cultural practices and expres-sions. They decontextualize them from the social relations in which they take place in order to recontextualize them, on the one hand, in national inventories with reference to other practices and expressions under the same national gov-ernment and, on the other hand, in international lists with reference to other heritage of humanity. As such, listing renders transferable the practices and expressions itemized and singled out for attention. This transferability is a cause for concern; at the meeting in June 2003, the Argentinean delegate expressed this concern with regard to the UNESCO lists of intangible heritage: "There is a dan-ger in publishing just a list per se, even though it is done with all good intentions: we are giving a shopping list for treasure hunters. In the case of this convention, we might end up with a free catalog for multinationals who want to appropriate intangible cultural heritage. We are all for transparency, but the problem with it is that sometimes others take advantage of it."

The Argentinean delegate noted that "this is a discussion we also had sur-rounding the Convention on Sub-Aquatic Heritage," and indeed the allusion to treasure hunters refers to real problems associated with the World Heritage List (see Schuster 2002, 14–15, and Gamboni 2001, 8–9). As J. Mark Schuster (2002, 8) has remarked, it is an interesting property of lists that "once someone compiles them others will use them, often not for the purposes for which they were originally intended." Such purposes can even be diametrically opposed to those intended by the lists' authors.

The story of the rescue of the Jemaa el-Fna marketplace in Marrakesh, Morocco, its inscription on the Representative List, and its role in the creation of the Intangible Heritage Convention opens the next chapter of this book. But there is a tragic postscript to this story. In 2011, a bomb tore through Café Argana, a popular second-floor roof café overlooking this marketplace in the Marrakesh Medina (the old city). Fifteen people died, most of them tourists, including a ten-year-old girl. Two weeks later, Moroccan police detained nine people: a prime suspect whose cell phone was allegedly found at the site of the bombing, and eight accomplices. The police suggest they were operatives of the terrorist network Al Qaeda in North Africa, which, however, denies responsibility for the bombing. The man charged with bombing the café, Adil Othmani, claims his confession was obtained by means of threats and torture. His family claims he is a scapegoat for what they believe was an attempt by Moroccan security police to defuse the protests of the "Arab spring" in the streets of Marrakesh. In October 2012, a Moroccan magistrate sentenced Adil Othmani to death and the other eight suspects to serve sentences in prison.

What actually took place and who is responsible, I will not speculate. But we know where it took place. And it is not unreasonable to ask why the bombing happened in Jemaa el-Fna, and not somewhere else: like city hall, for instance, or a ministry, an embassy, a hotel, or the Al Mazar Shopping Mall, outside the Marrakesh Medina. There are many ways to answer that—no doubt different levels of security have something to do with it—but one part of the explanation is surely that bombing Jemaa el-Fna grabs international attention in a way that other places just cannot match. Nearly every international news story I have come across about the bombing goes out of its way to mention UNESCO's recognition of Jemaa el-Fna as the intangible heritage of humanity.

One could draw a parallel here to the monumental Bamiyan Buddhas carved into a cliff in the Bamiyan valley in central Afghanistan in the fourth and fifth centuries CE: World Heritage destroyed in 2001 by the Taliban not least for its power as a tool of communication. A regime shunned by the international community, the Taliban reported receiving no less than thirty-six letters from UNESCO pleading with them to spare the giant sandstone statues, and hundreds of official and semi-official communications from governments around the world. With the support of Pakistan, the New York Metropolitan Museum of Art offered to send a team to Afghanistan to remove the Buddhist sculptures (CNN 2001); diplomatic missions from Sri Lanka and from Japan also offered to remove the statues and reassemble in their home countries; Japan suggested the

Fig. 3.3 Two women walk past the huge cavity left by one of the Buddhas of Bamiyan. Public domain via Wikimedia Commons.

alternative solution of covering "the statues from head to toe in a way that no one would recognize they had ever been there, while preserving them underneath" (Zaeef 2010, 127). The Taliban turned down these and other overtures, instead shredding the statues with tanks and artillery shells before deploying prisoners to plant dynamite in the statues and blowing them up bit by bit. Whatever else we have to say about this, the Taliban put the World Heritage List to effective use (see Elias 2007, 2013; Gamboni 2001; Holtorf 2006; Meskell 2002).

More dramatically still, the Islamic State has filmed and distributed propaganda videos of its destruction of cultural heritage in Syria, Iraq, and Libya, including ancient temples, tombs, towers, and statues in the city of Palmyra (a World Heritage site) as well as ancient mosques, churches, and libraries. In 2015 and 2016, Islamic state militants in Iraq reduced the ancient Assyrian city of Nimrud to rubble, systematically smashing statues of winged bulls and lions, destroying engraved frescos and the tombs of Assyrian kings with sledgehammers, dynamiting temples, and bulldozing a huge and spectacular stepped tower (McKernan 2016a and 2016b; Flood 2016).

This militant iconoclasm provoked intense response around the world and within the United Nations. Irina Bokova, UNESCO's director-general, condemned in the strongest terms the "destruction of humanity's cultural heritage," calling it a crime of war (UNESCO World Heritage Center 2015); indeed, the

UN General Assembly unanimously passed a resolution condemning the barbarism, expressing outrage, and suggesting that destroying ancient sites "may amount to war crimes" (United Nations General Assembly 2015). In a study of the rise of heritage diplomacy, sociologist Tim Winter observes that the "intentional destruction of cultural heritage in Syria and Iraq" illustrates that "the political work heritage is being put to continues to increase" (2015, 1011). Similar to the Taliban's destruction of the Bamiyan Buddhas and the bombing of Jemaa el-Fna, but on a much larger scale and taking full advantage of audiovisual technologies, the media, and the internet, the Islamic state has turned UNESCO's heritage lists to its own ends as technologies of communication (Smith et al. 2016; Harmanşah 2015; De Cesari 2015; Rico 2017; Gamboni 1997).

Yet another example is the campaign of destruction that Islamist militants, Ansar Dine (Defenders of Faith), waged in Timbuktu (listed as World Heritage in 1988) over ten months in 2012 when they controlled northern Mali. Attacking mosques, tearing down mausoleums, and reducing the tombs of Sufi saints to piles of rubble with pickaxes and shovels, Ansar Dine invited journalists to film the violent acts of iconoclasm, citing their particular puritanical strain of Islam (Apotsos 2017).

The World Heritage Committee met in Saint Petersburg from June 25 to July 5 that year. At the request of the Malinese government, the committee unanimously agreed on Thursday, June 28, to inscribe Timbuktu on the List of World Heritage Sites in Danger, a symbolic measure that focuses international attention on situations of emergency. Responding directly to this listing, Ansar Dine went on a fresh rampage over the weekend, storming multiple tombs in Timbuktu. To international reporters they declared their intention to "destroy every mausoleum in the city, all of them, without exception" and asked with contempt: "UNESCO is what?" (UNESCO c'est quoi?) (Morgan 2013, 127–142; Brumann 2016; Joy 2016; Viejo-Rose and Sørensen 2015, 285–286).

The move left the committee stunned. Expressing grief and alarm, it pleaded with the Islamic militants while rejecting the link between the committee's decision in St. Petersburg to add Timbuktu to the Danger List and Ansar Dine's subsequent campaign of destruction on the listed site (Brumann 2016). UN Secretary Ban Ki-moon and UNESCO Director-General Irina Bokova also appealed to the militants to "stop these terrible and irreversible acts" of "wanton destruction" (UN News Centre 2012). In response, an Ansar Dine spokesman assured an AFP (Agence France Presse) reporter that "from now on, as soon as foreigners speak of Timbuktu" they would attack anything referred to as a World Heritage site. "There is no world heritage, it doesn't exist. The infidels must not get involved in our business" (Al Jazeera 2012).

Adding his voice to those of Ban Ki-moon and Bokova, Fatou Bensouda, chief prosecutor of the International Criminal Court in The Hague, demanded that they "stop the destruction of the religious buildings now," and warned: "This is a war crime which my office has authority to fully investigate" (*Telegraph* 2012). The threat was not empty. In September 2016, the court sentenced Ahmad al-Faqi al-Mahdi, a former Malian civil servant who oversaw the destruction of the tombs and mausoleums of Timbuktu, to nine years in prison for war crimes. This was the first time the International Criminal Court had heard a case about the destruction of cultural heritage; one year later, the court also sentenced al-Mahdi to pay reparations of 2.7 million euros ($3.2 million) to victims, "primarily the people of Timbuktu, who depend on tourism" (Cook 2017).

While the court's rulings set new precedents, such list-based iconoclasm is not particularly novel. To name but one antecedent, in reprisal for the bombing of Lübeck, Hermann Göring is said to have instructed the Luftwaffe in 1942 to destroy "every historical building and landmark in Britain that is marked with an asterisk in Baedeker" (Boorstin 1992, 106, quoted in Schuster 2002, 15). These raids became known as the Baedeker Blitz, named for the authoritative German travel guidebook to Britain.

Indeed, another controversial use made of UNESCO heritage lists is to promote tourism (Winter 2010). As Manon Istasse remarks with regard to the Medina of Fez in Morocco, "In the view of most inhabitants and members of tourism institutions, the concrete benefit of World Heritage Listing is financial: tourists are coming" (2016, 43). Officially, this is not one of the lists' purposes, but it is universally acknowledged as a major motive for inscription (Caust and Vecco 2017). States nominate cultural and natural heritage sites for inscription on the World Heritage List and they nominate traditional practices and expressions for the Representative List of Intangible Cultural Heritage hoping to attract enlightened tourists who make their own use of these lists, checking them off against their travel plans (Tschofen 2007; Di Giovine 2009, 25–68). In this regard, the lists are no different from their ancient predecessors, the classical lists of remarkable monuments known in antiquity as the Seven Wonders of the World; indeed, the sole remaining of these ancient wonders, the Great Pyramid of Giza, is on the World Heritage List. As Peter Clayton and Martin Price have pointed out, these classical lists were actually not conceived of as enumerations of wonders but rather as a guide to sights; "not, in the Greek, *thaumata* (wonders), but as *theamata* (things to be seen), the dramatic monuments that fill the pages of modern guide books" (2013, 4). Thus, the Seven Wonders were the Baedeker guides of their time, the Lonely Planets of Hellenic travelers. UNESCO's heritage lists, as modern successors, are usually turned to the same end. Far from being an accidental consequence of listing, increased tourism is expected to boost local economies while guaranteeing the economic viability and survival of places and practices that have lost their former economic raison d'être.

There is nothing suspect about these purposes, which correspond well to a liberal conception of the role of the state in facilitating economic growth.

Cultural consumption by tourists is often a major incentive for preservation and helps to generate necessary resources. Even so, listing comes across as a questionable response specifically to the threat of "folklorization" as conceived of by UNESCO: a term used in publications, speeches, and internal documents to characterize the reification and commoditization of traditional practices for outside audiences (see more in chapter 5). In a sense, folklorization parallels the danger that tourism presents to World Heritage sites, threatening physical destruction through wear, tear, and erosion (Caust and Vecco 2017; Gamboni 2001).

A periodic report submitted by Morocco to the executive committee of the Intangible Heritage Convention in 2013 notes that "the substantial media coverage of inscription has greatly increased the visibility." While it enumerates some positive effects of listing ("it has raised awareness of the cultural and historic importance of the space [for locals and overseas visitors]"), the report warns that "inscription may also have negative results." It cites as an example that "for the Jemaa el-Fna it has raised concerns about the 'folklorization' of the Square, the negative impacts of tourism (and a progressive loss of authenticity), changes in attitudes among young people, the expansion of commercial activities, etc." ("Periodic reporting . . . Morocco" 2013).

Good intentions aside, the listing of traditional practices and expressions brings them to the attention of tourists and turns them into tools for local economic recovery. This is perhaps not particularly surprising. Heritage and tourism are collaborative industries, as Barbara Kirshenblatt-Gimblett has suggested, "Heritage converting locations into destinations and tourism making them economically viable as exhibits of themselves" (1998, 151).

The System of Heritage

After all the diplomatic maneuvering and deliberation, the Intergovernmental Meeting of Experts in June 2003 finally settled on a compromise. In spite of their successful rejection of the Caribbean proposal for an International Register of the Intangible Cultural Heritage, Japan and its allies could not rally sufficient support for the List of Masterpieces or Treasures. Instead, delegates settled on an instrument they named the Representative List of the Intangible Cultural Heritage of Humanity. This compromise still makes listing the central international instrument of the convention and it upholds the principle of selection; gone, however, is the highly charged vocabulary of treasures and masterpieces.

UNESCO's heritage lists are a prestigious form of display with wide circulation among powerful actors. In much the same way as museum walls, they are surfaces on which heritage may be arranged so that "its effects—however they might be construed—will be carried back out into the world and enabled to act on it" (Bennett 2000, 1424, on art museums). The arrangement of intangible heritage on such lists is designed to create state and community practice, channeling resources to its preservation and revitalization, but also transforming people's relationship to their practices and expressions.

The UNESCO list effects change not least because it provides an incentive to governments to "proclaim the richness of their cultural heritage" (Early and Seitel 2002, 13, quoted in Kirshenblatt-Gimblett 2006) or, to put it another way, to boast. The *Director-General's Preliminary Report on the Situation Calling for Standard-Setting and on the Possible Scope of such Standard-Setting* in the field of intangible cultural heritage, from 2002, thus stressed the importance of establishing such a list in association with the proposed convention "for its driving force for States Parties as proved by the 1972 convention experience" (UNESCO 2003b, paragraph 7).

From this point of view, UNESCO's lists of heritage emerge as a form of argumentation, but one whose powers of persuasion depend on flattery. Much like the Proclamation of Masterpieces, these lists parallel other international spectacles that make a people visible to itself by weighing its virtues against those of other peoples. The lists yoke pride to the plow of heritage preservation; or, as the Australian Department of the Environment and Heritage maintains regarding the World Heritage List, "Listing also promotes local and national pride in the property and develops feelings of national responsibility to protect the area" (Australian Department of Environment and Heritage, n.d).

In the previous pages, I have presented a key debate in the Intergovernmental Meeting of Experts that drafted the Intangible Heritage Convention concerning the use of the list as an instrument of the convention. This debate, I argue, goes to the heart of heritage practices, which are always predicated upon selection. Safeguarding certain sites or practices under the banner of heritage consumes limited resources and directs those same resources away from other sites and practices. Selection and (inevitably) exclusion are thus structural elements of the system of heritage—its designation, preservation, revitalization, promotion, display, and so forth. The allocation of resources is a political operation, and the same goes, mutatis mutandis, for the designation of heritage, intangible or otherwise. The particular criteria on which its designation is premised are important, but they never fully account for particular selections: it is never self-evident which particular practice, expression, object, or site is most excellent, outstanding, authentic, or, indeed, representative, for these terms are themselves indeterminate and open to debate.

Heritage as category and the list as instrument are alike in many ways. Both depend on selection; both dislodge their objects from previous contexts, rendering them discontinuous in some aspects from their surroundings; and both recontextualize them with respect to other objects similarly selected, according them a generality and value that derives from the authority of the persons or institutions that sanction the selection. The Representative List of the Intangible Cultural Heritage of Humanity is the outcome of a compromise of sorts between delegations that wanted a List of Masterpieces/Treasures and those who wanted no list at all, or else proposed a comprehensive register with no selection. The Representative List accepts selection as a structural element but rejects excellence as a criterion of selection in an attempt to get away from hierarchization and competition among states. However, representativity is even more indeterminate as a criterion of selection. It begs the question of what the list and the heritage it designates actually represent. A great deal of discretion is left to the Intergovernmental Committee responsible for inscribing intangible heritage on the Representative List (for insiders' critical assessments of how the committee exercises this discretion, see, e.g., Jacobs 2013, 2014; Kuutma 2012; and Smeets and Deacon 2017).

As defined by UNESCO's convention and its activities in this field, intangible cultural heritage *is* a list. Intangible heritage is a mechanism of selection and display. It is a tool for channeling attention and resources to certain cultural practices and not to others. Intangible heritage is both a hospital *and* a dance-band: a serious enterprise concerned with the life and death of traditions and communities *and* a fund-raising dinner dance party with colorful costumes, glaring spotlights, and rhythmic tunes. The professionals who run the programs at UNESCO are most concerned with the former; most national delegates concern themselves with the latter. Together, the hospital staff at UNESCO's secretariat and the bandmasters on the Intergovernmental Committee bring intangible heritage into being in (broken) dialogue with countless actors on the ground around the globe.

Notes

All direct quotations, unless otherwise cited, are all from my own ethnographic field notes made at the meetings discussed within the chapter.

1. Systems of Living Human Treasures were developed primarily in Japan and South Korea, along with the closely related category of the "intangible cultural heritage." Japan enacted the Law for the Protection of Cultural Properties in 1950, a comprehensive legislation for heritage conservation that replaced the earlier National Treasures Protection Act from 1929. In 1955, Japanese authorities appointed the first intangible cultural properties along with their "holders," defined as Living Human Treasures, that is, "those who have mastered or possess exceptional skills in arts and crafts" (UNESCO 2002a, 13). Such appointments have since been made annually. The "holders" are awarded grants, and funds are available to assist them in training disciples and to support public performances and exhibitions. A fifth category was added to the Japanese Law for the Protection of Cultural Properties in 1975, "Folk-Cultural Properties," comprising both tangible and intangible heritage. In distinction from the Living Human Treasures program associated with the official appointment of intangible cultural properties and holders, folk-cultural properties are always collective, and recognition for them is given only to groups, not to individual "holders" (UNESCO 2002a, 14).

The Republic of Korea's Cultural Property Preservation Law dates from 1962. It is based in part on the revised Japanese model and draws a distinction between four categories of cultural properties: important tangible cultural properties, important intangible cultural properties, folk-cultural properties, and monuments. The first Korean intangible cultural properties were appointed in 1964 together with "holders" or Living Human Treasures. These latter receive monthly stipends and are in return obliged to train successors and make intangible heritage available to the public at large (UNESCO 2002a, 14–15). Living Human Treasures systems were also set up in the Philippines and Thailand in the 1980s. In the United States, the National Endowment for the Arts established National Heritage Awards in 1982 on the model of the Japanese system, "as a way of honoring American folk artists for their contributions to our national cultural mosaic" (National Endowment for the Arts). Analogous programs focused specifically on handicrafts have been instituted in several countries of Europe, including France, the Czech Republic, and Poland (UNESCO 2002a, 16–18; see also Almevik 2016; Löfgren 2011; Palmsköld 2011).

2. Only three international conventions have done better for themselves in the same period: the international conventions against doping in sport, against corruption, and for tobacco control. It took thirty years for 177 states to ratify the World Heritage Convention.

3. The director-general is even more blunt in the French version of the brochure, where inevitability becomes full-fledged destiny: "Il est évident . . . qu'à terme, la complémentarité de ces deux volets est destinée à se resoudre dans leur union" (UNESCO 2001b, 3).

4. This is widely recognized within UNESCO; thus, for example, Laurent Lévi-Strauss, at the time the chief of UNESCO's Section for Tangible Heritage and deputy director for the Division of Cultural Heritage, speaks of the "very European-inspired definition of cultural heritage as set out in Article 1" of the World Heritage Convention (2001, 70; see also Droste and Bertilsson 1995, 14).

5. These carpentry techniques are documented in S. Azby Brown's *The Genius of Japanese Carpentry*, a detailed and interesting account of the work of Tsunekazu Nishioka, a master carpenter involved in the dismantling and reconstruction of the Horyu-ji temple between 1934 and 1955 (Brown 1998, esp. 25–35).

6. As Bernd von Droste and Ulf Bertilsson note, however, the World Heritage Committee had already in 1980 made an exception for the reconstructed city center of Warsaw: "More than 85 percent of the city of Warsaw was destroyed in August 1944, and much reconstruction work was carried out from 1945 to 1949. Warsaw's 18th-century historic centre—its churches, palaces and marketplace—has been meticulously reproduced. Today it is architectural evidence of a nation's will to preserve its culture" (1995, 9). The World Heritage Centre's website actually vaunts it as "an outstanding example of a near-total reconstruction of a span of history covering the 13th to the 20th century" (UNESCO World Heritage Centre, "Historic Centre of Warsaw").

7. Except the English, of course.

8. Zambia is not singled out here because it performs exceptionally poorly at sports or because its artists go completely unrecognized in galleries of great repute, but rather because its standing is fairly typical of poorer countries in these arenas where distinction and money so often go hand in hand.

9. This concern is not without basis; media coverage often confuses the Representative List with the World Heritage List, which is of course much better known and highly esteemed. The same holds true among diplomats at UNESCO, who refer indiscriminately to "world heritage" (Brumann 2013, 40). Even peer-reviewed articles in prominent scholarly journals do not always understand the distinction; see "Masterpieces of Oral and Intangible Culture: Reflections on the UNESCO World Heritage List" by Peter J. M. Nas (2002) in *Current Anthropology*.

10. There was not an official vote, but the secretariat kept a tally of states that took a position for and against the Caribbean proposal; like the text of articles under consideration at any

given time, the tally was projected onto a large white screen behind the stage where the chairman, the rapporteur, and the UNESCO secretariat sat:

For: Barbados, Denmark, Dominican Republic, Greece, Iceland, Jamaica, Sweden, and Uruguay.

Against: Belgium, Benin, Brazil, Cambodia, Central African Republic, Chile, Colombia, Congo, Democratic Republic of Congo, Ethiopia, France, Honduras, India, Japan, Morocco, Niger, Nigeria, Panama, Philippines, Rwanda, Senegal, Spain, Togo, Turkey, Uganda, United Republic of Tanzania, and Vietnam.

CHAPTER 4

Making Communities

Protection as Dispossession

The latest ambition of the bourgeoisie was to build a mall here, taller than the mosques. The bourgeois live off the square, off the tourism that the square brings, but they don't realize that tourists don't come here looking for malls. Well, what we are attempting—and UNESCO's decision will help us in this—is to change the way many of Marrakesh's own inhabitants look at the square. So they feel a justified sense of pride. (Goytisolo 2002; my translation)

"Justified Sense of Pride"

The square in question is Jemaa el-Fna in Morocco. The words are those of Juan Goytisolo, the Spanish author, dissident, and long-term resident of Marrakesh. He's describing the intended effect of the square's inscription on UNESCO's intangible heritage list. In the mid-1990s, Goytisolo spearheaded a group of Moroccan intellectuals in a coordinated effort to protect this busy marketplace by the entrance to the Marrakesh Medina, or old city (inscribed on the World Heritage List in 1985).

Jemaa el-Fna is the site of a myriad performances—storytelling, snake-charming, fortune-telling, glass-eating, preaching, acrobatics, dance and musical performances, to name a few. Gathering their audience into a circle, a performance space known as the *halqa*, these street performers are referred to as *hlayqiya*; they draw the crowds, foreign and Moroccan, to Jemaa el-Fna (Kapchan 1996). The square also offers diverse services and products: from fruit stalls and fresh meats to the finest barbeques and kebabs; from dental care to herbal medicine; and from tarot card readings to henna tattooing. In the evening, open-air restaurants take up a good deal of the space (Beardslee 2016; Schmitt 2005).

Fig. 4.1 Jemaa el-Fna Marketplace, Marrakesh, Morocco. ©Zharov Pavel/Shutterstock.

In the 1990s, as Goytisolo notes, city authorities, businessmen, and contractors planned to demolish several buildings around the square to make way for a glass-fronted, high-rise shopping center and an underground car park to serve the shoppers. Goytisolo argued that the cultural space of Jemaa el-Fna would not have survived that development.

You will recognize a familiar story here, told in many variants across the world. It is a narrative of loss and ruin. Nowadays, it recounts the destruction of heritage at the hands of forces of globalization. A hundred fifty years ago, the same story spoke of the destruction of tradition by forces of modernity. It was the creation narrative of my discipline, the field of folklore; it fueled the collection of tales and songs and tools, and it motivated the description of customs and rituals and folkways before the bulldozers of modernity would wipe out their every trace.

This is the story that cultural critic Walter Benjamin later recounted in allegorical form as he describes Paul Klee's painting *Angelus Novus*. "This is how one pictures the angel of history. His face is turned toward the past," but his wings are caught in the powerful storm of progress: "This storm irresistibly propels him into the future to which his back is turned, while the pile of debris before him grows skyward" (1968, 258). Enter the folklorist, the conservation professional, the heritage worker: "The angel would like to stay, awaken the dead, and make whole what has been smashed." Instead, the storm carries him against his will into the future, toward which he has turned his back. In front of him, the debris piles up. The past appears as a landscape of ruins: "one single catastrophe which keeps piling wreckage upon wreckage and hurls it in front of his feet" (258). In other words, a demolition ground—much like that envisioned for Jemaa el-Fna.

In Marrakesh, the angel of history took Goytisolo as a guide, along with his fellow artists and intellectuals who responded with alarm to the construction plans. They formed an NGO, Les Amis de la Place (Friends of the Square), and sought out the help of UNESCO. Their timing was perfect. In the mid-1990s, UNESCO had just set up a section for intangible heritage in its secretariat and the first preparations were under way for what would later become the Intangible Heritage Convention (see chapter 3).

In 1996, Goytisolo contacted UNESCO's director-general Federico Mayor, who was his fellow countryman, a poet, author, academic, and politician. Mayor and Goytisolo were already acquainted, and Mayor proved more than willing to support Goytisolo's campaign (Mayor Zaragoza 2010). As Mayor later put it, "I will never forget the visit that author and philosopher Juan Goytisolo paid me one evening in Paris to express his idea that, in the same way as has been so successful with cultural and natural heritage, we ought to showcase these musical, literary, and pedagogical expressions which reveal that distinctive capacity of the human species, creativity—the capacity to reflect, invent, imagine, anticipate, innovate. Humanity as a whole would be richer if it valued and appreciated what these fruits represent, so precious yet so underappreciated" (232; my translation).

With the support of the director-general and with a little help from the "Friends of the Square," UNESCO's Cultural Heritage Division and the Moroccan National Commission for UNESCO organized an International Consultation on the Preservation of Popular Cultural Spaces in Marrakesh in 1997. Assembling scholars of ethnology, anthropology, sociology, and oral history as well as actors, writers, and politicians, this meeting served both to elaborate an international program to protect intangible heritage and to spotlight the plight and the value of Jemaa el-Fna, valorizing the marketplace through international recognition (Schmitt 2008).

In other words, Goytisolo and like-minded intellectuals in Marrakesh enlisted the aid of UNESCO's critical gaze (to borrow a felicitous turn of phrase from Michael Dylan Foster 2015, 229) to save Jemaa el-Fna. The key to saving the square, in Goytisolo's analysis, was to reform the relationship of the local population—and in particular of its wealthier, more powerful elements—to Jemaa el-Fna by teaching them to see it through other eyes (see Gauthier 2009). With the help of UNESCO, Goytisolo and his colleagues turned international attention to Jemaa el-Fna, if only for a moment. Influential foreigners sang the praises of Jemaa el-Fna, suggesting it is so remarkable that it ought to be recognized as the heritage not only of Moroccans but of humanity. According to geographer Thomas Schmitt (citing Goytisolo), once the king was on board, it became easier to persuade other influential Moroccans. City authorities in Marrakesh finally got it; instead of evacuating the square, they preserved it (2008, 103).

Symbol of Backwardness and Decay

This is where the story gets interesting. Together with UNESCO experts, Moroccan authorities surveyed the dangers that threatened to undo Jemaa el-Fna as living heritage; they cited socioeconomic transformations as a "serious obstacle to the preservation and flourishing of this cultural space," compounded by the advance of modernization, urbanization, and the growth of tourism, all of which threaten "the authenticity of the acts and performances." In an interview with Arcadi Espada, however, Juan Goytisolo himself offers a rather different perspective on the menace facing the Marrakesh marketplace: "The bourgeois 'society' of Marrakesh looks at the square with disdain and has on various occasions attempted to do away with it because they think it is a symbol of backwardness and decay. This attitude is by no means rare: often, it is the alien gaze that returns beauty and integrity to places. Alhambra, for example, was discovered by English writers and travelers. Borrow recounts that when he asked people from Granada about Alhambra they referred to it as 'these little Moor things.' Something like that is happening in Marrakesh" (2002; my translation).

The principal threat to Jemaa el-Fna, it turns out, was not from the outside, and not from faceless modernization and urbanization or other suspects from the litany of modern ills cited above, nor even from the growing number of tourists. Instead, the principal threat came from local inhabitants who wield political and economic power. The purpose of reimagining the marketplace as intangible heritage, therefore, was to transform the relationship of Marrakesh's own inhabitants to what goes on in Jemaa el-Fna.

Goytisolo's explanation of exactly what inclusion on UNESCO's list can help to achieve illustrates how an international roster of merit provides incentive to national and local governments to preserve particular expressions or spaces of traditional culture. In Marrakesh, a local commission implemented a ten-year protection plan that included an urban planning study, the creation of a research facility, the identification of traditional knowledge holders, and provisions to strengthen the customary law relevant to the square's management (UNESCO 2001a). In addition, an early analysis of the impacts of UNESCO's recognition identified plans for weekly storytelling sessions, the creation of prize competitions for storytelling, and a fund-in-trust for the benefit of old storytellers to encourage them to transmit their skills to young apprentices (UNESCO 2002b). A fine idea, this fund was ultimately not created, however, and the resources provided by UNESCO for this purpose were returned to the UNESCO/Japan Fund-in-Trust (Beardslee 2016). On the other hand, the Medina governor did take the following measures: "destruction of two buildings unsuited to the popular and traditional aspect of the square, removal of illuminated advertising boards, transformation of streets converging on the Square into pedestrian zone, reduction of car traffic" (UNESCO 2002b, 7).

The preservation measures amount, then, to a concerting of efforts to guard against change, to ensure the perpetuation of the ways in which the cultural space is orchestrated, and to promote uninterrupted continuity in the associated practices and expressions. This coordination (and the provision of requisite resources) is facilitated by the support of local and national authorities. By changing how the Marrakesh elite looks at the square, adding to its value through international recognition, its incorporation into a patrimonial regime solicits the interest of the upper echelons and encourages their active participation in safeguarding this heritage.

This participation may well be a precondition for the success of undertakings such as these. But it comes at a price. That price is the vertical integration of vernacular culture: its incorporation into the administrative structures of official culture and compliance with the logic of policy and bureaucracy. The programs and prize competitions in Jemaa el-Fna afford an example of particular ways in which administrative structures turn vernacular practices into objects for the government to act on. The actions taken by the Medina governor, destroying buildings "unsuited to the popular and traditional aspect" of Jemaa el-Fna and removing illuminated billboards, demonstrate how this compliance with administrative logic can serve to museify everyday practices, reimagining habitat and habitus as heritage. The intervention thus retains the association of the square with backwardness, to which Goytisolo objected, but the language of heritage refigures backwardness as authenticity. As a token of authenticity, this "backwardness" needs to be maintained. More than maintained, actually, for it is actively reconstituted—in this case, with bulldozers and dynamite.

Through safeguarding programs, local councils, administrators, national bodies, and the international community attempt to act on the social field. Their interventions transform the cultural space into a resource for administering populations, a resource through which communities can police and reform themselves so they can conduct themselves in accordance with the way they have been, or will be, trained to see the square, that is, with "a justified sense of pride."

This "alien gaze" symbolically reforms Jemaa el-Fna from a rogue element to a public theater of power and Marrakesh-ness. Existing customs, habits, pastimes, and expressions are transformed, as Barbara Kirshenblatt-Gimblett would have it, to "representations of themselves" (1998, 151) as they become objects of conservation through plans developed by local, national, and international experts with reference to officially sanctioned criteria of excellence.

Fostering the Sense of Community

To be clear, I do not want to give the impression that the customs, expressions, and spaces in question were previously unaffected by the practices and policies of local and national governments. But what is new here is the direct interest taken in the customs and expressions as such and their refiguration as cultural heritage to be safeguarded through government intervention from threats to their continued existence. By means of new social institutions (councils, committees, juries, networks, organizations, associations) and using genres of display characteristic of intangible heritage (lists, brochures, competitions, exhibitions, school programs, and especially festivals), existing practices and expressions have become objects of safeguarding, as in Jemaa el-Fna.

To ethnomusicologist Thomas Beardslee, it "is no surprise that the first of the larger, more formalized multi-genre [associations]. . . , the *Association des Maitres du ḥalqa*, was formed in 2002 following the first of these festivals, in part as a way of negotiating collectively over the pay for the festival and anticipated benefits coming from the UNESCO designation" (2014, 276). In addition, several smaller associations have formed on the square after it gained UNESCO status, "dedicated to a particular genre or ethnicity—one Berber association, two Aissawa, two with assorted musicians and other performers, four Gnawa, and one of storytellers. Most hlayqiya [i.e., performing artists] claimed to have membership in an association" (266–267; Beardslee 2016; see also Schmitt 2005, 187). Thus, as Beardslee recognizes, intangible heritage has proven an effective technology of reformation in Jemaa el-Fna, "fostering the growing sense the hlayqiya have of themselves as being a community—a body that is more readily able to act upon and be acted upon by government than would be a population of ungrouped individuals" (2014, 224).

"And the Square Is Still There"

The story of how Jemaa el-Fna was rescued from the blade of the bulldozer is one of the success stories that UNESCO tells about its efforts to safeguard intangible heritage. It is frequently told as a story of origins—an etiological narrative—adding yet another origin for intangible heritage to the Andean and Japanese etiologies (see chapters 2 and 3). The 1997 consultation in Marrakesh was certainly a catalyst; it gave boost to UNESCO's programs in the field and helped to usher in negotiations for what became the Proclamation of Masterpieces of the Oral and Intangible Heritage of Mankind and later the Intangible Heritage Convention.

As a creation story, it sets the register in which UNESCO likes to describe its efforts in this arena. Like other stories of origins, the narrative of Jemaa el-Fna claims to tell us something essential about the object it originates. The story often ends with the phrase: "And the square is still there," offered as a resolution to the narrative. And indeed, it is still there; instead of a shopping center and a parking lot, storytellers and glass-eaters still perform to the crowds in Jemaa el-Fna; astrologists and water sellers still hawk their services. Instead of one voice, there are many; instead of sameness, difference. Geographer Thomas Schmitt describes the story of Jemaa el-Fna "as a *local-global* success story with a

Fig. 4.2 Standardized carts selling orange juice, Jemaa el-Fna, Marrakesh, Morocco.
©Salvador Aznar/Shutterstock

happy ending (at least for the time being)," although not everyone, he adds, will accept this narrative. "Because it was important to prevent the building of tower blocks in the old city of Marrakech," Schmitt writes, "an international convention was born that offers protection for endangered local cultural traditions all over the world" (2005, 180).

"And the square is still there." Yet, all is not as it was. Something has happened. It is important to understand that safeguarding is a tool of transformation. It transforms people's relationship to their places and practices, and that transformation also affects the places and practices themselves. The square is still there, but a standardized cart on wheels with a traditional look and feel is now mandatory for food vendors, a nostalgic design introduced by the Agence urbaine de Marrakech in 2005 (Schmitt 2005, 188–189; Bessmann and Rota 2008, 125). Moreover, the city government agency ordered shops around the square to harmonize their storefronts and use uniform, large, green parasols (Choplin and Gatin 2010, 26–28). With a ten-year plan, a local commission, weekly storytelling sessions, competitions, funds, and inventories of performers, Marrakeshi authorities have left no stone unturned in their effort to orchestrate difference, to organize Jemaa el-Fna as a safe cultural space characterized by harmony and a pleasant distribution of colors and sounds and products and services. An administrative grid has been superimposed on the square. Invisible to the human eye and intangible to the human hand, it is real in its effects. City authorities and bourgeois society are finally succeeding where before they had failed: in bringing order to Jemaa el-Fna.

To say the fox is guarding the henhouse is perhaps to overreach, but not in the wrong direction. In safeguarding the square, they have changed it. Sure enough, Jemaa el-Fna is still busy with life, still teeming with people selling, buying, performing, watching, listening, taking part, or passing through (Tebbaa 2010). But fire swallowers and musicians, food stalls and preachers are now—increasingly—each in their proper place. Chaos makes way for order as performances and services are zoned.

Folklorist Deborah Kapchan began her ethnographic work on the square in 1994, well before UNESCO held its international consultation there and before Goytisolo and other artists and intellectuals formed the "Friends of the Square" association. Twenty years later, she recalls the changes that came with its proclamation as the intangible heritage of humanity: "In preparation for the rehabilitation of the square, Moroccan authorities relocated all the herbalists to another, single section of the square; what's more, they were told to cease their verbal performances. Obviously, the cleaning up and 'preservation' of Jma' al-Fna in Marrakech required a codification of roles in the square, and since herbalists are not in the UNESCO categories of 'storytellers, acrobats, or musicians,' their own brand of verbal art was not recognized and was ultimately silenced" (2014, 187).

There is more. As noted above, to safeguard Jemaa el-Fna the Medina governor has reduced car traffic and created a pedestrian zone in the streets that converge on the square. These measures may sound helpful to the performing artists, the hlayqiya, on the square, taking away the noise, smell, and distraction of motor traffic. Instead, they proved devastating, especially to the storytellers. Already in 1985, when the Marrakesh Medina was added to the World Heritage List, the bus station that had been on Place Jemaa el-Fna moved away. That still left shared taxi ranks on the square, but as part of the governor's measures, that too moved from the square as motor traffic through Jemaa el-Fna was more or less closed off. This changed the cultural space of the square, but not as the safeguarding plan intended. In his interviews with storytellers in Jemaa el-Fna, Thomas Beardslee found that they blamed the demise of their trade on the removal of the bus stop and the taxi ranks:

These storytellers—even more so than musicians, magicians or acrobats—depend on pedestrian traffic, specifically on Moroccan-Arabic-speaking audience members with a bit of time to kill. The presence of these transportation hubs meant that the storytellers had a fairly regular supply of audience members coming from the crowds waiting on buses and taxis. Once they were removed, that supply dwindled dramatically: there is no longer the flood of workers leaving the tanneries in the afternoons, no more daytime traffic and waiting crowds from the inter-city bus station, and no morning and evening rush of workers reaching other parts of the city in shared taxis. For most of the day, the Square in 2014 is a vast, hot, empty space (save for a few snake charmers and henna women) that relatively few people visit, aside from wandering foreigners looking puzzled as to why the Jemaa el Fnaa is so famous. (2014, 96)

Hegemony on the Surface, Domination Below

In 2013, the hlayqiya went on strike. An American tourist commenting on TripAdvisor on his visit to Morocco in March that year wrote: "The square was lovely. When I visited the first time, there were tons of people and performers. It was great to be able to interact with them. Unfortunately, on this trip the performers were on strike so they weren't out to be seen" (TripAdvisor User Review 2013). In Finnair's in-flight magazine that same year, a journalist noted that "tonight this UNESCO World Heritage site is quiet. The spot in the middle of the town square where men recant their ancient stories is now occupied with wide banners. Slogans are written in Berber and Arabic and a cardboard sign in English sums up the protesters' concerns: 'Where are the rights of artists in Djemaa el-Fna?'" (Palonen 2013, 19). The artists had two principal demands: first, that a commission be set up to investigate what happened to the money that the Japan/UNESCO Funds-in-Trust made available and was in part supposed to help support them and guarantee the future of their arts on the square; second, that they regain some measure of control over their square, where they are now, they said, confined to 5 percent of the surface while food carts and merchants occupy 95 percent of it with the blessing of city authorities. After several days and many disappointed tourists, the city government promised to produce a benefits program for the performers (see Beardslee 2016, 95–99).

There is one more story about the square that begs to be told here. It may inform our reading of the etiological narrative that officials and delegates and diplomats and specialists in the United Nations tell each other about the Marrakeshi origins of the Intangible Heritage Convention: the success story of Goytisolo's inspiration and UNESCO's salvage of Jemaa el-Fna. This other account takes us beneath the surface; literally so, underneath the marketplace. It is the story of Ilham Hasnouni, a young student activist who took part in protest rallies at Cadi Ayyad University in 2008. At about the time the Arab spring protests began to spread through northern Africa in 2010, Hasnouni was arrested by Moroccan security police and became Morocco's youngest political prisoner. Blindfolded and handcuffed, she was transferred to the Marrakesh Medina, the old city within the walls: "I was taken to a dark, damp basement, where I spent the night" (El Rhazoui 2011). To begin with, she had no clue where she was but then, slowly, it dawned on her. Through the ceiling of her subterranean cell, she heard the din of celebration, the rhythms of drums and dancing on the square above her.

Shortly before Hasnouni's arrest, another student, Boudkour Zahra, was stripped naked for three days in the notorious police prison underneath Jemaa el-Fna, humiliated in front of her classmates, and beaten in the face and the genitals with an iron bar. Her screams went unheard on the square, at ground level, where flutes and chants, banter, and drums fill the sonic spectrum. Also arrested for political protest, Zahra was Morocco's youngest political prisoner before Hasnouni joined her. Various interrogators took turns beating Ilham Hasnouni, she tells us, time and again in the subterranean chambers below Jemaa el-Fna: "A few hours after I arrived there, the door opened and new jailers made their appearance. Again, the questions started. But this time they didn't even bother to wait for my non-answers. They beat me until I passed out." As she regained consciousness, the first sound she heard was the heavy, dull thud of blows landing on her body. "Back in my cell," she adds, "I desperately needed to sleep. I was shaking with fatigue. But sleep was impossible because of the dampness of the cell and constant rumble of drums from Jemaa al Fna" (El Rhazoui 2011).

So what is this? Intangible heritage as an instrument of torture? Context is everything, is it not? Antonio Gramsci, the Italian political theorist and activist imprisoned by Mussolini's fascist regime, would have us distinguish between hegemony and domination. In his prison diaries, he describes hegemony as a soft form of power that consists in moral leadership and rule by consent, in part through modern institutions of culture, education, and the media. Conversely, domination makes use of force and the threat of force, in part through institutions like the police and the courts. In modern societies, the two go together. Where consent is denied, force is used (1999). Jemaa el-Fna testifies to both forms of modern power: hegemony on the surface, domination below.

The story of the rescue of Jemaa el-Fna is told in a narrative genre known in folkloristic taxonomy as the etiological legend, that is, a story that takes place in the world more or less as we know it, claims to tell the truth, and describes the origins of objects or institutions that may still be observed. Usually, etiological narratives purport to tell us something essential about the institution or object; its origin is key to understanding it. That is the case with the rescue of Jemaa el-Fna, as the story is usually told. It is a success story told in UNESCO circles about the organization's project to safeguard intangible heritage, and it demonstrates how the concerted efforts of local visionaries and international experts may save a rich cultural space and traditional practices from annihilation by commercially driven globalization and modernization, in the shape of the shopping center and the parking lot (recall Joni Mitchell's "Big Yellow Taxi": "They paved paradise/ And put up a parking lot/ With a pink hotel, a boutique/ And a swinging hot spot"). The story of "El Condor Pasa," recounted in the second chapter of this book, is another etiological narrative, also explaining UNESCO's efforts in the field of intangible heritage through an account of their origins, justifying international norms to counter the international exploitation of local culture. These stories not only give us (participants in the storytelling events) the origins of UNESCO's programs for safeguarding intangible heritage but also a rationale, an explanation, and a justification: they convey a vision of what cultural heritage is, what it is good for, and how to go about protecting it.

You may ask: so what is the argument here? Taking a story of origins from the halls of UNESCO and transporting it back to its narrative setting, an anticlimax now follows on from the original resolution: "And the square is still there." We have undone the closure of this authoritative account, denied it the last word. We have opened up narrative space. That is a powerful form of critique. As Pierre Bourdieu argues in an essay on the genesis and structure of the bureaucratic field, "There is no more potent tool for rupture than the reconstruction of genesis: by bringing back into view the conflicts and confrontations of the early beginnings and therefore all the discarded possibles, it retrieves the possibility that things could have been (and still could be) otherwise" (1994, 4).

We have commanded the halqa, so to speak, and countered story with story. There are other stories to be told beside the ones with widest circulation in the meeting rooms, corridors, and publications of the UN. These stories give context to one another. That, after all, is a central task of critical scholarship: to add context, to tell other stories, to counter simplification with complexity, to imbue homogeneity and order with difference, possibility, alternatives. The rest of this chapter puts the lesson of Jemaa el-Fna into broader theoretical and comparative context, studying intangible heritage as an instrument of reform and considering the relationship between those practices designated as intangible heritage and the social collectives designated as communities: the objects and the subjects of heritage.

Deterioration, Disappearance, and Destruction

Contrary to the UN's narrative tradition with its stories of origins, there had been attempts to protect folklore at the international level well before the Marrakesh meeting of 1997, before Japan joined the World Heritage Convention in 1992, and even before the Bolivian letter of 1973. The first coordinated attempt to provide folklore with international legal protection was at the Diplomatic Conferences of Stockholm in 1967 and Paris in 1971 for the revision of the Berne Convention for the Protection of Literary and Artistic Works. Moreover, as early as 1971—two years before receiving the letter from Bolivia—UNESCO administrators prepared a study titled the "Possibility of Establishing an International Instrument for the Protection of Folklore" (UNESCO 1971). This document made no specific policy recommendations but stressed that the situation of folklore was "rapidly deteriorating" and insisted that further efforts for its protection were "of the utmost urgency" (Sherkin 2001, 44).

This sense of urgency has animated international negotiations for half a century, but it has a longer history going back to the twin ages of European Enlightenment and Discovery. The rapid deterioration of popular tradition has been part and parcel of the concept ever since doctors and priests began to record "vulgar errors" in the European countryside while attempting to eradicate them, and since the days when missionaries and colonial administrators recorded the supposedly moribund customs of the colonial populations they were charged with civilizing. For better or worse, folklore and its synonyms have never quite shaken off connotations of decline and disintegration, and this alarm of the eleventh hour has always fueled both research and policy debate (Anttonen 2005; Bauman and Briggs 2003; Kirshenblatt-Gimblett 1996; Dundes 1969).

Irrespective of the initiatives from 1967 and 1971, seldom cited in UNESCO documents, the better-known 1973 request from the government of Bolivia (see chapter 2) appears to have been a major catalyst for the inscription of folklore on the international agenda. After decades of deliberations, it is extraordinary to consult the letter from 1973 and to find how closely the work still being conducted follows its formulation and how little the problems seem to have changed, despite hundreds of expert meetings, workshops, roundtables, consultations, and fact-finding missions. The "process of commercially oriented transculturation" is still cited as a major threat requiring immediate attention from the international community, though it is now spoken of in terms of globalization. Thus, part of the rationale for the Convention for the Safeguarding of the Intangible Cultural Heritage, cited in its preamble, is that "the processes of globalization and social transformation, alongside the conditions they create for renewed dialogue among communities, also give rise, as does the phenomenon of intolerance, to grave threats of deterioration, disappearance and destruction of the intangible cultural heritage, in particular owing to a lack of resources for safeguarding such heritage" (Convention for the Safeguarding of the Intangible Cultural Heritage 2003). In spite of the compromises palpable in its qualifications, this passage paints an ominous picture of deterioration, disappearance, and destruction. These threats loom large in all of UNESCO's work in the past decades through which the concept of intangible cultural heritage has been brought into being. As a rule of thumb, one can expect one or more references to globalization and its damaging effects in any document, debate, or presentation on intangible heritage within UNESCO.

This sense of danger shadows the notion of intangible heritage in UNESCO discourse. In fact, the menace of globalization is so consistently associated with intangible heritage that it seems intrinsic to the concept. In this, the concept brings with it connotations of urgency always associated with folklore and popular tradition, but it adds a distinctly global twist. Indeed, intangible heritage appears forever to be on the verge of destruction.

Looming threats provide grounds for intervention. As ministers of culture from UNESCO member states declared at the close of a top-level meeting in

Istanbul in 2002, "the extreme vulnerability of the intangible heritage . . . requires that governments take resolute action" (Istanbul Declaration—Final Communi-qué 2002).

Culture and Governmentality

In June 2003, as a member of the Icelandic delegation to UNESCO, I observed the third session of the Intergovernmental Meeting of Experts that drafted the Intangible Heritage Convention. In what follows, I draw on disputes in this meeting, as well as interviews and archival sources. I juxtapose these with theories of heritage and governmentality to argue that the orchestration of differences and government through community are central goals of the convention.

Of course, it is important to remember that although select traditional practices and expressions are canonized, people continue to rework residual representations and create emergent ones in ways "that have little to do with the canonized repertoires and sometimes even serve to subvert them." As folklorist Barbro Klein points out, "Folklore lives through a flow of creative reshapings in daily life at the same time as it is utilized for a host of political and related purposes" (2006, 69). Nevertheless, the broadened scope of heritage, extending into the realm of the intangible and the popular, redefines such marginal practices (marginal to the dominant culture, that is) as objects of cultural policy and administration. While this broadened scope may be more democratic, such "aesthetics of marginalization" (Kirshenblatt-Gimblett 1988, 149) also remap the territory of government, extending it further still into the habitus and habitat of populations (Collins 2011).

The history of UNESCO's work in this field in the 1970s and 1980s is documented elsewhere (e.g., Blake 2001; Bortolotto 2008; Sherkin 2001). In the 1990s, these endeavors shifted away from an archival paradigm of European pedigree. Documentation and research moved down the agenda while intergenerational transmission became the new priority—the attempt to ensure continuity of the traditions targeted. Japanese and Korean programs on "living national treasures" and laws for the protection of "intangible heritage" (on the books since 1950 in Japan and 1962 in the Republic of Korea) provided new blueprints for UNESCO's activities in this field (see chapter 3). From this paradigm shift emerged the so-called Living Human Treasures program in 1993, and the Proclamation of Masterpieces of the Oral and Intangible Heritage of Humanity adopted in 1997 (Nas 2002), and it culminated in the adoption of the Convention for the Safeguarding of the Intangible Cultural Heritage in 2003 (Bortolotto 2008).

The paradigm shift of the 1990s is significant. Instead of preserving textual or audiovisual recordings of performances, UNESCO's declared objective is now to preserve the enabling conditions of performances—the social fabric and habitat—and to provide incentives for transmission from one generation to the next. Making sure that people keep singing their songs tomorrow is a very different task from archiving the songs they sing today.

The insinuation of government into vernacular practices—practices that were previously only of incidental interest to administrators—gives rise to greater regulation of public life. What intangible heritage interventions do, in effect, is to create instruments to act on populations—not so much to shape their conduct directly from above as to influence people to reform their conduct of their own accord. In this, heritage parallels previous uses of art and esthetics in liberal governance. Historically, they have served as instruments to involve individuals as active agents in the processes of their own transformation and self-regulation (Bennett 2000, 1415). Likewise, intangible heritage provides government with a means to intervene in the regulation of social life while also keeping a distance from it.

My argument here is indebted to a body of work published since the 1990s that constitutes a field of inquiry around the concept of "governmentality." Taking its cue from Michel Foucault's essay "On Governmentality" from 1978 (Foucault 1991), this work concerns the rationalities and arts of governing by means of what Foucault describes as "the conduct of conduct." Such "government at a distance" (Rose 1999, 49) is characteristic of liberal political formations that emerged in the eighteenth and nineteenth centuries. In contrast to other forms of rule, liberalism seeks not to crush the capacity for action of its subjects but rather to recognize that capacity and act on it (3–4). The conduct of conduct takes place at thousands of scattered points and requires a profusion of techniques and programs for connecting agendas in political centers to those dispersed sites where operations of power connect with the population and its customs, beliefs, health, hygiene, security, and prosperity (18).

Foucault refers to this proliferation of programs and techniques as the governmentalization of the state. It encourages an equal proliferation of independent authorities and experts (demographers, sociologists, folklorists, anthropologists, doctors, psychologists, managers, social workers, and so on) and of fields of knowledge and expertise relating to the population. It also depends upon ways of aligning political aims and the strategies of experts, and upon establishing lines of communication between the calculations of authorities and the aspirations of free citizens (Rose 1999, 49).

The perspectives of governmentality theory were brought to folklore, anthropology, and cultural studies in the 1990s and have proven particularly fruitful in the critical analysis of cultural policy. Indeed, many techniques for the conduct of conduct belong to what is usually referred to as "culture." With the benefit of governmentality theory, Tony Bennett has argued, we are equipped to move beyond the two culture concepts—the esthetic and the anthropological—to a third understanding of culture as a specific set of instruments for acting on the social with particular ends in view. In this view, culture as a concept and category is a historical formation that has emerged alongside governmental forms of rule. It constitutes a complex of relations between what were previously considered unrelated practices, forging from these a new effective reality (Bennett 2003, 58). Much as "society" and "the economy" have come to be seen as historical formations emerging out of governmental forms of rule that take the population as their object, Bennett shows how "culture, too, can be approached as consisting of a range of particular forms of expertise arising out of distinctive regimes of truth that assume a range of practical and technical forms through the variety of programs for regulating 'the conduct of conduct'" (56).

It is customary to account for the prevalence of the "anthropological" sense of culture as a whole way of life over earlier formulations of culture as "the best that has been thought and known in the world" (Arnold 1998, 8) in terms of a democratic extension of the culture concept. However, when culture is understood historically as instruments for acting on the social, Bennett argues that "this development presents itself in a different light: that is, as a result of the incorporation of ways of life within the orbit of government and, thereby, the production of a working interface between culture and the social" (2003, 59). Folklore may be understood in the same fashion, as a subset or parallel set of instruments for acting on the habitus and habitat of particular segments of the population: the peasants, the *Volk*, the "people," the subaltern, or, conversely, "any group of people whatsoever who share at least one common factor" around which a sense of identity can be organized (Dundes 1965, 2; see also Dundes 1977).

Heritage and Community

Following Barbara Kirshenblatt-Gimblett, to recycle "sites, buildings, objects, technologies, or ways of life" as heritage is to give these things a new lease on life, not as what they once were, but as their own representations (1998, 151). To label a practice or a site as heritage is not so much a description, then, as an intervention. We must recognize cultural heritage as a field of governance, as Tim Winter has stressed, "one that has emerged in the modern era, involving the governance of space, of people, of cultures and natures, of material worlds, and of time" (2015, 998). In fact, heritage reorders relations between persons and things, and among persons themselves, objectifying and recontextualizing them with reference to other sites and practices designated as heritage. Heritage assembles previously unrelated buildings, rituals, paintings, and songs, and it addresses them as something to be safeguarded, that is to say, acted upon through programs, schemes, and strategies carried out and evaluated by experts whose operations connect the calculations of authorities with the desires and ambitions of citizens.

In an interview with the *World Heritage Newsletter*, Joseph King of the International Centre for the Study of the Preservation and the Restoration of Cultural Property (ICCROM) argues that the "conservation of heritage can be a very important aspect" of development on the African continent. Even in "those places facing more serious problems," he continues, "conservation of cultural heritage can play a part (even if small) in improving the situation" (*World Heritage Newsletter* 2001). Together with Jukka Jokilehto, chief of ICCROM's architectural conservation program, King explains this in greater detail in their jointly authored "Reflections on the Current State of Understanding" of authenticity and conservation in the African context. Here, they clarify that it may not always "be possible to insist on continuing traditional habitat as a 'frozen entity'" for "it may sometimes be taken as arrogance to insist on conservation of traditional ways of life if the population does not appreciate this." The question then arises, they go on, "of how to control and guide such modifications in life patterns." In response, they urge that "the present community should be given every opportunity to appreciate and respect what is being inherited from previous generations." "This is a learning process," they explain, "which may require incentives and examples, and which is especially founded in a close collaboration between the population and authorities." The goal, they conclude, is to "identify ways to generate a cultural process that desires such heritage, and therefore takes care of its safeguarding" (Jokilehto and King 2001, 38).

These directions are a fine example of how heritage-making and safeguarding serve as instruments for acting on the social field to "control and guide modifications in life patterns" and to "generate a cultural process." They also underline that heritage is a both a pedagogic project and a transformative process. It transforms the relationship of people with their practices and, as a consequence, their relationship with each other (mediated through those practices). It does so by appealing to their civic duty and moral responsibility for maintaining a particular alignment between the past and the present, in which strong emotions and identities are invested. As William Mazzarella observes, "Any social project that is not imposed through force alone must be affective in order to be effective" (2012, 299). In this sense, heritage is a technology for acting on the social, giving rise to changed behavior.

In 2008, when presenting the first Representative List of the Intangible Cultural Heritage of Humanity, UNESCO's director-general, Koichiro Matsuura, declared his confidence that "with time, this List—designed to give more visibility to our living heritage—will contribute to raising awareness of its importance and instill a sense of pride and belonging to custodian communities" (UN News Centre 2008). Compare that with the words of Juan Goytisolo with which this chapter opened: "Well, what we are attempting—and UNESCO's decision will help us in this—is to change the way many of Marrakesh's own inhabitants look at the square. So they feel a justified sense of pride." The prestige of international recognition that comes with listing is thus designed to elicit the self-recognition of communities as the inheritors and custodians of their own heritage. It is supposed to induce in people a desire to have a heritage and to take care of it; to curate their own practices, or those of other segments of the local population.

The alignment of the past with the present is central in generating a cultural process "that desires such heritage." To quote Kirshenblatt-Gimblett again, "The possession of heritage—as opposed to the way of life that heritage safeguards—is an instrument of modernization and mark of modernity" (2006, 183). By cordoning off certain places and practices as sites of continuity with a cultural tradition or a historical past, everything else is in effect severed from that tradition and history. Inheriting marks the passing away of the social relations that heritage objectifies; it signals a radical disjuncture between the past and the present. Hence, to possess heritage is to be modern; it is a modern way of relating to the past. This past, as given material form in heritage sites and performed in intangible heritage, is inevitably a product of the present that appoints, organizes, and represents it (see Bendix 2009; Klein 2006; Rastrick 2007; Smith 2006; Thompson 2006; Tornatore 2011).

Historically, heritage played a significant role in the creation of modern nation-states. As heritage that was held in common, monuments, landscapes, and folklore were invested with national symbolism, focusing the political imagination on particular representations of the national community (see Anttonen 2005; Anderson 1991; Abrahams 1993; Bendix and Hafstein 2009; Hansen and Martins Holmberg 2016; Klein 2006; Löfgren 1989; Mathisen 2009; Ó Giolláin 2000; Palumbo 2003, 2011; Smith 2006; Thompson 2006). The appointment of cultural and natural treasures conveyed a sense of common responsibility for their transmission to a collective future rooted in a particular territory. This common responsibility gave rise to a series of national institutions, including parks, archives, and a variety of museums. These new institutions required their own dedicated personnel and their own forms of expertise; they were constructed according to a transnationally diffused matrix and appointed with the task of reforming citizens, instructing them, and instilling a consciousness of their responsibility and allegiance to the national community (Bennett 1995, 2001a).

Heritage continues to be an important instrument for representing the nation, rallying citizens around a common identity and sense of belonging. The uses of folklore for this purpose have been documented in a wide range of contexts (see, e.g., Abrahams 1993; Anttonen 2005, 2012; Baycroft and Hopkin 2012; Christiansen 2005, 2007; Dundes 1985; Gunnell 2010, 2012; Herzfeld 1982; Hobsbawm and Ranger 1983; Hopkin 2012; Leersen 2007, 2012; Ó Giolláin 2000). However, it is more difficult now than ever before to imagine national monocultures, what with the multiplication of diasporas and cross-border communities and the resurgence of regional identities and indigenous peoples. The modern national subject came at a price: it glossed over difference; it demanded allegiance to a uniform national culture and history, through selective oblivion, and at the expense of alternative loyalties.

It is hardly a coincidence that under circumstances of intensified migration and visible difference cultural heritage is all at once everywhere (see Rodenberg and Wagenaar 2016; Rana, Willemsen and Dibbits 2017; Harrison 2010; Klein 1997; Coombe and Weiss 2015; Logan 2012; Ashworth, Graham, and Tunbridge 2007; Littler and Naidoo 2005, esp. Hall 2005 and Khan 2005). Cultural heritage creates a discursive space in which social changes may be discussed and it provides a particular language for discussing them (see Klein 2006; Rastrick 2007). It enables people to represent their own understandings of their histories and identities. Yet at the same time, the terminology of heritage is a mechanism of power: it curtails expression by defining the sort of things it makes sense to say.

Ironically perhaps, in the important political transformations of our times it is once again folklore (now under the mantle of intangible heritage) that is instrumentalized, much as it was in the rise of nationalism in the nineteenth and twentieth centuries. Under these circumstances, many governments have come to acknowledge and even promote "communities" as cultural and administrative units. Although such communities represent a slippery slope for the project of the nation-state, a new form of government rationality is emerging that focuses on "the organization of self-regulating and self-managing communities that are, in some respects, disconnected from the larger wholes of nationally defined societies or, in the case of diasporic communities, cut across them" (Bennett 2000, 1421).

According to sociologist Nikolas Rose (1999), governing through community is part of an important turn in liberal government. It represents a shift in focus away from the individual in society toward communities as mediating entities to which individuals owe allegiance and through which they reform and manage themselves. This turn responds, in part, to new forms of identity politics emerging out of civil and human rights movements, in addition to diasporic migrations and the newfound vocality of indigenous groups. However, it is also closely related to processes of economic and cultural globalization and to the generalization of neoliberal policies through trade agreements and aid programs enforced by bodies like the International Monetary Fund, the World Bank, and the World Trade Organization.

Such processes and policies make it possible to speak of an emergent global governmentality or a governmentalization of international relations, in which states play a diminishing role but transnational organizations, corporations, coalitions, and diasporic networks steadily assume greater responsibilities. This delegation of responsibility to the citizenry is an aspect of the neoliberal political project, integrating individuals into their own government and giving them responsibility for conducting themselves individually and each other in communities (Árnason and Hafsteinsson 2018). This move also characterized "third way" politics in various guises; from Great Britain to Taiwan, third way politicians identified community as a "third space" between the state and the individual that proposes itself as a solution to the problems of excessive state interference in the lives of citizens but also to the anomie and insecurity associated with excessive individualism.

At various levels of government, from local to international, we observe this new emphasis on communities as an innovative way to make sense of collective existence and to make it calculable and administrable. Over the last twenty-five to fifty years (beginning at different times in different places), but especially in the last decade, "a whole array of little devices and techniques have been invented to make communities real" (Rose 1999, 189). Within a fairly short period, there has been a phenomenal upsurge of new sorts of expertise through which "community"—which began as a language of resistance—has been transformed "into an expert discourse and a professional vocation" (175). As Rose points out, "Community is now something to be programmed by Community Development Programmes, developed by Community Development Officers, policed by Community Police, guarded by Community Safety Programmes and rendered knowable by sociologists pursuing 'community studies'" (175).

We can add to this list the many institutions and programs of community heritage: community museums, community archives, community heritage festivals, community heritage registers, community heritage centers, community heritage commissions, and community heritage grants. And there is a parallel profusion of experts and professionals, such as community curators, community heritage commissioners, community historians, community folklorists, community exhibition designers, and community heritage development officers. This trend is not limited to the public sector; past decades have witnessed a great variety of public-private partnerships in this area with a concomitant mushrooming of interdisciplinary consulting firms, such as Community Heritage Partners in Pennsylvania, who help "property owners, local governments, and community organizations develop realistic solutions to preserve and renew their architectural heritage, strengthen their community character, and enhance their quality of life." Not content merely to provide technical assistance in preservation, they also "develop strategies for community participation and private initiatives to build awareness and change attitudes" (Community Heritage Partners, n.d.).

Every claim of community refers to something that already exists and to which we owe allegiance. Yet our allegiance to these communities is something we need to be made aware of and requires "the work of educators, campaigns, activists, [and] manipulators of symbols, narratives and identifications" (Rose 1999, 177). Despite or indeed because of its central role in the conception of governing, as Tony Bennett remarks, "community has constantly to be rescued from its imminent disappearance or, because the perceived need for community often precedes its existence, to be organized into being" (2000, 1422–1423).

In much the same way as a common heritage is invoked to forge national community, it is also central to the constitution of local, indigenous, and diasporic communities. The communalization of heritage and cultural policy helps to form and to reform population groups and to orchestrate differences in the state. It is a strategy for coping with difference. From this perspective, intangible heritage emerges as an instrument in the production of a strong (but not exclusive) sense of belonging for community members. Population groups subjectify themselves as "communities" and objectify their practices and expressions as "intangible heritage." Government can then act on the social field through communities and by means of, among other things, intangible heritage policies.

This corresponds to developments in environmental conservation, where there is widespread preoccupation with community, and programs proliferate that devolve to communities the responsibility for putting environmental policy into practice. Political scientist Arun Agrawal coined the term "environmentality" to describe this governmental rationality in which communities are interpellated as "environmental subjects" (2005). Populations learn to conceive of their habitat as "the environment" and to appreciate the need for its conservation, and—through an infusion of expertise and in cooperation with state, nongovernmental, and intergovernmental organizations—are charged with administering themselves and their environmental practices (e.g., Agrawal and Gibson 2001; Li 2001; McDermott 2001). Contemporary approaches to heritage conservation may be described in similar terms, and we might speak of a patrimonial governmentality, or "patrimoniality," that interpellates individuals and populations as "patrimonial subjects"; that teaches them to conceive of some of their practices and material culture in terms of heritage and to appreciate the need to safeguard these; and that, through cooperation with state, nongovernmental, and intergovernmental organizations and experts, inducts them into a patrimonial regime.

Whose Heritage?

Much like the hot button issue of the list (see chapter 3), questions regarding communities, their proper place in an international convention, and their relations to states and intergovernmental organizations were debated intensely in the meeting of experts that drafted the Convention for the Safeguarding of the Intangible Cultural Heritage. Member states differ, of course, in whether and to what extent they govern through community, and relations between official and minority cultures are differently structured in different states. Indeed, along with the creation of lists, the question of communities was the most contentious issue at the meeting's third session in June 2003 at UNESCO headquarters at Place Fontenoy in Paris. The delegate from Hungary, more than anyone else, spoke out for community rights in the convention and for maximal requirements for consultation with practicing communities and nongovernmental organizations (NGOs). He took every opportunity to do so, and opportunity presented itself in connection with several articles drafted and approved at this session, in particular with respect to various provisions on safeguarding at the national level (articles 11–15 in the final text). He was far from isolated in his position, however; among others, the representatives of Vanuatu, Papua New Guinea, Zimbabwe, Peru, and Finland expressed similar points of view.

This issue had been debated at previous meetings and it resurfaced immediately on the first day of the June session. The preliminary draft convention distributed to delegations stated (in article 4) that "each State Party recognizes the duty of safeguarding its intangible cultural heritage." As soon as the floor opened, the Hungarian delegate raised his sign and made the observation that "there is a difference between speaking of 'its' intangible cultural heritage and intangible cultural heritage 'present in its territory.' It is *not* the state's intangible cultural heritage. It is not created by the state but by communities and groups. This is a point of principle!"

The point here concerns different ways of imagining community and locating culture, and the Hungarian principle holds that these are not isomorphic with the state, though the state has duties toward communities within its borders. In response, the South African delegate warned that "many issues will arise from the phrase 'present in its territory'" and asked the committee to retain the term "its."

The delegate from Papua New Guinea followed him and objected to the homogeneity presumed by the notion of a state's heritage: "We don't talk about 'our national heritage,' but about different cultures in our territories. We are against the notion of national cultural heritage. We therefore support using the phrase 'present in its territory.'"

Several other delegations expressed their preference for one or the other of these formulations before a Chilean delegate intervened with the preposterous suggestion to use both: "to safeguard *its* intangible cultural heritage *present in its territory*." Perhaps this proposal is best understood as an example of deliberate misreading—not an uncommon tool of diplomacy—for it clearly retains the idea of the state's own heritage and makes the qualifier "present in its territory" more or less superfluous (or else refigures it from an inclusive to a restrictive sense).

This debate over a possessive pronoun is typical of the often convoluted process of transnational consensus-building in UN organizations. I have observed the same tortuous process in the World Intellectual Property Organization in Geneva. Moreover, anthropologist Sally Engle Merry describes similar debates in the UN's Commission on the Status of Women in New York, and as she notes, "Although the wording debates seemed trivial, they revealed political differences in subtle ways" (2006, 40). Negotiating terminology—debating the use of pronouns—is the UN way to circumvent irreconcilable differences in order to reach consensus in a roundabout style. It is easy to agree with Merry that one is deeply impressed observing "people from countries all over the world trying to put together some words that every one of them could live with, despite their differences" and actually coming up with a binding agreement (47).

Predictably, the most vocal critics of the emphasis on consultation with communities were states in which conspicuous ethnic and cultural minorities present a serious challenge to the state's monopoly on the moral resources of community, states like Russia, Turkey, India, and Spain. Although their specific concerns remained unspoken, it was evident that these states were reluctant to take on international commitments in a convention that could conceivably be used as an instrument of separatism, sedition, or minority rights struggles by Chechens and Ingush in the Caucasus, Kurds in Kurdistan, Assamese and Khasis in northeast India, or Catalans in Catalonia and Basques in Euskadi, to name but a few examples.

In response to a UNESCO questionnaire in the year 2000 (on the application of its 1989 Recommendation for the Safeguarding of Folklore and Traditional Culture), Spain's UNESCO commission stressed that Spanish legislation "does not allow for any conceptual confusion between the terms 'traditional communities' and 'cultural minorities'"; cultural minorities receive no special protection under Spanish law whereas it makes provisions for fostering and promoting the practices of traditional communities (Blake 2001, 43). A revealing example of the political uses of taxonomy, this sort of legal sensitivity undergirds the opposition to international obligations to protect the cultural heritage of all communities in the state's territory and to involve communities actively in policy decisions and safeguarding.

Conversely, in some cases equally palpable circumstances account for an emphasis on consultation with communities and their role in the convention. For instance, the most outspoken champion for community rights, Hungary, has its own ax to grind. Hungary lost two world wars, and the resulting changes to the map of Europe left ethnic Hungarians dispersed among nine of its neighboring states: Romania, Slovakia, Serbia, Ukraine, Russia, Austria, Croatia, the Czech Republic, and Slovenia (in descending order of importance). It goes without saying that the position of these Hungarian minorities is of great concern to Hungarian authorities. Thus, one and a half million people of Hungarian descent make up one-third of the population of Transylvania, a province of the Austro-Hungarian Empire that reverted to Romania at the end of World War I. For most of the twentieth century, Romanian authorities saw them as an unruly minority and attempted to assimilate them by means of their so-called Romanianization policy (involving, e.g., forcible relocation, job reassignments, and school mergers). Disputes over this minority are at the root of protracted hostilities between the governments of Hungary and Romania.

In a spirit of compromise, article 5 in the preliminary draft convention distributed to participants at the June session stipulated that "each State Party shall endeavour insofar as possible, in a manner which enriches cultural diversity in the context of national life as a whole" to implement a number of safeguarding measures at the national level (UNESCO 2003a, Appendix 2, 7). Not only does this tortuous phrase twice remove the obligation of *shall* (with *endeavour* and *insofar as possible*); it also stipulates that the manner in which that obligation is fulfilled shall conform to a unity-in-diversity vision of the state. This stipulation was ultimately dropped, but not without a good deal of debate. As the meeting's chairman, ambassador Mohammed Bedjaoui (who went on to become Algeria's minister of foreign affairs in 2005), explained on the first day of the session: "The ambassador of India, who I see is not present today, was very insistent at previous meetings and fought to use the phrase 'in a manner which enriches cultural diversity in the context of national life as a whole.' India is of course a very multicultural country and there are lots of things to balance there."

To be sure, there are many manners of safeguarding, transmitting, revitalizing, and promoting traditional practices and expressions that do not situate them within "the context of national life as a whole." To name but one example from the northeastern states of India—a cauldron of contending ethnic communities with a number of insurgency movements against the rule of the New Delhi government—folklorist Desmond Kharmawphlang recounts in *Indian Folklife* (newsletter of the National Folklore Support Centre in India) how rebels abducted a close colleague from his home and took him to a clandestine training camp operated by a Khasi insurgency group. "They asked him to stay there for two weeks," Kharmawphlang relates, "to talk about folklore of the Khasis in order to inspire some sort of unity among the cadres" (Kharmawphlang et al. 2004, 19).

Conversely, folklore training also serves in a great number of instances to promote allegiance to national unity and to inspire its forces. By way of illustration, the Lithuanian Law on the Principles of State Protection of Ethnic Culture from 1999 (amended in 2006) provides that the "Ministry of National Defence along with the Ministry of Education and Science shall include ethnic culture in training of military personnel and patriotic education programmes" (WIPO Lex 2010, art. 9, para. 8).[1] Such state protection of ethnic (or traditional, folk) culture, with its military aspect and patriotic pedagogy, is not insignificant in a small state with sizable Polish, Russian, and Belarusian minorities, where ethnic Lithuanians account for only about 32.5 percent of the population of Vilnius District Municipality, which includes the capital Vilnius (but 63 percent of the city proper and 83 percent of the country's population) (Statistics Lithuania, 2013). Indeed, the preamble to the law in question argues for its necessity based on "the fact that ethnic culture constitutes the essence of national existence, survival and strength" while "the various forms of Lithuanian ethnic culture and particularly its living traditions are in obvious danger of extinction" (WIPO Lex 2010, preamble).

Back in the meeting room at Place Fontenoy, Bedjaoui urged the meeting to keep the phrase "in a manner which enriches cultural diversity in the context of national life as a whole" and not to "take advantage of India's absence to delete it in one fell swoop." Korea and France, however, suggested dropping the phrase for the sake of a shorter and clearer text, for, as the French delegate said, "This is a legal document and generations of young lawyers will interpret it." He hastened to add, "No one will suspect France of not favoring cultural diversity," but "the whole convention is about cultural diversity; why say it in one article rather than another?" The Chilean delegate agreed and suggested that a note on cultural diversity be put in the preamble to the convention. The delegation of Honduras, however, said it supported the article as it stood and in particular the phrase in question. Moreover, the Turkish delegate insisted, "We should retain the phrase we are discussing" because "it promotes tolerance within the community towards the intangible cultural heritage of other communities and groups" (and "we should also show some respect to India even though they are absent").

Some raised questions regarding the relevance of "national life as a whole" to the duties undertaken by states in the article, and there was clearly a measure of discomfort surrounding this phrase among some delegations. Reacting to this, the delegate from the Dominican Republic frankly suggested that the committee stop skirting the issues with vague phraseology and just come out and use the term "nation-state," since that was clearly what was meant by "the national life as a whole." "Ah, non," chairman Bedjaoui was quick to rebut, "the 'nation-state' is an explosive term!" "If we say 'nation-state,'" he went on, "the political scientists will gut us!"

In the final text of the convention, States Parties to it take on the (conditioned) obligation to "endeavour to ensure the widest possible participation of communities, groups, and, where appropriate, individuals that create, maintain and transmit such heritage" in the framework of their safeguarding activities at the national level "and to involve them actively in its management" (article 15).

Sovereignty, Territory, Community

This debate may seem, at first glance, far afield from the topic of intangible heritage. In spite of appearances, however, it speaks directly to the sort of intervention constituted by that heritage and its safeguarding—the manner in which it is instrumental in acting on the social. Neither the degree and modalities of community involvement in this intervention nor the conditions imposed on expression are extraneous to the manner in which traditional practices of cultural communities are selected, promoted, and protected as intangible cultural heritage. These are crucial factors affecting how heritage is used to imagine community, to structure allegiance, to channel or suppress dissent, and to orchestrate differences so as to organize either homogeneity or cultural diversity within political unity. The debates and negotiations in UNESCO's drafting committee thus afford important insights into the international politics of heritage and how these correlate with national politics, global governance, and human rights.

A recurring issue in global governance is the tension between national sovereignty and the mandate of international organizations. Sovereignty is constantly asserted and "rescued" from subordination to supranational authority, even as intergovernmental organizations depend for their legitimacy on the sovereign powers of their constituent governments. This relationship is negotiated anew in the creation of nearly every international instrument.

The Convention for the Safeguarding of the Intangible Cultural Heritage is no exception. During the debates on community involvement and on mechanisms for civil society representation in the convention's execution (e.g., through NGO consultations), the Colombian delegate reminded the drafting committee that "this is a convention between states and they are responsible for it," and the Zambian delegate warned that "the committee may be infringing on national sovereignty." Although their objections did not meet with approval, concerns about potential infringements of sovereignty were still rife in the committee.

German diplomats emerged during the June meeting in 2003 as ardent defenders of national sovereignty against supranational incursions. They received strong support especially from their colleagues from Turkey, Austria, Japan, Grenada, and the Czech Republic. I confess that I had a hard time making sense of some diplomatic alliances, this being one of them. It is important to bear in mind, however, that a great deal of horse trading went on outside the meeting room. Discussions and negotiations took place during coffee and lunch breaks, and over linen-and-china decked Parisian dinner tables. Over coffee or drinks or steak frites, alliances were formed and broken over the major issues at stake in this convention, but in many cases such alliances also involve affairs completely foreign to intangible heritage. As Lynn Meskell and her coauthors note in their analysis of multilateralism in UNESCO, "Transgovernmental networks comprised of informal horizontal peer-to-peer interactions, including vote exchanges, have become the norm" and "pressures from private interests whether individuals, companies and NGOs are also becoming more common, especially as regards World Heritage Properties" (2015, 430; see also Meskell 2014).[2]

A lengthy sovereignty debate at the June meeting revolved around the power to place particular items of intangible heritage on the heritage lists created through the convention (see chapter 3). Should the convention's executive committee be able to do so of its own accord or should the initiative in all instances come from the State Party involved? The Italians spoke out in favor of the former position: "We favor a solution which allows the committee to place intangible cultural heritage on a list at its own initiative. Therefore, we favor deleting the phrase 'at the request of the State Party concerned.' Italy believes the intangible cultural heritage is the heritage of humanity." The Hungarian delegate concurred and likewise emphasized that "we are concerned here with the general heritage of humanity."

Responding to this perceived threat to national sovereignty in the name of humanity at large, Germany stressed that it was crucial that the committee not be given powers to act without the consent of the state party involved: "Do we want to invite States Parties to ratify a convention which might entail as a consequence that political pressure will be applied to them because of intangible cultural heritage in their territory? . . . This is dangerous." And Germany was not alone in smelling danger. The Chinese delegate took the floor next and stressed that China agreed with Germany: "It is very important to China to keep the phrase 'upon the request of the State Party concerned'" (consider Tibetan traditions and you'll know why). And the Indian delegate insisted on the retention of this condition, cautioning that its deletion "would be very dangerous" (consider the Khasi insurgents who kidnapped a folklorist to inspire the cadres).

Germany and its allies in the protection of national sovereignty won the day. The final text makes listing of heritage contingent on its proposal by the States Parties concerned. The principle of territorial sovereignty cited by the German delegate, though its invocation is a leitmotif in the negotiation of most international instruments, is particularly notable for the consideration of heritage and sheds light on what is new in this convention.

The World Heritage Convention from 1972 defined heritage in spatial terms, as monuments, groups of buildings, and sites, and as natural reserves and parks. In contrast to the more recent "environmentality" model of conservation, the convention's conception of "natural heritage" has been criticized for being all too spatial in its lack of attention to human populations that live in areas designated as parks and reserves, or whose subsistence depends on them, alienating these populations from their administration if not expelling them (see chapter 3). World heritage is thus by definition expressed as territory; territory that can be "delimited, measured, mapped" (Pressouyre 1997, 57; Brumann and Berliner 2016, 3).

This spatialization of heritage is recognizable in innumerable heritage maps and geographies that belong all at once to statecraft, the tourism industry, and global governance. In *Imagined Communities*, historian Benedict Anderson remarks that maps were used to classify and create spatial reality in the colonies, marking out territory through abstract delimitations to put space under surveillance. Old sacred sites were incorporated into the map of the colony, lending time depth to newly created territorial unity. In this way, the mappers would drape themselves in ancient prestige, and, Anderson notes, "If this had disappeared, as it often had, the state would attempt to revive it" (1991, 181–182).

Heritage has thus long been central to the conception of territory: it aligns present claims of territorial sovereignty with past authority; it lends itself to easily recognizable representations of the territory and its unity; and it infuses such claims and representations with prestige and legitimacy. Conversely, territory is a defining characteristic of heritage. In fact, it is so central that it is fair to say that in certain respects heritage is territory. It is other things besides, but whatever else it may be, *heritage is territory.*

Of course, that applies primarily to the cultural and natural heritage of the World Heritage Convention. A distinction needs to be drawn between monuments, groups of buildings, and sites, on the one hand, and intangible cultural heritage on the other. Intangible heritage shifts away from territorial definition. The relationship of intangible heritage to populations is not mediated through land or territory. Instead, intangible heritage objectifies the practices and expressions of human communities. It is defined ethnographically rather than topographically. Intangible heritage emerges out of an intervention in community practices, and this intervention defines and delimits the community. If tangible heritage is then territory in some sense, by the same token it stands to reason that *intangible heritage is community*.

Safeguarding Community

The safeguarding of intangible cultural heritage represents a subtle innovation in governmental rationality, disciplining populations through a conversion of their customs, practices, and expressions into heritage (the threatened nature of which makes it morally imperative to intervene). Ultimately, this shift makes community itself subject to conservation in the face of its purportedly steady decline in the modern world. Community is thus the most fundamental intangible heritage that UNESCO's 2003 convention sets out to safeguard. In this sense, it is an important objective of the convention to build communities with which their members identify, even if many states are careful to circumscribe the terms of such empowerment. This desire to empower communities is apparent in the convention's definition of intangible heritage: "The 'intangible cultural heritage' means the practices, representations, expressions, knowledge, skills—as well as the instruments, objects, artefacts and cultural spaces associated therewith—that communities, groups and, in some cases, individuals recognize as part of their cultural heritage" (article 2, paragraph 1).

This is perhaps better described as an indefinition; the relative clause that follows the second dash defers the power to define intangible cultural heritage to the communities themselves (and groups and, in some cases, individuals). In this way, the convention "endeavours to ensure" that the community is involved in any safeguarding measures or that such measures are at least not conducted without the community's approval—it delegates responsibility to communities as collective subjects (Blake 2009; Bortolotto 2009; see also Tolia-Kelly, Waterton, and Watson 2017).

The convention's circular formula—that "intangible cultural heritage" means the practices that communities recognize as part of their cultural heritage—begs the question of what the term "community" denotes. In fact, it requires the definition of the communities with which state actors consult and cooperate. To involve communities in safeguarding it is necessary first to delimit them, to define membership in them, and to designate a mechanism for consultation or cooperation (a "competent authority").

Part of the political attraction of communities lies in their apparent naturalness (Noyes 2003). Despite appearances, however, and like nations before them, communities need to be made up. Boundaries and distinctions have to be put into place. Communities have to be visualized, surveyed, and mobilized. Intangible cultural heritage does just that: it converts cultural practices into resources for administering populations. In this way, empowerment depends on subjection. This is the classical paradox of subjectification for, as Foucault argues, subject formation takes place in the element of power (in the double sense of the French *pouvoir*: the noun "power" and the verb "to be able to"). The moment at which we attain status as subjects (the subjects of our thoughts, words, and deeds, and subjects in our relations with ourselves and others) is also the moment of subjection in which we become subject to a set of rules and norms of behavior, and to definitions, boundaries, and exclusions already imposed on the discourse in which we assume a subject position.

Thus, the communities to which UNESCO's concept of intangible heritage refers itself are all positioned squarely as collective subjects within states and subject to states. Their empowerment cements their administrative bonds to central government, even as it loosens their cultural bonds. By defining community, providing it with outside expertise, and conferring official prestige on its marginalized practices and expressions, this process demonstrates how residual and interstitial cultural representations—craftsmanship, oral traditions, rituals, performing arts—are incorporated into the hegemonic order of representation.

Orchestrating Difference

In a comment on UNESCO's Proclamation of Masterpieces of the Oral and Intangible Heritage of Humanity (a predecessor to the convention and its lists), Henri J. M. Claessen (2002) expresses misgivings about the induced survival of moribund cultural practices: "Governments will pay people to dance dances the use of which no one sees any longer, to sing incomprehensible songs that have long since lost their meaning, to perform mystery plays in which no one now believes." Claessen asks: "Why do this? Why spend a lot of money and work to make a list of such endangered masterpieces?" (2002, 144).

Why indeed? One answer might be that in many cases practicing communities would very much like to see their traditions represented on such a list, which confers honor on them and draws attention, not least from local and national authorities. If these communities find it meaningful, if they see the use in it, and they believe it is worthwhile, then their desire to safeguard certain practices provides a partial answer to Claessen's question, "Why do this?" I have argued here that the desire to safeguard and strengthen communities is another partial answer. The third piece in this puzzle is the will to safeguard and promote cultural diversity. These three answers are entirely consistent; they address the question at micro, meso, and macro levels, respectively (the same question was often asked of those who advocate revitalizing endangered languages and is answered in Dorian 1987).

The Istanbul Declaration, issued by UNESCO ministers of culture in 2002, emphasizes that "the multiple expressions of intangible cultural heritage constitute some of the fundamental sources of the cultural identity of the peoples and communities" and maintains that they are "an essential factor in the preservation of cultural diversity" (Istanbul Declaration—Final Communiqué 2002). This reciprocity between cultural identity and cultural diversity has been the backbone of UNESCO's rationale for its activities in the field of intangible heritage and in particular for the creation of the 2003 convention. In fact, the Istanbul Roundtable was held under the banner "The Intangible Heritage: A Mirror of Cultural Diversity."

There is more than one way to understand diversity, however, and more than one way to give it policy expression. There are not many states left that do not pay at least lip service to such diversity and that have not implemented a policy at the national level to promote cultural diversity, though those policies conceive in different ways of the sort of diversity desirable and how it is to be managed (Bennett 2001b; Bonet and Négrier 2011; Zapata-Barrero 2016; see also Stenou 2003). Such policies rely on a range of practices and techniques to govern subject formation in the new multiple field of identity and allegiance. Organizing communities as spaces of emotional relationships and of strong, but not exclusive, identifications is a subset of these practices. Government through community and the orchestration of difference should be seen as aspects of one enterprise.

Differences between communities are arranged, celebrated, and often overstressed and exoticized in media structured according to a global grammar of festival and exhibition. Usually, these integrate the communities into some program or other of unity in diversity. Through such heritage politics, differences are orchestrated as cultural diversity, as groups within a state are given a voice but also given a score to sing in harmony. These politics play out in a remarkably uniform fashion across the globe, as Arjun Appadurai explains: "Typically, contemporary nation-states do this by exercising taxonomic control over difference, by creating various kinds of international spectacle to domesticate difference, and by seducing small groups with the fantasy of self-display on some sort of global or cosmopolitan stage" (1996, 39).

The Convention for the Safeguarding of the Intangible Cultural Heritage sets just such a cosmopolitan stage. As suggested in chapter 3, its lists highlight and promote, they bring attention to select local practices and expressions, and they rally resources to their safeguarding. Although modeled on the World Heritage

List, these lists differ in that the heritage inscribed on them is embodied by living persons in practicing communities and has no existence apart from these communities. In effect, UNESCO's intangible heritage lists showcase communities in a manner that owes as much to the global grammar of multicultural festivals as it does to the World Heritage List. Indeed, the festival is itself one of the principal genres of display in the safeguarding of intangible heritage (see chapter 5). Organizing esthetic markers of difference in lists, brochures, documentaries, web pages, and spectacles, UNESCO's intangible heritage initiatives display the diversity of cultures and coordinate it under the sign of humanity—as unity in diversity.

Homogeny and Hegemony (or, Danishness Transposed)

Koichiro Matsuura, UNESCO's director-general (1999–2009), missed no opportunity to stress the importance of the intangible heritage for the promotion of cultural diversity worldwide. In an address in Copenhagen in June 2004, Matsuura posed the question, "Why has the protection of intangible cultural heritage become a matter of urgency in recent years?" (UNESCO 2004b, 1). Responding to his own query, he continued: "The answer, I believe, comes in large part from a growing recognition that accelerating globalization is placing enormous new pressures upon cultural diversity. These pressures have given rise to fears of greater cultural homogenization and associated threats to the world's cultural diversity, especially in its local, indigenous and living forms. These fears, which are widely shared, have stimulated the demand that something must be done before it is too late. The convention is a vital part of this process of urgently addressing the cultural challenges of globalization" (1).

Fear of the global homogenization of culture can put a peculiar spin on international policymaking under the aegis of UNESCO. Matsuura himself illustrated this peculiarity with his subsequent remarks in the Copenhagen address: "This very meeting is part of a process of national self-reflection in Denmark on the question of intangible cultural heritage. Such reflection can be both stimulating and unsettling. It may provoke some hard questions. For example, what is at the core of Danish identity and culture? What is it that you do not want to lose at any cost? . . . Can this distinctive feature be defined and labeled? Do you want to preserve it? Can you imagine Denmark and 'Danishness' without it? These are the kinds of questions, transposed to all the countries of the world, that are shaping the agenda of intangible cultural heritage" (UNESCO 2004b, 1).

Leaving aside, for present purposes, the problematic notion of culture as essential expressions of difference, it is primarily the national inflection of this notion that troubles me. I find it disconcerting that a process of "national self-reflection," designed to define "Danishness" and label "the core of Danish identity and culture," should stand, in the director-general's opinion, at the center of "the agenda of intangible cultural heritage." Although it is meant to respond to perceived threats to the world's cultural diversity and to mitigate fears of homogenization, such a process—"transposed to all the countries of the world"—would inevitably defeat its purpose.

In an interview at UNESCO headquarters in Paris, a member of the UNESCO secretariat expressed views similar to those of the director-general. When I queried him as to why he thought it was important to safeguard intangible heritage, he asserted that this heritage is needed to maintain cultural diversity in the world because "that's what makes Colombia different from Bolivia, and so on!" (personal communication, November 25, 2003). In an important article on the politics of heritage, Regina Bendix has remarked on this elastic capacity of heritage "to hide the complexities of history and politics" (2000, 38). As my interlocutor's remarks make evident, intangible heritage can highlight certain differences while occluding others—say, in the case of Colombia and Bolivia, the differences between militia and electoral politics, which at the time of the interview surely distinguished Colombia from Bolivia as effectively as their respective popular traditions.

To be fair, I should add that later in the same interview, my informant acknowledged that intangible heritage "also problematizes national identity, especially in cross-border communities" (personal communication, November 25, 2003). This observation gestures toward what should be obvious: a world where cultural difference is expressed as a collection of coexisting nationalnesses—"Danishness," "Japaneseness," "Indianness," "Zambianness," "Colombianness," and so on—is less diverse, not more diverse, than the one we inhabit. International policy that imagines such a world as its objective, if it were to have any effect, might be more perilous to global cultural diversity than the "cultural challenges of globalization" that occasion it.

There is good reason to be skeptical. As Appadurai has remarked, fears of homogenization can be "exploited by nation-states in relation to their own minorities, by posing global commoditization (or capitalism, or some other such external enemy) as more real than the threat of its own hegemonic strategies" (1996, 32). For an illustration, one need merely recall one of UNESCO's etiological accounts of how it came to concern itself with folklore: the Bolivian minister's alarm in the face of the "process of commercially oriented transculturation destructive of the traditional cultures," and the simultaneous suppression of indigenous identities and appropriation of indigenous culture by the Bolivian state (see chapter 2).

A UNESCO-sanctioned imperative for cultural diversity that foregrounds international diversity and backgrounds cultural differences within states can, will, and certainly has been used to justify the suppression of minorities. The director-general's peculiar spin on cultural policy is perhaps best understood, therefore, as cooptation of human rights discourse on diversity. Distributing difference between states rather than within them, it legitimizes the eradication of difference in the name of defining, labeling, and, ultimately, bringing into being an orderly collection of internally consistent national identities and cultures.

The director-general was not wrong in his conviction that intangible cultural heritage and the convention for its safeguarding can be useful instruments for addressing "the cultural challenges of globalization." He was right, but for the wrong reasons. Their importance is not that they get at the core of national identity or that they help to label distinctive features of national character. What is significant is how the concept and the convention enable a reimagination of heritage and encourage the relocation of culture in communities. Intangible heritage, as defined and instrumentalized in the 2003 convention, enfranchises and invests capacities in practicing communities; it contributes to their organization as partially self-regulating administrative entities.

The model of communalization, as analyzed by Nikolas Rose, is undoubtedly most applicable in states characterized by advanced liberalism—whether in its neoliberal, social-democratic, or "third way" inflections. It is important to note, however, that this model does not apply equally or consistently to all liberal states even in the "developed world." Rather than conceive of communalization as a single model of government, it is probably better to admit of a range of different degrees, modes, and methods of governing through community. This is even more important with reference to "developing" countries, for globalization and liberalization do not produce the same results everywhere. There are certainly many liberalisms, and citizens are integrated into their government to various degrees (see Grossberg, Miller, and Packer 2003, 34; Ong 2006).

Voicing Community

If the communalization of government delegates many tasks of social governance to the community level, it maintains all the while a loose affiliation of all communities in the sovereign territory with each other and with the state; this affiliation is organized around the common citizenship of the individual members of different communities rather than around their cultural ties. The intangible cultural heritage, as conceived of by UNESCO, is appointed, assembled, and interpreted in part by or in consultation with practicing communities, whose identities are intertwined in its representation. To the extent that community members are integrated into and made responsible for the work of representation, intangible heritage enfranchises and gives voice to communities. In so doing, however, an attempt is made to fix particular sets of relations and authority as relatively stable units—communities—that can speak with one voice.

Inevitably, such attempts instigate jockeying for power at ground level (see, e.g., Berliner 2010; Bortolotto 2009; Kuutma 2009; Lowthorp 2007; Noyes 2006;

Fig. 4.3 Patum de Berga, Catalonia, Spain. Creative Commons via Wikimedia Commons.

Tauschek 2009; Tornatore 2011). In a discerning analysis of some early conse-quences of the nomination of the Patum festival in Berga, Catalonia, for UNES-CO's Proclamation of Masterpieces, folklorist Dorothy Noyes recounts how attempts to fix the community can play out locally. A popular street festival and collective performance with a long history, the Patum has always been a vehicle of intense contestation among Berguedans, but it has also fostered a delicate sort of social equilibrium through its multivocality and indirection. Moreover, the festival has helped incorporate new inhabitants into full membership in Berga's social life, and its importance in this regard has grown in the last few decades with new waves of immigration into the city (Noyes 2006).

As Noyes, explains, "In the early 1990s, a certain group of festival partici-pants well-connected in City Hall created a foundation, a Patronat for the pro-tection of the Patum: a festival with thousands of passionate adherents that is in no conceivable danger of dying or losing its formal integrity" (2006, 38). This foundation controls some of the material elements of the festival—instruments, effigies, costumes—but its board is not directly elected, there is no explicit struc-ture of rotation in office, and it includes members of some groups of festival par-ticipants but not of others who have different views. And yet outsiders, if they look no further, have no reason to doubt that the Patronat represents the community. In practice, UNESCO and the Catalan Department of Culture both seem to regard it as the "competent authority" for administering the Patum festival (38).

Berguedans are divided about this state of affairs. While some contest the Patronat's authority, others have instead opted to withdraw their labor and retreat from participation. In a town of 16,000 inhabitants, where the effort of all is needed to maintain local vitality, "some of the most talented actors have surrendered control to the bureaucrats" (Noyes 2006, 39). The exit and exclusion that have accompanied the festival's institutionalization carry consequences that are important for the organization of community and the administration of the social field in Berga, as Dorothy Noyes demonstrates:

> The members of the Patronat stem from the "respectable" wing of Patum opinion, and in many incidents over the years this wing has attempted to control participation with a view to controlling the Patum's potential for social change. There are indications that this control . . . is part of the Patronat's agenda. For example, recently a system of "points" was created for designating the festival administrators, an honorific office accorded every year to four newly married couples. Among other things, points are given for having been born in Berga and having been married in church. In a city with a large immigrant population and in which the working class is historically anti-clerical, these are highly divisive criteria. (2006, 40)

From Marrakesh to Berga and beyond, it is evident that the language of intangible heritage—its programs of preservation, protection, documentation, research, promotion, education, and revitalization, and its specialist knowledge and expertise—offers tools and techniques that communities can use to organize themselves as spaces of identification, to conduct the conduct of their members, and to find their voice in the polyphony of contemporary, pluralistic societies. The danger is that in finding their voice, these communities, in cooperation with administrators and experts, will suppress their own multivocality, will amplify one voice and drown out dissent. To the extent that this is the case, the convention safeguards not only cultural heritage but also a political heritage of subjection. In principle, UNESCO's slogan of "unity in diversity" represents harmony and understanding. In practice, it runs the risk of enforcing conformity within the diverse communities it designates.

Notes

All direct quotations, unless otherwise cited, are from my own ethnographic field notes made at the meetings discussed within the chapter.

    1. The law defines this culture as "the sum total of cultural properties, created by the entire nation (etnos), passed from generation to generation and constantly renewed, which makes it

possible to preserve the national identity and consciousness and uniqueness of ethnographic regions" (WIPO Lex 2010, art. 2, para. 4).

2. See also Lynn Meskell's insightful analysis of political pacting, voting blocs, and the politics of inscription on the World Heritage Committee (2014). On lobbying and horse trading behind the scenes in the World Heritage Committee, see a particularly nuanced account by Brumann 2013, 41.

CHAPTER 5

Making Festivals

Folklorization Revisited

The scientist asks: Why does it work?
The engineer asks: How does it work?
The economist asks: How much should it cost?
The folklorist asks: Do you want fries with that?

ARE FESTIVALS INTANGIBLE heritage? You could ask the Japanese government. In 2016 UNESCO added no less than thirty-three Japanese float festivals "held by communities annually to pray to the gods for peace and protection from natural disasters" (UNESCO Intangible Cultural Heritage Lists 2016) to its Representative List of the Intangible Cultural Heritage of Humanity in a single new inscription. I have no argument with that but would add nuance: calling a festival "intangible heritage" is not to describe it but to intervene in it. It is to impose upon the festival a particular relationship and to bring to bear on it a certain brand of expertise and set of tools. These are known as "safeguarding," and they transform their objects.

One of the central tools in UNESCO's tool kit for safeguarding cultural practices and expressions is precisely the festival. The festival is a hallmark of the intangible heritage regime, which fosters the development of festivals for everything from healing rituals to foodways. I propose therefore to reverse the terms. Instead of considering festivals as intangible heritage, consider intangible heritage as a festival. In this chapter, I propose to tease out the meaning and logical consequences of that proposition and to examine it in the light of three interlinked processes that folklorists study and in which we take part: festivalization, heritagization, and folklorization.

Working with examples of practices nominated to and/or showcased on UNESCO's Representative List, in what follows I will make a case for reclaiming the term "folklorization" from authenticity discourses. I argue that the current heritagization of social practices is the latest phase in the long-term infusion of folkloristic perspectives, knowledge, and concepts into the public sphere, as part of society's reflexive modernization. Aptly named folklorization, this infusion marks the success of the field of folklore (broadly conceived) in what has always been its ultimate objective: to change how people look at their own culture, how they define and practice it; to reform the everyday life and expressive culture under study.

Safeguarding as Reflexive Modernization

Heritage and safeguarding go together like tea and biscuits or, more accurately, like subject and predicate. Once a cultural practice is interpreted as heritage, the stage is set for its safeguarding. To safeguard intangible heritage means to create new social institutions (like intangible heritage councils, committees, commissions, networks, foundations, and so on) and to curate certain expressive genres (festivals, but also lists, workshops, competitions, prizes, documentaries, promotional materials, and so on). The social institutions administer these expressions in practices referred to as safeguarding.

One productive way to understand safeguarding is to consider it as the cultural inflection of what sociologist Ulrich Beck calls the "risk society" and defines as "a systematic way of dealing with hazards and insecurities induced and introduced by modernisation itself" (1992, 21). It is in this sense that Beck, Anthony Giddens, and Scott Lash (1994) speak of an era of reflexive modernization, as modern technologies proliferate for dealing with the consequences of modernity itself. If a surge in heritage is a consequence of modernity (consider how buildings turn into heritage once threatened by redevelopment, or practices turn to intangible heritage once social changes render them vulnerable), then safeguarding is a modern technology for addressing those consequences, a systematic way of "dealing with hazards and insecurities" introduced by modernization itself in the cultural domain.

When deemed successful, safeguarding (1) *reforms the relationship of subjects with their own practices* (through sentiments such as "pride"), (2) *reforms the practices* (orienting them toward display through various conventional heritage genres), and ultimately (3) *reforms the relationship of the practicing subjects with themselves* (through social institutions of heritage that formalize informal relations and centralize dispersed responsibilities).

Beginning with the last point, the heritagization of traditional practices brings into being new social institutions and concentrates in them responsibilities that were previously distributed among a number of social actors. Thus in 2007, for example, a national center, Kutiyattam Kendra, was founded in the capital of Kerala, a state in India, to administer a national "action plan" for safe-guarding the Sanskrit theatrical tradition after its inscription on UNESCO's Representative List (Lowthorp 2013, 2015). In China, the Hongtong Center for the Safeguarding of Intangible Cultural Heritage was charged with safeguarding the Hongtong Zouquin Xisu (i.e., the custom of visiting sacred relatives in Hon-gtong) and this new center took over many competences previously dispersed among local populations (You 2015). And in Malawi in east Africa, following the inscription of the Vimbuza healing dance on UNESCO's list, the Ministry of Culture "convened an official body, the National Intangible Cultural Heritage Committee that comprises cultural workers, academics, and ethnic association members among others." A special "Vimbuza Healers and Dancers Association of Malawi" was also formed, which forthwith established a code of conduct for its members with the proclaimed purpose of countering "the negative image of Vimbuza caused by inappropriate practice" (Gilman 2015, 206).

I have pulled these three examples from an illuminating, comparative vol-ume, *UNESCO on the Ground: Local Perspectives on Intangible Cultural Heritage*, edited by Michael Dylan Foster and Lisa Gilman (2015), but they could be multi-plied by almost random selection from the Representative List. Thus, in Mada-gascar, a coordination committee was formed to oversee the safeguarding of the wood crafting knowledge of the Zafimaniry, and in parallel, an association of Zafimaniry artisans was created, the Fikambananan'ny Zafimaniry Mpiangaly Hazo, to safeguard, promote, and transmit their craft ("Periodic reporting . . . Madagascar" 2012). And in Vietnam, according to the government's report on safeguarding activities submitted to UNESCO, cultural authorities have invested in the management capacity of preexisting Ca trù clubs to safeguard traditional Ca trù poetry singing, and as a result, "the number of Ca trù clubs that hold regular practices and other activities and have a growing number of members has increased from 20 to 60" ("Periodic reporting . . . Vietnam" 2013). In all these cases (and countless others), we are witness to an institutionalization of social relations and the emergence of new social actors: centers, councils, associations, clubs, committees, commissions, juries, networks.

This reformation of the subjects of intangible heritage goes hand in hand with a reformation of the objects of intangible heritage: the practices, represen-tations, expressions, knowledge, and skills to which the 2003 convention refers in its definition. Translation into the language of intangible heritage is subject to generic conventions associated with what we might call the intangible heri-tage genres. These genres promote the traditional practices and in the process they orient them toward display. Thus, besides forming an association and set-ting a code of conduct, the safeguarding plan for the Vimbuza healing dance in Malawi includes a new book about Vimbuza, a museum exhibit about Vimbuza, an inventory of Vimbuza practitioners, and, last but not least, the regular organi-zation of Vimbuza dance festivals.

Vimbuza: Heritagization as Modernization

A bit more context: Vimbuza is a popular healing ritual among the Tumbuka in the north of Malawi. Showcased on UNESCO's Representative List of Intangible Heritage, it is part of a larger dance-and-drum based healing tradition (ng'oma) found throughout Bantu-speaking Africa. Vimbuza was an odd candidate for the Representative List; for one thing, it is the only disease that figures on it—for Vimbuza names an illness as well as the cure. By means of traditional rituals, Vimbuza healers diagnose and treat spirit-related illnesses, resulting from spirit possession. The healing dance is one of its principal therapeutic rites. Accompanied by drumming and bells, the dance has an active audience made up mostly of women, who take part in the therapy. They sympathize and display solidarity with the possessed dancer by singing and clapping with increasing intensity, while the dance becomes more and more frenzied, until it reaches its peak and the spirits release their grip on the patient (Gilman 2015, 201–202).

UNESCO describes Vimbuza in the following words on its intangible heritage web page and in its pamphlets:

> Most patients are women who suffer from various forms of mental illness. They are treated for some weeks or months by renowned healers who run a temphiri, a village house where patients are accommodated. After being diagnosed, patients undergo a healing ritual. For this purpose, women and children of the village form a circle around the patient, who slowly enters a trance, and sing songs to call helping spirits. The only men taking part are those who beat spirit-specific drum rhythms and sometimes a male healer. Singing and drumming combine to create a powerful experience, providing a space for patients to "dance their disease." Its continually expanding repertoire of songs and complex drumming, and the virtuosity of the dancing are all part of the rich cultural heritage of the Tumbuka people. The Vimbuza healing ritual goes back to the mid-nineteenth century, when it developed as a means of overcoming traumatic experiences of oppression, and it further developed as a healing dance under British occupation, although it was forbidden by Christian missionaries. . . . Vimbuza is still practised in rural areas where the Tumbuku live, but it continues to face oppression by Christian churches and modern medicine. (UNESCO Intangible Cultural Heritage 2008b)

Based on fieldwork in Malawi, folklorist Lisa Gilman (2015) has analyzed the inscription of Vimbuza. She found the principal motive for its nomination seems to have been expediency: compiling a nomination dossier is an arduous task, but Vimbuza was already well documented in several ethnographic studies. That made life easier for functionaries in the Malawi Ministry of Culture charged with getting something onto UNESCO's Representative List, preferably right away. As Gilman found out, however, local practitioners of Vimbuza by and large do not regard it as heritage at all. To them, it is a medical practice. Several healers whom Gilman interviewed remarked that if the government wanted to take an interest

Fig. 5.1 Vimbuza, Rumphi District, Malawi. ©Lisa Gilman.

in Vimbuza, it should be through the Ministry of Health, and not the Ministry of Culture.

However, as UNESCO's description acknowledges, the medical establishment in Malawi is critical of Vimbuza as a healing practice. And in a predominantly Christian country with a strong Pentecostal element, the religious establishment is also antagonistic toward Vimbuza. Some call it Satanic (Gilman 2015; Soko 2014). In this context, it is rather remarkable that some of those whom Gilman found to be most supportive of Vimbuza's recognition as intangible heritage are in fact fundamentalist Christians and medical doctors. They are pleased to see it recognized and showcased as Malawian heritage—as a dance and as an expression of cultural identity—if that means it is divorced from the ritual setting. As such, Vimbuza figures as heritage, not as habitus (Gilman 2015).

To invoke Barbara Kirshenblatt-Gimblett's theorization of cultural heritage, to recycle "sites, buildings, objects, technologies, or ways of life" as heritage is to give these things a new lease on life, not as what they once were, but as "representations of themselves" (1998, 151). As a metacultural practice, cultural heritage points beyond itself to a culture it claims to represent. With Vimbuza, it is evident that this metacultural relationship (to Malawi culture *through* Vimbuza) comes at the expense of preexisting relations to the practice, which are medical or spiritual. It stands to reason, therefore, that those Malawians who would prefer to eradicate Vimbuza seem more favorably disposed to its standing as intangible heritage than many of its practitioners.

In Malawi, then, a popular medical practice has become the object of safeguarding, for which it has no need. As one part of the action plan for safeguarding Vimbuza, Malawi now organizes an annual festival for a disease and its treatment, where the dance is detached from its ritual ends and transformed into pure, metacultural display—where it stands as its own representation (Gilman 2015). It is not hard to see why the healers with whom Gilman spoke feel that the concept of heritage misrepresents their healing practices. Translating the ritual into intangible heritage functions as a counterritual, draining it of its powers and substance, leaving the dance as display, the ritual experts on the festival stage going through the motions, acting as-if, for an audience that is not looking to be healed but rather just looking. In fact, safeguarding has emerged as the single greatest threat to Vimbuza's continued vitality. It is when Vimbuza is treated as heritage that it becomes endangered; its heritagization seems to prefigure and perhaps to hasten its obsolescence.

Folklorization

UNESCO divides intangible heritage into five separate domains and refers to one of these as "Social practices, rituals and festive events." A third of the elements inscribed on the Representative List of the Intangible Cultural Heritage of Humanity belong to this domain, including a dozen carnivals and a generous assortment of other festivals, feasts, fiestas, festivities, and celebrations.

Many of these are popular, enjoying broad participation and economic success. Ironically, their success presented something of a challenge in the early phase of UNESCO's intangible heritage programs, when candidature files for what was then called the Proclamation of Masterpieces of the Oral and Intangible Heritage of Humanity (see chapter 3) actually included a section in which imminent threats to proposed heritage elements had to be detailed and safeguarding measures proposed to counter those threats. Administrators writing the files sometimes had to be creative to imagine looming dangers and suggest appropriate interventions to thwart them; indeed, they often still do such creative somersaults even though this is no longer strictly required.

Sometimes other festivals pose the purported threat and are presented as illegitimate copies of the proposed original—another example of the dangers of success. Such was the case, for example, in the town of Berga in Catalonia where, according to Dorothy Noyes, "many locals have long insisted that the fire festivals in other Catalan towns are 'copies' of their festival, the Patum" (2006, 36). This discourse of authenticity and plagiarism is reinforced by UNESCO's recognition, and realized among other things through such intellectual property strategies as trademarking the name, symbol, and image of the Patum festival and its "most distinctive elements" (36).

In other cases, the files conjure up an impending threat to the authenticity of the festivals because of their popularity. What is deemed dangerous to intangible heritage in these cases is a surfeit of interest from outsiders, however conceived. UNESCO's shorthand for this is "folklorization," a notion predicated on a conception of authenticity that associates practices and expressions with communities, identity, and belonging. UNESCO's second Proclamation of Masterpieces in 2003 gave recognition to at least three different traditional festivities (subsequently incorporated into the Representative List of Intangible Cultural Heritage) that had in this way fallen, or were in danger of falling, victim to their own success. The official Proclamation brochure warned, for example, that even though la Día de los Muertos in Mexico "faces no major threat nowadays, its significance for practitioners could easily be lost." Hence, the candidature file promises intervention to safeguard this wildly popular festival: "The festivity's metaphysical and aesthetic dimensions will be protected from the growing number of non-indigenous commercial and recreational activities that tend to obscure its spiritual character. It is for this reason that the action plan recommends improved legal protection for this tradition" (UNESCO 2004a, 29; my translation).

In much the same way, the Proclamation depicted the Carnival of Binche in Belgium as endangered by an excess of interest: "Binche's carnival enjoys immense popularity today. Nevertheless, the pressures exerted by industrialization and increased media coverage over the years have resulted in the loss of certain traditional aspects of the carnival. In addition, the image of the Gille has been somewhat distorted by the media and other commercial interests eager to exploit the carnival's striking emblem" (UNESCO 2004a, 11; my translation). This sense of aggrieved ownership led the town council in Binche to seek intellectual property protection for the festival and its distinctive features in order to suppress copies and prevent distortion, mutilation, and modification (Tauschek 2010).

The Carnival of Barranquilla in Colombia came into its own because of Barranquilla's position as a busy trading center. As the Proclamation text put it, the city's commercial character "made its inhabitants very open to new trends and ideas, and the fact that it had no cultural traditions to really call its own, led to the easy adoption of those brought in by immigrants, turning it into a veritable

Fig. 5.2 Gathering of Gilles, Carnival de Binche, Belgium. ©Markus Tauschek.

melting-pot of indigenous, African and European cultural heritages" (UNESCO 2004a, 17; my translation).

In spite of this understanding of the carnival as a festival on commercial crossroads, UNESCO presents excessive commercialization as a major hazard threatening the traditionality of the carnival: "With its growing success in the twentieth century, Barranquilla's carnival took on the trappings of a professional event, receiving wide media coverage. This development generates economic benefits for many low-income families, but the growing commercialization may at the same time constitute a potential threat to many traditional expressions" (UNESCO Intangible Cultural Heritage 2008a). As part of Barranquilla's candidature, the Colombian government put in place an action plan to protect "this time-honoured celebration," including legislation to protect the "popular and traditional aspects of the carnival that have been adversely affected by commercialization" (UNESCO 2004a, 17; my translation).

UNESCO's Convention for the Safeguarding of the Intangible Cultural Heritage from 2003 is modeled on the earlier Convention concerning the Protection of World Cultural and Natural Heritage, adopted by the General Conference of UNESCO in 1972. Likewise, the Representative List of the 2003 Convention is modeled on the World Heritage List of the 1972 Convention (see chapter 3).

But whereas UNESCO (i.e., its member states and secretariat) has been eager to reproduce the success of the 1972 convention and list (for which the organization is best known in many parts of the world), it has also made an effort to avoid reproducing some of its failures, even if that effort is not always successful. Thus, questions of authenticity have plagued the World Heritage Convention from the outset. In the evaluation of monuments, buildings, or sites nominated for inscription on the World Heritage List, the convention's so-called test of authenticity has largely been based on the "authenticity of materials," judging the value of heritage by the presence of original materials and the absence of new ones. Formulated in the 1960s by a European conservation profession, this test reflects an ideal of permanence that is literally set in stone and developed in civilizations with stone monuments and historical stone buildings. No surprise then that the World Heritage Convention's notion of authenticity has proved less than accommodating to alternative ways of conceiving of the relationship of the past to the present, including those that construct this relationship in perishable, organic materials or embody and perform it in practices, expressions, and know-how (Bortolotto 2010; Brumann 2014; Gfeller 2017; Labadi 2013).

One of the political motivations for creating a second heritage convention in UNESCO was to counterbalance the Eurocentric, monumentalist, and materialist bias of the World Heritage Convention with an alternative conception of cultural heritage, valorizing other ways of relating past to present. For this reason, the Intangible Heritage Convention eschews any direct reference to authenticity (Bortolotto 2013). However, it has not been easy to get away from authenticity, which folklorists Richard Bauman and Charles Briggs aptly qualify as "one of the key tropes of modernity" (2003, 16). If truth be told, the field of folklore has had more than a little to do with its persistence, as Regina Bendix shows in her comparative examination of German and American folklore studies, *In Search of Authenticity: The Formation of Folklore Studies* (1997); from the Ossian controversy in the eighteenth century to the condemnation of fakelore and the criticism of folklorism in the twentieth, folklorists have taken an active part in the politics of authenticity from the founding moments of the field until the present day (see Dundes 1989, 40–56). The ghost of authenticity haunts the convention's implementation and returns in the specter of folklorization. We've seen it haunting festivals in Spain, Mexico, Belgium, and Colombia, but in the last analysis the ghost is in the machine, so to speak; it lurks in the intangible heritage regime itself.

As conceived of in the discourse surrounding the convention, folklorization threatens intangible heritage with objectification and, once objectified, with commodification, exoticizing heritage for consumption by outsiders and alienating it from the practicing community, or at least transforming the community's relation to its practices. This threat is a factor of the shifting spheres of circulation of the practices and expressions in question; the circulation affects the circulating culture itself, changing the modes of its representation to respond to the tastes and expectations of a shifting audience. In other words—those of the Bolivian minister of culture and religion quoted in the second chapter—this is the danger posed by "a process of commercially oriented transculturation destructive of the traditional cultures."

The gist of this notion of folklorization is that the increasing circulation of such practices and expressions is self-defeating. It suggests that their representation on the interface between the community's inside and outside undermines and threatens to end their circulation within the community—at least as the *same* practices and expressions. Recall, for example, that "wide media coverage" and "growing commercialization may . . . constitute a threat to the many traditional expressions" in the Carnival of Barranquilla; that the popularity and proliferation of activities related to la Día de los Muertos mean that "its significance for practitioners could easily be lost"; and that over the years increased media coverage has "resulted in the loss of certain traditional aspects of the carnival" of Binche (UNESCO 2004a, 17, 29, 11; my translation). It is worth noting here, however, that the report submitted to UNESCO by Belgium in 2012 on the implementation of the convention acknowledges that "since inscription, the profile of the Carnival of Binche has been higher, with a larger number of visitors (including from overseas) and more media coverage" ("Periodic reporting . . . Belgium" 2012). To say this might have been anticipated would be an understatement, but it would also miss the point: it was always the idea.

From this perspective, objectification of the practices and expressions makes them transferable and is the first step toward their alienation from the source community. Consequently, the first line of defense against the threat of folklorization is to curtail the circulation of the practices and expressions involved. The paradox here is that the principal incentive for inscription on national and international heritage lists is precisely to promote these festivals (and other practices singled out for listing), to attract more tourists, and to increase rather than limit their circulation. Many of the tools used to safeguard intangible heritage are geared to these ends, including, notably, the festival.

Condensation

Promotion and awareness-raising carry various implications for the practices recognized as intangible heritage. One observes, for example, their condensation, which helps to make them transportable outside community boundaries, whether physically through traveling performances, virtually through their mediatization, or socially through the inclusion of tourists as spectators. In Galichnik in Macedonia, for example, a traditional village wedding ceremony that used to be up to eight days long is now enacted as a staged recreation in a two-day condensed version over a weekend, with thousands of people in attendance, an event that is "heavily promoted by the Ministry of Tourism" and extensively covered by the media under the banner of "intangible heritage" (Silverman 2015, 241).

As Swedish folklorist Owe Ronström has noted, condensation is an integral part of the process of festivalization and may be understood as economic and cultural rationalization and an "efficient means to process the local for global export" (2016, 75–79). Thus, based on her decade-long engagement with the people of Cheju Island in South Korea, folklorist Kyoim Yun reports that once the Yongdung Rite (a Korean shamanic ritual) had been inscribed on UNESCO's Representative List in 2009, shamans from Cheju Island were mobilized to stage the ritual in an intangible heritage festival for a cosmopolitan audience in Seoul. A media blurb for the event even highlighted "the advantage of observing the island's ritual without actually having to go there." On another occasion, a shaman complained that the organizers "kept requesting that the ritual be shortened to fit the time frame for the whole event" and in the end they were "pushed to perform for twenty minutes total, a situation that the shaman compared to abbreviating Shakespeare's play *Romeo and Juliet* to four words, 'Oh Romeo!' 'Oh Juliet!'" (2015, 190).

Something similar happens with Vimbuza. In the traditional ritual context, as Gilman notes, the dance may last anywhere from two to twelve hours or more, all depending on the number of spirits involved and on how long it takes for each spirit to pass through (2015). But in the festival frame, since no one is possessed nor anyone healed, the Vimbuza dance is easily condensed and performed within a standardized time frame.

As noted previously, the Place Jemaa el-Fna was among the first items inscribed on UNESCO's list of intangible heritage (see chapter 4). Condensed to make it transportable, the cultural space of Jemaa el-Fna has moved around from the square itself within the old Marrakech medina to various cities in Europe. The current phase in the heritagization of this old marketplace began in 1997 when UNESCO organized a symposium in Marrakech that paved the way for the Proclamation of Masterpieces of Intangible Heritage and later for the Intangible Heritage Convention (Schmitt 2008; Tebbaa and Skounti 2011). Two years later, in 1999, with the Proclamation program under way at UNESCO and Jemaa el-Fna as its poster child, "Place Jemaa el-Fna" was recreated in the Tuileries Gardens, and several performers were given visas to create a cross between a festival and an outdoor museum in Paris, performing exoticism in a display genre that speaks more of intangible heritage than it does of the marketplace itself. For linguistic reasons, much of the audience in the Tuileries Gardens related mostly visually to the performances; for tax reasons, the herbalists could not sell the goods they brought with them, but only act as if they were trying to sell them to an audience that itself was not looking to buy, but rather just looking (Kapchan 2014).

Fig. 5.3 Jemaa el-Fna transported to the Tuileries Gardens in Paris, France. ©Deborah Kapchan.

In 2001, the artists from Jemaa el-Fna were back in Paris, invited this time by UNESCO's director-general to stage the cultural space of Place Jemaa el-Fna at UNESCO's headquarters. It was part of a festive event orchestrated by UNESCO over three consecutive evenings in the Place Fontenoy. The event showcased six cultural practices on the occasion of their proclamation as the intangible cultural heritage of humanity. A festival celebrating universal heritage, the event transported to Paris condensed versions of Kutiyattam theater from India, Kunqu opera from China, Nogaku theater from Japan, Gelede ritual from Benin, and Mandingue music and epic poems from Guinea, in addition to the cultural space of the Jemaa el-Fna marketplace. All of this was staged for a public of diplomats and dignitaries invited to partake of the spectacular feast in the 7th arrondissement of Paris. Those of us who missed this production may find consolation in visiting instead the Jemaa el-Fna Food Festival in the Netherlands; known as the "Eetplein Djemaa el Fna," it takes place every September in Rotterdam's Museum Park (Proef de Cultuur Djemaa el Fna Rotterdam 2017).

Festivalization

A critical, comparative approach to the implementation of the Intangible Heritage Convention brings to light the dominance of certain expressive genres in the activities called safeguarding: lists, competitions, prizes, documentaries, and especially the festival, most important for our discussion here. It is not just that traditional festivals are heritagized, though that happens on a wide scale and, we may add, folklorists, ethnologists, and anthropologists take an active part in that process (Leal 2016). More important still for my argument here, as part of their safeguarding, those practices and expressions that are framed as intangible heritage are festivalized. Indeed, the festival as a genre of display is so closely associated with the safeguarding of intangible heritage that in Malawi an illness and a medical practice for its treatment have been festivalized. Lisa Gilman cites Malawi healer Lestina Makwakwa, who she says was, like many of her colleagues, "especially critical of the idea of a Vimbuza festival . . . or other occasions where Vimbuza is performed outside of the ritual context, because these displays strip it of its significance" (2015, 208).

To a man with a hammer, everything looks like a nail. From the Vimbuza disease and healing ritual in Malawi to shamanic rites in Cheju Province in South Korea to the cultural space of Jemaa el-Fna, safeguarding traditional practices as intangible heritage involves creating festivals dedicated to them—even when that makes no sense. As a rule of thumb, where we have intangible heritage, we will find festivals. Another way to put this is to say that intangible heritage is a festival. It is other things besides, granted, but whatever else it may be, it is a festival.

Beyond Malawi, Korea, Macedonia, and Morocco, the examples could be multiplied; and of course, one could always provide counterexamples, for there are certainly exceptions. Be that as it may, I think the pattern is clear and striking. I suggest, therefore, that the heritagization process of recent years may be understood in the context of the festivalization process of the same period. It is an oft-commented fact that the number of festivals worldwide has grown exponentially (Laville 2014; Négrier 2015; Boissevain 1992, 1–19). Especially since the 1980s and 1990s, cultural festivals have moved beyond the arts to festivalize a miscellany of expressions, practices, and identities, from pastries to pétanque, from costumes to crafts, from fishing to rituals, and from ethnicity to locality— moving out from the institutionalized arts to the domain nowadays increasingly known as the intangible heritage (Laville 2014; Négrier 2015; Boissevain 1992, 1–19; see also Ronström 2016).

At the same time as new festivals emerge, existing festivals are marketed to tourists; indeed, festivals have always attracted the attention of travelers. As folklorist Roger D. Abrahams remarked, festivals are occasions for the festive community to show off: "resounding times and elaborated places for excited exchange, for bringing out, passing around, for giving and receiving the most vital emblems of culture in an unashamed display of produce, of the plenitude the community may boast, precisely so that the community may boast" (1982, 161). Festivals are "geared toward deliberate display" (Picard and Robinson 2006, 2), offering a "boastful" reflection of the community to locals and visitors alike. As David Picard and Mike Robinson observe, festivals "draw our attention as participants, tourists and scholars precisely because they provide moments of time and space to reflect upon our being in the world and questions of collective meaning and belonging" (2006, 26).

The surge in festivals in general and the festivalization of intangible heritage in particular may be understood in the context of reflexive modernization (Beck, Giddens, and Lash 1994) as modern technology for dealing with the consequences of modernity: economic (providing financial incentive in the festival context for arts, crafts, and activities that have lost their former economic basis), social (forging a sense of community in times when its dissolution is commonly decried), and political (staking claims on the allegiance of participants and showing off to neighboring cities/towns/villages).

Like heritage itself, festivals are tasked with turning place into meaningful location and defining its uniqueness as a destination (Kirshenblatt-Gimblett 1998)—for inhabitants and visitors alike. In the words of Richard Bauman, "They are cultural forms about culture, social forms about society, in which the central meanings and values of a group are embodied, acted out, and laid open to examination and interpretation in symbolic form, both by members of that group and by the ethnographer" (1986, 133). Thus, festivals nowadays help to stage modern societies' reflexive awareness of themselves while reforming the relationship of people to their own culture and to themselves as a social collective. When festivals come under the sign of intangible heritage, they fit like a glove on the hand of the safeguarding project. The processes of heritagization and festivalization can therefore work in tandem, each assisting in and accelerating the other.

Safe for Consumption

The festivalization of popular culture has a longer history, however, one in which folklorists have been involved for a long time. Michel de Certeau has outlined a compelling history of this engagement in France, dwelling in particular on two critical moments in the development of the field of study variously known as folklore studies, ethnology, or "les arts et traditions populaires" (popular arts

Fig. 5.4 King Louis XVIII crowns the "rosière" in Mittau, 1799. Public domain via Wikimedia Commons.

and traditions): the end of the eighteenth century and the last decades of the nineteenth century (1986, 119–136). Noting that the "liberal, enlightened aristocracy of the end of the eighteenth century developed a passion for the "popular"" (121), de Certeau relates the early formation of the discipline to a "rusticophilia" that fomented the development of village festivals in which a virgin ("rosière") was crowned for her chastity. "The vogue for 'rosière' celebrations, which began in the 1770s, represents a return toward the people, whose words had been silenced, to domesticate them more completely," de Certeau writes, adding that the "idealization of the "popular" is all the easier if it takes the form of a monologue. The people may not speak, but they can sing" (122; see also Abrahams 1993).

In 1789, the French people spoke; giving voice to the threat that was always the undercurrent in the liberal aristocratic idealization of the popular. A centerpiece in the cultural program of the revolutionary government was to study vernacular languages and dialects across France with the express purpose of stamping them out; they were thought to give cover to the enduring remains of the feudal order in the provinces. But folklore or popular, vernacular culture came once again into focus during the days of the Third Republic (1870–1940) in France, with the organization of festivals, a proliferation of collections and editions of folklore and folksong, and the formation of a science dedicated to its study. The same held true across much of Europe and the Americas in this period. This was the heyday of folklore; from the concert hall to the university, composers, artists, and scholars from the new middle classes adapted cultural expressions from the "folk," transferring them between social classes, from the rural proletariat to their cultured bourgeois or petit-bourgeois readers and audience.

In the economic boom and large-scale social projects that followed World War II in Western societies, their previous class structure changed profoundly. The unprecedented growth of the middle class cast folklore in a new light, with new audiences enjoying it in new media. Thus, according to Pierre Bourdieu's analysis of taste in his magnum opus, *Distinction*, which he based on French mass surveys from the 1960s, folk dance is "one of the spectacles most characteristic of middle-brow culture (along with the circus, light opera and bull-fights)" (1984, 52). The "spectacle of the 'people' making a spectacle of itself, as in folk dancing," Bourdieu hypothesized, "is an opportunity to experience the relationship of distant proximity, in the form of the idealized vision purveyed by aesthetic realism and populist nostalgia, which is a basic element in the relationship of the petite bourgeoisie to the working or peasant classes and their traditions" (58).

This nostalgic idealization of popular culture reinforced the identities of the audiences as modern, progressive, and cultured. Its study and its spectacularization both perform the stories that modern societies tell themselves about themselves. Their effect is not innocent. "It is precisely the "popular" halo . . . that formed the foundation for an elitist conception of culture," argues Michel de Certeau (1986, 122), through a contrastive exoticism. This contrast stands at the origins of the field of folklore/ethnology: separating the scholar, his readers, and the spectators of popular arts, on the one hand, from their practitioners, on the other; a condescending symbolic violence that displays and festivalizes expressions and customs in "a castrating cult of the people" (123). The folklorist, concludes de Certeau, arrives "at the moment a culture has lost its means of self defense" (123). As part of the dominant regime, the discipline's task has been to incorporate subaltern expression into dominant culture, so it may stand there as its own translation, its own representation, under generic conventions of display that render it enchanting, exciting, innocuous, and/or exotic but unthreatening, safe for consumption. Depoliticizing the distinction between the popular and its counterpart (which, after all, is a political distinction), scientific writings, collections, spectacles, and festivals alike may serve as pliers for pulling sharp teeth and fixing an innocent smile on the face of the popular.

Taking a leaf from de Certeau's book, I urge that the proliferation of festivals and the proliferation of heritage since the 1980s are not entirely distinct trends with distinct explanations. On the contrary, they are interlinked expressions of the same social, economic, and cultural conditions, two overlapping results of the same forces at work (see Ronström 2016, 72). We could invoke in this context all the usual shorthand expressions, or buzzwords, that we throw around to describe macrotrends and forces in contemporary societies: from globalization to neoliberalization, or from the postindustrial society of services, tourism, and the spectacle to governmentality, responsibilization, and identity politics. I do not think we would be wrong to invoke any of these though admittedly we would not be very specific. But as a folklorist, I would suggest we look again in another direction: our own.

Folklorization Revisited

The jeans I'm wearing have a large stamp inside, on the backside of the left, front pocket. It elucidates the history and cultural significance of the blue jeans: "For over 140 years, our celebrated high quality denim riveted jeans have been before the public. This is a pair of them! Created by Levi Strauss in 1877—has become an American tradition, symbolizing the vitality of the West to people all over the world." Wearing this pair of jeans means something and the company making them would like me to know it: I have stepped into American tradition, clothed with rich symbolism. Lest I forget it, my place in Western cultural history is wrapped against my thigh.

This is but one example, well known; for others, just look around you. You read about it on labels and menus, or you learn about it from advertisements and in-room literature: from Levi's to Marlboros and from slow food to hotel chains, consumer goods now present analytical notes on their origins and cultural meanings. "Less and less remains uninterpreted in our society, while more things seem to gain meaning only through interpretation," writes Austrian folklorist Konrad Köstlin: "Our behavior and the objects with which we surround ourselves come complete with self-justifying, explanatory, and interpretive histories of reference" (1997, 261).

As Köstlin teaches us, the particular charge, perspective, and language of ethnology or folklore studies has been popularized to the extent that the disciplines themselves are nearly irrelevant; we are all folklorists nowadays. In contemporary societies, an ethnological understanding of everyday life is integral to everyday life itself, diffused by media, marketing departments, and oral tradition.

"If it were not so pompous-sounding, we could call it a popularized 'cultural scientification' (*Verkulturwissenschaftlichung*) of the world," Köstlin muses (1997, 261). I have another idea. Let's call it folklorization. After all, the cultural science to which Köstlin refers is the one known in the United States as folklore (and in many other countries as ethnology). Appropriating the concept of "folklorization," so frequently invoked by UNESCO to describe purported threats to intangible heritage, I would suggest that we expand it to refer to this reflexive capacity of modernity that turns the folk into folklorists.

Bear with me.

UNESCO did not conjure the concept of folklorization out of thin air, of course. We may trace its lineage through analyses and critiques from the last decades of the twentieth century of state-sponsored folklore festivals, troupes, and ensembles in Latin America and Eastern Europe, and of the hegemonic adaptations and commercial reworkings of cultural traditions (see Bendix 1997; Feldman 2006; Habinc 2012; Hagedorn 2001; Kaneff 2004; Klekot 2010; McDowell 2010; Turino 2003). According to John McDowell's reading of such critiques, "'to folklorize' means to move traditional expressive culture from an original point of production and relocate it in a distanced setting of consumption" (2010, 182), and folklorization constitutes "a processing of local traditions for external consumption" (183). Polish ethnologist Ewa Klekot notes that folklorization, in this sense, is a tool used extensively in modern states to deal with potentially dangerous differences: "Folklorize and rule seems to have been a tacit motto of both the British empire and the Soviet Union, with its folkloristic parades celebrating 'the unity of over 100 nations'" (2010, 80, note 5). But as ethnologist Mateja Habinc writes in the postsocialist context of Slovenia, "Folklorization is not a specific characteristic of socialist times; it is part of the more general project of modernization" (2012, 193).

The genealogy of the concept of folklorization extends back to an essay from 1962 in which German folklorist Hans Moser coined the term *Folklorismus*, or folklorism, to describe "second-hand mediation of folk culture" (1962; my translation) or secondhand folklore, that is, to refer to shifting spheres of circulation of performances, customs, and expressions. The companion concept to "Folklorismus" in Moser's writing is that of *Rücklauf* (feedback or backflow), coined to describe the recycling of scholarly interpretations of popular expressive and material culture into the expressions and materials themselves; thus the interpretation advanced by folklorists of a particular festival or costume tradition becomes part of the festival or tradition itself; the fieldworker who comes along a generation later to study the festival or the costume may recognize in her interviews and observations the theories of her predecessors, whether they explain its origins, function, structure, or symbolism. For Moser, this presented a conundrum: an ersatz layer of culture, requiring the vigilance of folklorists who had to separate the wheat from the chaff, folk culture from folklorismus (Moser 1964).

Already in 1966, Hermann Bausinger, the leader of a new generation in the field in Germany, called such distinctions into question. In a brilliant essay, Bausinger observes that first- and secondhand traditions are intertwined, implying that their analytical separation is a distortion of social facts. The criticism of folklorism, Bausinger (1986) argues, is in effect directed at the democratization of attitudes that were previously exclusive. Such attitudes are characterized by Pierre Bourdieu as arising out of social distinction; their democratization reflects a shift away from an aristocratic sensibility (the "passion for the popular," of which Michel de Certeau spoke, among the liberal, enlightened aristocracy of the end of the eighteenth century) to the "populist nostalgia" of the middle class according to Bourdieu's analysis of the French mass surveys of the 1960s (Bourdieu 1984, 58–60). In other words, the concepts of folklore and folklorismus both arise out of social and cultural processes for which the usual shorthand is modernity—from shifts in social structure and their cultural performance in books, spectacles and festivals (Bendix 1997).

In fact, Bausinger suggests that at closer look the supposedly distinguishing characteristics of folklorism are actually part and parcel of any representation of traditional culture: "the do-just-as-if, the conjuring up of new expressions for ancient forms, the stamp of tradition even among regressive forms, the artificial patina, and the presumption of wholeness and originality" (1986, 121). These, Bausinger points out, and in particular the "presumption of wholeness and originality," also characterize the criticism of folklorism, which thus appears to rest on the same premise as that which it criticizes. He concludes that "folklorism and the criticism of folklorism are in the long run identical" (122).

Both are an integral part of reflexive modernity, highlighting its progress and innovation through contrast while also channeling the critique of a litany of modern ills, like the disintegration of the community, the dissolution of the family, or, indeed, the leveling force of globalization. As Konrad Köstlin remarks, "Modernity's main characteristic is . . . the synchronic presence of that which is historically asynchronic" (1999, 290). Folklorization, then, is a process integral to modern societies (see Anttonen 2005). In other words, the scholarly field dedicated to popular expressive and everyday culture developed as part of the reflexive mechanism of modern societies: "As a discipline concerned with the domain of the unquestioned and taken-for-granted, Volkskunde has always wanted to inform its own people in their own language about their own habits. . . . As the study of one's own culture, Volkskunde always wished for 'Rücklauf,' the replanting of that which it described. That which had been collected was to be returned to the folk, the recorded folksong was to be sung again and recognized as a 'typical' folk product" (Köstlin 1999, 292).

The names of the field may provide a clue in this context. Both the English term folklore and the German term *Volkskunde* were coined to designate at once the discipline and its object: the lore (i.e., learning/science) or *Kunde* of the folk/*das Volk* as well as the lore/*Kunde* about the folk/*das Volk*. In the English-speaking context, this has been a continuing source of apprehension for folklorists, especially as the term's semantic range in popular usage has gradually narrowed down to the frivolous and erroneous while the field which it names has expanded and diversified its scope (see, for example, contributions to the special issue of the *Journal of American Folklore* edited by Ilana Harlow and published in the summer of 1998, "Folklore: What's in a Name?";

see also Kirshenblatt-Gimblett 1996 and Hafstein and Margry 2014). However, if Köstlin is right, then the ultimate objective of the study of folklore has always been a full merger of the science about the folk with the lore of the folk; after all, the point of modern society's reflexivity is to absorb its knowledge of itself into social practices.

A New Wave of Folklorization

For the past couple of centuries, writes Köstlin, "the business of this discipline has been to label 'special' what people have regarded as normal, to declare the everyday as something particular" (1999, 293), worthy of attention, in need of interpretation, and asking to be displayed, whether in books, journals, catalogues, exhibitions, spectacles, or festivals: from plows, dresses, and lullabies to cigarettes, blue jeans, and jokes. Our attention changes its objects. Our theories become part of everyday life itself, for as Köstlin notes: "The rites of passage of Arnold van Gennep or the liminal theories of Victor Turner already are being read as contentious movie scripts for the practice of modern living," heralding "a joyful retribalization of society" (293). Actually, this is the particular charge of the field as part of society's reflexive capacity, its purpose: "The discipline will continue to do so. It will bespeak the normal, the routinized, the customary—thus changing its character completely. It will offer to decipher that which thus far has simply 'been there.' There will be less and less that will not be spoken of" (293).

In an article on the ethnologization of Provence, French folklorist and anthropologist Laurent-Sébastien Fournier describes the process I refer to as folklorization as "a slow sedimentation of folkloristic knowledge that winds up influencing both how local populations look at their own culture and how they define it to those people (temporary and permanent residents) who discover it" (2016, 2; my translation). According to Fournier, "the 1970s marked the beginning of a new wave of ethnologization" or folklorization, in which ethnologists, folklorists, anthropologists, and their students "take more and more part in administering local cultural projects, which in turn breathes new energy and meaning into the field" (10–11; my translation).

Fournier's insight extends far beyond Provence, of course. In the United States, as Robert Baron and Nick Spitzer artfully demonstrate, "a national infrastructure of public folklore and folklife programs crystalized" during the 1970s and '80s and "quickly grew into a well-articulated network of federal, state, and local programs" (2010, vii; Baron 2016). The work of public folklorists involves "the staging of folklife festivals, curating of exhibits, production of documentary videos and films, and coordination of folklife in education programs" (Hansen 1999, 35) in addition to radio production, web curation, and the coordination of prize, fellowship, and apprenticeship programs for vernacular artists. As Baron and Spitzer define it, public folklore "is the representation and application of folk traditions in new contours and contexts within and beyond the communities in which they originated, often through the collaborative efforts of tradition bearers and folklorists or other cultural specialists" (2010, 1). Folklorist David Whisnant describes the work of public folklorists as one of "systematic cultural intervention" (1983, 13) designed to bring about cultural change (see Whisnant 1988; Hansen 1999).

But this folklorization of the public sphere extends well beyond the work of people trained in folklore, ethnology, or anthropology. We are witness in the past decades to an incredible success: the success of our field of knowledge (broadly defined) in shaping contemporary society's reflexive understanding of itself. It is, however, an uneven success; the perspectives, the craft, and the vocabularies of folklorists and ethnologists suffuse society, but often without the critical edge; reflexivity is rallied to the causes of celebration and marketing more often than it serves to strengthen critical awareness and promote change (see Köstlin 1999; Mugnaini 2016).

The ubiquity of heritage is, I would suggest, one concomitant of this folklorization of public space and of everyday life. The heritage subject has a reflexive relation to the objects and practices she recognizes as her heritage. As part of our reflexive understanding of our material culture and social practices, we have learned to have a heritage; having a heritage is to be different from that heritage, it is to be modern.

The heritage relation creates a sense of distance by imagining a vista outside one's own self from where one may observe one's own customs and expressions with, as it were, an alien gaze. Recall Juan Goytisolo's observation, quoted in chapter 4 in the context of the rescue of Jemaa el-Fna, that "often, it is the alien gaze that returns beauty and integrity to places." Michael Dylan Foster refers to this part of the heritage relation as defamiliarization; the most telling example is precisely how UNESCO's recognition of heritage sites or practices changes local perspectives by prompting local populations and authorities to see "one's own tradition through the eyes of another" and to take pride in it, an important part of what Foster terms the "UNESCO effect" (2011, 66).

For our purposes, the heritagization of recent years and decades may be considered an aspect of or a phase in the folklorization of the past two centuries. Safeguarding practices and expressions as cultural heritage routinely involves translating them into heritage genres of display, such as the list, the prize competition, and in particular, the festival, which promotes condensation, transportability and spectacularization, attracting tourists, cultivating a reflexive relationship between populations and their practices, and giving the latter a "second life . . . as representations of themselves" (Kirshenblatt-Gimblett 1998, 151). This is folklorization in more or less the sense that the term is used within UNESCO discourse (itself extensively informed by folklorists and the field of folklore). Ironically, when reference is made to folklorization in that discourse, it is presented as the problem while safeguarding is the solution; I submit instead that the two go hand in hand.

Moreover, heritagization is one aspect of folklorization in the second sense I propose to give the term, that is, of the infusion of folkloristic knowledge, perspectives, and concepts into the public sphere where they shape the public's understanding of and relation to expressive culture and social practices, and indeed reform those expressions and practices as part of society's reflexive modernization. In the context of intangible heritage, such reform is referred to as safeguarding. The festival, a genre of display characteristic of intangible heritage, provides a stage for performing this reflexive modernity.

Coda: Do You Want Fries with That?

Just in case it did not register, the whole argument of this chapter runs counter to the punch line in the opening joke. However, as emblems of modern culture, fries are themselves not immune to folklorization. I conclude therefore with another example, complementing the Vimbuza ritual with which the chapter opened: the Belgian potato fry. In 2014, the National Union of Fryers (Navefri/Unafri) ran an advertising campaign presenting potato fries as cultural heritage. It collected over 50,000 signatures for its petition to add the culture of the *fritkot*, the Belgian "fry hut," to the national inventories of intangible heritage (RTBF 2016). Ironically, many English speakers refer to these fries as French, but in a small federal state divided into linguistic communities and regions with strong separatist movements, the potato fry is unusual in its ecumenical capacity to denote pan-Belgian identity across linguistic and political differences. According to statistics from the National Union of Fryers, 95 percent of Belgians visit a fry hut at least once a year. Together with the Red Devils (the national soccer team) and the royal family, potato fries might be described as part of the mysterious trinity uniting Belgians into one nation.

Make that a quaternity: let's not forget Belgian beer. In 2016, "Beer Culture in Belgium" was inscribed onto UNESCO's Representative List of the Intangible Heritage of Humanity in a rare display of national cultural unity, following on from its listing in the three Belgian inventories of intangible heritage: *De biercultuur in België* (Flemish community, 2011), *La culture de la bière en Belgique* (French community, 2012), *Die Bierkultur in Belgien* (German-speaking community, 2013). Likewise, on the waves of the successful campaign and petition, the culture of the *fritkot* was formally added on the Flemish inventory of intangible heritage in 2014. Under the government's federal structure, cultural issues are devolved to the Flemish, French-speaking (Walloon), and German-speaking communities, and therefore each community maintains its own inventory. In 2016, potato fries found their way onto the inventories of intangible heritage in the other two communities as well; another important symbol of their unity-in-diversity.

In the nomination dossier, the National Union of Fryers argues that "the delicious scent of fries, the unique social atmosphere, and the know-how of our fryers make potato fries not only an irresistible delicacy, but also a unique cultural treasure." Indeed, the dossier explains, making fries is an artisanal trade and the fries themselves are a testament to cultural diversity. The fry hut, we learn, is a social microcosm and a public assembly, gathering bus drivers, students, and bankers to partake of their favorite fries. The dossier goes on like this:

> In contradistinction to the fries at McDonalds, which taste the same in Helsinki, Madrid, and Chicago, every Belgian fry has its own flavor. There are over 5000 fryers in Belgium, but one of the key traits of the fry-hut culture is the way in which two fryers in the same village make fries with distinctive flavors, and each one of their respective customers prefers the fries of his or her own "fry-hut tribe." It is important to continue to cherish this diversity and to cultivate the social experience surrounding the fry hut. Many households have a fry day, a particular day of the week when the family goes to the fry hut. Exiting the film theater, the football stadium, the concert hall, or after work, people go there together, socializing with a cone of fries. (Semaine de la frite 2016; my translation)

I do not know whether folklorists, ethnologists, or anthropologists took part in making this dossier. I would not be surprised. But I enter the quotation above into evidence that Belgian fryers have successfully adopted the mode of knowledge production distinctive of these disciplines. They speak my language. They have folklorized potato fries and the art of frying them. Not only that; they've figured out how to fry folkloristic knowledge. They dip it in the frying pot at just the right temperature and serve it up hot and perfectly golden: crisp on the outside, soft on the inside.

It seems to me that this is a prime example of folklorization, illustrating how scholarly interpretations of material and expressive culture are recycled to become part of the object interpreted. Less and less remains uninterpreted in modern societies, as Konrad Köstlin claims, while more and more the commonplace comes furnished with cultural histories and ethnographic frames of reference. An ethnological understanding of everyday life has been integrated into the practice of everyday life. Not only is eating fries from your local fry hut a ritual pledge of allegiance to your "fry-hut tribe," but it also cultivates a distinctive social experience with a long history, sustains family values, celebrates diversity, and upholds the community of Belgians. Through extensive media coverage and promotion, the folklorization of the fried potato comes to shape the public perception of the fry hut, and to some extent people's relation to their foodways, perhaps even the flavor. And since this process happens under the sign

Fig. 5.5 "Now we have to make certain they continue to exist!" Demolition of the fry-hut Maison Antoine in Place Jourdan, Brussels, Belgium, April 2017. ©mlopez /Shutterstock.

of intangible heritage, it comes complete with a tool kit for safeguarding the fry hut and the potato fry, including the usual expressive genres and the social institutions to curate them—modern technologies for dealing with the consequences of modernity.

Not only does Belgium have its National Union of Fryers (Navefri/Unafri); two museums have opened dedicated to potato fries, in Brussels and Brugge, with exhibitions on fry culture and history. A trilingual publication educates the public on fry culture and promotes its Belgianness; the Week of the Fry (*Week van de Friet* or *La semaine de la frite*) honors the "potato fry, Belgium's cultural and gastronomic heritage" in a media campaign and series of live events (Semaine de la frite 2016). And not only are there fry-huts at every festival that takes place in Belgium; to complete the recipe for intangible heritage, a dedicated "Fry-hut Festival" (*Festival de Fritkot*) was organized in Brussels, complete with the popular selection and crowning of the city's best fry hut, a prize competition in the traditional template of the rosière street festivals of the eighteenth century.

Presenting the candidature of fry-hut culture for the national inventories of intangible heritage, the president of the National Union of Fryers, Bernard Lefèvre, explained to journalists that "the fry huts have long been so commonplace that no attention has been paid to them." Belgians had to see their traditions through the eyes of another in order to declare the everyday as particular, requiring interpretation, valorization, and safeguarding: "It is only thanks to the interest of foreign visitors that we have learned to value them," said Lefèvre, before adding the inevitable conclusion: "Now we have to make certain they continue to exist!" (RTBF 2014; my translation).

Postlude

**Intangible Heritage as Diagnosis,
Safeguarding as Treatment**

The Doctor's Office

PATIENT: "What is it, doctor?"

DOCTOR: "There's no easy way to break it to you: you have heritage."

PATIENT: "Heritage? That's rough. What kind?"

DOCTOR: "Intangible. I'm sorry."

PATIENT: "Ouch! How bad is it?"

DOCTOR: "It is in urgent need of safeguarding. It's already metacultural."

PATIENT: "What's the prognosis?"

DOCTOR: "Intangible heritage is chronic, I'm afraid. It is often terminal, but in
    your case, we have reason to be optimistic. You may be able to live with
    your heritage for a long time, provided we take immediate measures to
    safeguard it."

PATIENT: "Is it painful?"

DOCTOR: "I won't lie to you. The treatment is not pleasant. You will have to
    learn to relate differently to yourself and to your heritage from here on out.
    It will change you."

PATIENT: "Should we get a second opinion?"

DOCTOR: "I recommend contacting UNESCO. If they agree with the diagnosis,
    we might even get you on their list."

PATIENT: "How would that help?"

DOCTOR: "Well, if you're listed, we may get voluntary funds to bring in specialists from Japan, and UNESCO's help to draw up a five-year safeguarding plan."

PATIENT: "From Japan? Is that really necessary?"

DOCTOR: "No one knows more about intangible heritage than the Japanese. They've been dealing with it for a long time."

PATIENT: "OK, but five years? Really?"

DOCTOR: "Listen to me, without proper treatment, you may lose what authenticity you have left. Worst case scenario, we might be looking at a full-blown case of fakelore."

PATIENT: "Wait a minute, doctor! That's what they said when our grandparents came down with tradition in the sixties."

DOCTORS: "Yes?"

PATIENT: "Yes, but they beat that!"

DOCTOR: "They did, with a lot of drugs. Back in those days, tradition responded to drugs."

(ENTER UNESCO)

Diagnosis

Recall the Vimbuza healing dance, referred to in chapter 5, and Lisa Gilman's (2014) study of its inscription on the Representative List of the Intangible Cultural Heritage? It took a couple of readings before it occurred to me. If it is true that "intangible heritage," with all that the term entails, is not an apt description of Vimbuza in Malawi, then Vimbuza, on the other hand, describes rather well what intangible heritage is and what it does. If Vimbuza names a spirit-related illness causing a variety of ailments, intangible heritage may likewise be described as the technical term for a cultural malady brought on by social, economic, and demographic change. If Vimbuza refers "to the rituals that are used to diagnose and heal these spirit-related illnesses" (Gilman 2014), intangible heritage may also be described as a diagnosis and its safeguarding as a form of treatment. If Vimbuza healers diagnose and treat spirit-related illnesses, much the same may be said of experts who administer intangible heritage. In this analysis, the people who perform Vimbuza and the people who would safeguard Vimbuza are doing the same thing; ironically, that is why their actions are at cross-purposes.

Revisiting other cases from across the globe in the light of this one, it is plain to see that intangible heritage offers in each case a broad diagnosis of what is wrong. Be it economic development, migration, depopulation, or social upheaval, intangible heritage names a cultural condition requiring the metacultural intervention of experts. Thus, intangible heritage is, first of all, a diagnosis. It gives a

Fig. 6.1 Vimbuza, Rumphi District, Malawi. ©Lisa Gilman.

name to a condition increasingly common in industrial and postindustrial societies under circumstances of economic, political, technological, and demographic change—for which the shorthand is usually globalization. Among the symptoms of intangible heritage is a sense of alienation and imperilment. If left untreated, the prognosis is usually estrangement, endangerment, and imminent loss.

Treatment

Known as safeguarding, the treatment is a long-term, intensive intervention requiring advanced expertise to obtain the desired results. Developed by heritage professionals under the auspices of UNESCO, modeled on experimental twentieth-century forms of cultural therapy from Japan and South Korea, the condition of intangible heritage is generally treated with a combination of social institutions (intangible heritage councils, committees, commissions, networks, foundations, and so on) and genres of display (intangible heritage lists, festivals, workshops, competitions, prizes, documentaries, and so on), with the former administering the latter in practices that are jointly termed "safeguarding."

Along with display, compensation is the key measure taken to safeguard intangible heritage. To ensure the continued viability of cultural practices, safeguarding attempts to compensate for the change in social and economic circumstances that create the condition diagnosed as intangible heritage. Thus, for example, safeguarding may replace previous modes of administration with

Fig. 6.2 Kutiyattam, Kerala, India. From left to right: Margi Raman as Rama, Kalamandalam Hariharan on mizhavu drum, and Margi Usha as Sita in *Surpanakanka*. ©Leah Lowthorp.

state patronage as in the cases of Kutiyattam theater in Kerala and the custom of visiting sacred relatives (Zouquin Xisu) in Hongtong. It substitutes tourists and other spectators for local participants as in the case of the shamanic diving women in the Yongdung rite in Cheju Island (Yun 2015). The same holds true for the villagers in Galichnik and neighboring villages in Macedonia, replaced by foreign tourists and spectators from the city (even if in this case the local diagnosis of intangible heritage has not been upheld by UNESCO's "second opinion"; Silverman 2015). The Malawi case is the exception that proves the rule: the Vimbuza ritual, a popular medical practice in great demand, is actually in no need of compensatory remediation. It needs neither state patronage nor the substitution of spectators for local participants to ensure its continued viability; yet, true to form, safeguarding brings both. In fact, these safeguarding measures emerge as the greatest threat to Vimbuza's continued practice.

Safeguarding cultivates and changes the relationship of practitioners and local populations with their practices. Cases analyzed from around the world reveal the common emotional register of intangible heritage. Recognition by UNESCO and national authorities, we find, very often elicits a response that people themselves describe variously as pride, confidence, self-respect, or self-belief. Thus, in Kutiyattam theater, the greatest effect of the recognition bestowed by UNESCO, according to one of the practitioners whom folklorist Leah Lowthorp interviewed, was that "working artists had an awakening, they found a belief in themselves; now we're really proud to be in Kutiyattam. It has gained value." In a similar vein, the listing of Toshidon masking traditions on the remote Japanese island of Shimo-Koshikijima is, according to one of Michael Dylan Foster's local informants, not "a reason for pride, but rather for confidence or *jishin* . . . [which] implies a deep trust that what one is doing is meaningful." The examples could easily be multiplied. To pick another, on the occasion of the inscription of thirty-three Japanese float festivals on the Representative List, the Fukuoka Convention and Visitor's Bureau announced: "The registration of Hakata Gion Yamakasa means that the culture of Fukuoka has gained an international recognition. We should really be proud of it and have to hand down to our future generations the important cultural assets of Fukuoka!" (FCVB 2016).

With recognition, then, and with the self-recognition it elicits, comes a duty to safeguard one's own practices. Foster's study (2015) of Toshidon and Kyoim Yun's study of shamanic ritual tradition on Cheju Island in Korea's southern sea (2015) are both set against the background of dramatic social change, spurred on by depopulation, on the one hand, and economic development, on the other. In both cases these transformations have all but eliminated the traditional audience for these rites and their very raison d'être: within a few years, there will be no children left of the appropriate age for whom to perform Toshidon, and the diving ladies in Cheju, the "real owners" of the shamanic ritual, have lost their jobs and are therefore no longer in need of the shamans' services.

Having internalized the global recognition of their traditions, Foster's informants "feel a certain 'burden' . . . , an increased sense of responsibility for the future of the tradition" (Foster 2015, 224), to the extent even that UNESCO's recognition "compels them to keep the tradition alive in some form" (224) despite the fact that there soon will be no more children on the island for whom to perform it. Yun adds that perhaps the most important effect of UNESCO's recognition in Cheju Island is that it "strips the shamans and their clients of the option to cease the ritual, which many seashore villages on Cheju have already done" (Yun 2016, 194).

Curiously, the alternative to safeguarding heritage is never not to safeguard heritage; the alternative to safeguarding heritage is always to destroy it (Poulot 2006, 157). The discourse of heritage frames safeguarding in ethical terms; once we accept the subject position this discourse devises for us, we have severely limited the choice of verbs with which it makes any sense for us to act on our heritage. We may choose between the synonyms of safeguarding (preserve, promote, transmit, celebrate, and others).

Side Effects

If intangible heritage is a diagnosis and safeguarding is the treatment, it is not without its side effects. Some case studies give warning that the side effects may sometimes be worse than the condition. Thus, You concludes from her study of the ramifications of UNESCO's recognition of the custom of visiting sacred relatives in Hongtong that "attempts at safeguarding ICH have caused a series of transformations that disempower local communities and people" (2015, 264).

As Leah Lowthorp explains, considerable funds have been invested in safeguarding Kutiyattam as a result of its UNESCO listing. Among other things, this has meant, in the words of one of the artists with whom Lowthorp worked in Kerala, that "Kutiyattam became a profession with a salary-base. . . . Ramesh was able to marry, because he could say he works here. That's a real social change" (2015, 168). The funds come with strings attached, however. They are disbursed through institutions, and artists who are lucky enough to earn a salary are now "required to reside at their institution six days per week, to formally request time off thereby reducing their salary, to take attendance for both students and artists, and to submit paperwork detailing their monthly activities" (169). Another artist whom Lowthorp spoke with reflects: "Now we have a condition of normal working people. It is good for an office but bad for art" (170).

Lowthorp and You are not alone in drawing such conclusions. Various other studies, some of them cited in previous chapters, record similar findings: consider the Patum of Berga or the cultural space of Jemaa el-Fna (see chapter 4), or recall the Bolivian dictatorship's efforts to protect traditional culture in the story of "El Condor Pasa" (chapter 2). They live in many places in different parts of the world, but they share the same complaint: as part of the safeguarding of intangible heritage, local actors are asked to surrender to experts and councils and administrators the control over their cultural practices.

Epidemiology

Intangible heritage is spreading fast. At the time of writing, UNESCO has recognized 399 elements of the intangible heritage of humanity, with more coming soon. The numbers rise every year. That list is merely representative, however. At the national level, the numbers are far higher. National inventories of intangible heritage each identify elements in the dozens or hundreds, depending on the country. Switzerland alone (population eight million), for example, officially recognizes 167 elements of intangible heritage, while Peru (population thirty million) recognizes some 150 elements, and India (population 1,210 million) recognizes thirty-four.

Unconfirmed cases of intangible heritage are potentially far more numerous. At the expert meeting that drafted the convention text in UNESCO headquarters in Paris in 2003, I listened to a Japanese diplomat who claimed that "in my country alone it is said that there are more than sixty thousand items of intangible cultural heritage." On the other hand, at a meeting of the convention's Executive Committee in Algiers in 2006, I witnessed a diplomat from Luxembourg claiming (straight-faced) that there is only one intangible heritage in his country;

hence, listing and safeguarding it was imperative, he continued, lest the people of Luxembourg be left with none.

As may be surmised from this last pair of numbers (and as explained in chapter 3), an epidemiology of intangible heritage traces it back to Japan and Southeast Asia; it is a relative latecomer to Europe and the Americas. Formally recognized by the international community only in 2003, intangible heritage is, however, highly communicable. Intangible heritage has since been diagnosed in 178 of the world's 195 states. It is already universal.

Conclusion

If Intangible Heritage Is the Solution, What Is the Problem?

THE PRECEDING CHAPTERS have brought out both positive and troubling outcomes of making intangible heritage, the lists it brings into being, the festivals it animates, the communities it summons into existence, and the way it orchestrates difference in contemporary societies. UNESCO's Convention for the Safeguarding of the Intangible Cultural Heritage signals a reformation of heritage as a category and concept. At the same time, it begs the question why: why this reformation and why now? What problems do people set out to solve with the concept of intangible heritage and with the convention for its safeguarding? With what effect?

There are several ways to answer these questions, depending on where one begins to unstitch the concept and convention and which threads one unravels. One predicament that intangible heritage seeks to remedy is the lopsidedness and bias of world heritage. Though it broke new ground in 1972, the World Heritage Convention turned out to be too narrow in its conception to keep up with the proliferation of heritage. The associated World Heritage List is supposed to represent cultural and natural heritage of such outstanding value that it is the duty of humanity as a whole to protect it. This list and the maps that plot it portray just what is wrong with the convention: half the world's outstanding cultural heritage appears to be in Europe, most of it in central and southern Europe, gathered in a plot of land that in the bigger scheme of things is relatively small and sparsely populated. In comparison, the cradle of humankind—sub-Saharan Africa—is home to 6 percent of its cultural heritage; the same proportion as Italy alone. Even that moderate representation of African culture includes many remnants of European trade and rule from the colonial era. Professing a cosmopolitan ethics of preservation, the underlying worldview of the World Heritage Convention turns out to be rather more parochial.

Its definition of cultural heritage as monuments, groups of buildings, and sites plays an important part in enclosing its scope; until recently, the Operational Guidelines for the convention limited its pertinence further by imposing a "test of authenticity" that focused on building materials. In practice, these conditions modeled world heritage on monumental stone architecture like the Acropolis, the Palace of Versailles, and the Cologne Cathedral. World heritage thus conceived excludes most material traces of nonmonumentalist civilizations, most traces of peoples who build their environment out of wood and other organic materials, and, of course, all "immaterial" culture through which the present is related to the past. To be sure, world heritage is subject to revisions these days, and the Operational Guidelines have been revised since 2005 to expand and relativize the criteria of authenticity. This widening of horizons is, however, a slow and partial process, itself under the influence of the Intangible Heritage Convention of 2003.

The concept of intangible cultural heritage is intelligible only in this context. Its basis is difference—that which it is not: *in*tangible. The Convention for the Safeguarding of the Intangible Cultural Heritage is born out of an alliance of those whom the World Heritage Convention excludes or whose relationship to generations past has been stretched or trimmed to fit its Procrustean definitions. Sponsored by Japan, Korea, and a coalition of African states, the 2003 convention presents itself as a solution of sorts to the disproportionate representation of the World Heritage List and to the skewed, Eurocentric conception underlying the 1972 convention—it complements, corrects, extends, and augments it.

In this regard, the Intangible Heritage Convention illustrates the new balance of power in the United Nations. Many of the states that threw their weight behind this convention were not sovereign in the 1960s when the World Heritage Convention was crafted. The world economy has also seen great changes since, evidenced by the fact that Japan is the largest contributor to UNESCO's regular budget and to its voluntary funds for heritage preservation. These political and economic developments were preconditions for the making of intangible heritage. It is hard to imagine the new convention coming into existence without the support of countries that gained their independence in the latter half of the twentieth century. But even that would not have been an issue had Japan not paid for the meetings of the drafting committee, subsidized the attendance of developing countries, established a trust fund to pay for the projects of the Intangible Heritage Section, and had the section's director from 1993 to 2003 and UNESCO's director-general from 1999 to 2009 (both Japanese) not put the convention at the top of their agenda.

Taking the concept of intangible heritage as an organizing principle, Japan and its many allies in East Asia, Africa, and beyond have challenged Western hegemony in international heritage policy. Refashioning universal categories, the leaders of this coalition thus make their own bid for hegemony. Given that the new convention is modeled on heritage practices in Japan and Korea, its success to date has already showcased Japanese and Korean approaches to preservation as best practices in the field and made the expertise of their intangible heritage specialists sought after. That leads us to another answer to the opening question: if intangible heritage is the solution, what is the problem? For Japan, it solves the problem of how to win friends and influence people in the cultural sphere—it is an instrument of cultural diplomacy, carving out new terrain in the world system, in which Japan is preeminent (and the Korean Republic a close second).

The rationale most often cited for the convention is a third way to answer the same question. The intangible cultural heritage—not the concept but the stuff it circumscribes—is said to be precarious. Associated with the adverse effects of globalization, vulnerability is in effect a constitutive element of the concept of intangible heritage. It is endangered almost by definition, and its endangerment is believed to have global causes and repercussions. Stories circulating in and around UNESCO speak of threats posed by commercialization, export, urbanization, and so on and they motivate policy making. The vulnerability of intangible heritage is the basis of a moral imperative to intervene; governments must do their part to safeguard this heritage before it is too late. To do so, various measures have been devised to guard against change and to promote continuity in traditional practices and expressions. The common denominator is an attempt to transform how practicing communities and local elites relate to traditions, teaching them to take pride in their practices and expressions. This transformation and valorization constitutes the different dances, songs, plays, stories, crafts, skills, and cultural spaces *as* the community's heritage. This designation of vernacular culture as heritage is not so much a description as an intervention; the concept of intangible heritage is normative, not analytical. Such designation justifies official efforts to safeguard practices and expressions; by kindling interest in these traditions among those in a position to make a difference, efforts to safeguard vernacular culture inevitably involve its integration into official structures.

However, it is not the practices and expressions alone that heritage interventions restructure. These interventions entail an attempt to fix practicing communities as loci of culture and as units of administration. Organizing the identification and allegiance of populations around the principle of community, intangible heritage should be understood as an aspect of the communalization of government that has come to characterize (neo)liberal governance in the last decades. In much the same way as states invite their citizens to imagine themselves as national communities by manipulating symbols, consecrating national cultures, and designating common heritage, so invoking intangible heritage gives symbolic substance to local, indigenous, or diasporic communities.

The Convention for the Safeguarding of the Intangible Cultural Heritage defers even the definition of intangible heritage to practicing communities: the concept of intangible cultural heritage refers to those "practices, representations, expressions, knowledge, skills" that communities "recognize as part of their cultural heritage." It also directs governments, policy makers, heritage experts, museums, and others to involve communities as active partners in safeguarding their heritage. Community members are thus integrated into the work of representation, and the intangible heritage becomes an instrument for enfranchising and giving voice to communities. To enable this, however, communities need to be stabilized, that is, a particular set of social relations and authority needs to be fixed as a unit capable of speaking with one voice. In fact, this is a major objective of the Intangible Heritage Convention. At closer inspection, intangible heritage is practically synonymous with community. A major rationale for its protection is to counteract the erosion of identity in a globalizing world and to reclaim emotional investment in community. In this sense, intangible heritage is an ethical concept—it refers to interpersonal relations, loyalties, and social organization. The purpose of the convention is not only to safeguard traditional practices and expressions but also, and just as important, to safeguard communities.

To safeguard communities—through programs of intangible heritage promotion, display, festival, preservation, documentation, education, and revitalization—is to organize the conduct of community members. Delegating responsibility for the conduct of conduct to the level of community, such communalization of government creates and capitalizes on a third space between the state and the individual, multiplying collective subject positions in which individuals may be addressed and from which they can speak. These communal subjects are, however, firmly defined as subjects *to* states, as complementary rather than alternative to national subjects. In fact, enfranchising communities cements their bonds to central government through relations of administration and dependence on expertise, funding, and technical support. Superimposing communities organized around various principles (locality, indigeneity, ethnicity, religion, diaspora, and so on) in the intangible heritage genres of display (lists, inventories, festivals, documentaries, pedagogical resources, and exhibitions), states celebrate a unity-in-diversity vision of their population: an assortment of nonexclusive identities, heritages, and communities all colorfully coexisting within the same territory and under the same government. This is yet another way to understand intangible heritage. If it is a solution, one of the problems it helps to solve is that of cultural difference in contemporary societies. Intangible heritage offers a way to organize such difference as manageable diversity that does not undermine political unity.

The Intangible Heritage Convention universalizes this same technique. UNESCO's lists, brochures, multimedia presentations, website, and other promotional programs juxtapose local practices from all over the globe, creating a montage of manifold particularities onto which we are invited to project an imagined global community. The Representative List of the Intangible Cultural Heritage of Humanity illustrates this triangulation between local, national, and global levels. It represents heritage defined by communities and in terms of community, nominated to the list by states parties to the convention, and attributed to humanity as a whole. Intangible heritage is an instrument for cultivating the civic virtues of people as good neighbors in local communities, good citizens in national communities, and good cosmopolitans in the global community of humankind. In other words, intangible heritage is a tool for reconciling the politics of difference with a politics of congruity and harmony.

This last thread unraveled ties back to the basic mission of the United Nations, founded in the aftermath of World War II to prevent future wars. As noted in the opening chapter, UNESCO's constitution, as the cultural, educational, and scientific branch of the UN, begins with the celebrated passage: "Since wars begin in the minds of men, it is in the minds of men that the defenses of peace must be constructed." The Intangible Heritage Convention is ultimately a means to this end.

The concept of intangible heritage and the convention for its safeguarding are thus called upon to solve a number of problems: to flout the materialistic doctrine enshrined in the World Heritage Convention; to challenge and assert international hegemony in the cultural sphere; to redraw the balance of power in international heritage forums; to face up to the challenges of globalization; to safeguard communities; to fix them as cultural, political, and administrative units; to organize difference as cultural diversity at national and international levels; to replace discord with concord; to make peace.

The Republic of Korea proposed in 1993 to UNESCO's Executive Board the creation of an international system of Living Human Treasures—in hindsight, a watershed moment that set UNESCO on track toward the Intangible Heritage Convention, adopted a decade later. The Korean proposal argued that intangible heritage has a number of advantages over tangible heritage, protected by the World Heritage Convention. One of the proposal's central arguments to recommend the Living Human Treasures paradigm is that intangible heritage is "ideology-proof" (UNESCO 1993, 3). According to the proposal, whereas "tangible cultural properties evoke ideological arguments, intangible cultural properties do not" (3).

In retrospect, the claim seems farfetched. Whether they concern listing, excellence, and outstanding quality; authenticity and revitalization; ownership, sovereignty, and community involvement; cultural difference, homogeny, and hegemony; or the moral solidarity of humanity, the debates, deliberations, and negotiations that went into making intangible heritage belie the guarantee that it is "ideology-proof." So too does the convention's implementation around the world. Intangible heritage is nothing if not a site of contestation.

Indeed, one need look no further than to Korea itself. In 2013, the Republic of Korea had its fifteenth nomination rubberstamped on the Representative List of the Intangible Heritage of Humanity: the making and sharing of kimch'i, a culinary-social process also known as "Kimjang." As described by the Representative List, kimch'i "forms an essential part of Korean meals, transcending class and regional differences" and the "collective practice of Kimjang reaffirms Korean identity and is an excellent opportunity for strengthening family cooperation" (UNESCO Intangible Cultural Heritage Lists 2013). Apparently, such affirmation of identity does not transcend the 1953 border drawn in the armistice between North and South Korea. UNESCO's recognition of kimch'i as the intangible heritage of South Korea was not well received north of the border. Snubbed and aggrieved, Pyongyang promptly put forth its own kimch'i heritage nomination. It is not every day that North Korea receives international honors; its regime is more used to rebuke than recognition from the United Nations. At its meeting in 2015, however, the Intergovernmental Committee for the Safeguarding of the Intangible Cultural Heritage added the "Tradition of kimchi-making in the Democratic People's Republic of Korea" to UNESCO's Representative List.

So much for the claim that intangible heritage is "ideology-proof" and does not evoke arguments. How could it not? Indeed, even traditional narratives that rationalize the convention tell a different story, when probed. These stories of origins and success circulate within and through the United Nations, among diplomats, experts, lawyers, and scholars on national delegations and in the secretariat of UNESCO, WIPO, and other UN organizations that have inscribed folklore on the international agenda. This book considers several such stories. Three in particular, set in Bolivia and Peru, Morocco, and Japan, narrate the importance of international cooperation for safeguarding local culture worldwide: the stories of the melody known as "El Condor Pasa," of the Jemaa el-Fna marketplace, and of the Horyu-ji Temples and the Ise Shrine. These narratives are told to explain, educate, and motivate, as charters for action.

I tell them differently. I refuse to stop at their "happily ever after." Following up leaves us with different lessons to draw from those usually offered, as in the case of the Jemaa el-Fna marketplace in Marrakech. On the one hand, under the sign of intangible heritage, the effort to safeguard the square was successful. The square is still there, still a cultural space animated by myriad performances, goods, services, people. It wasn't turned into a construction site or a parking lot as planned. On the other hand, Jemaa el-Fna encapsulates the paradox of intangible heritage: as part of its safeguarding, the square has been zoned, scheduled, and regulated; the performers inventoried; the sales carts standardized; the herbalists silenced; and the bus stop and taxi stand moved to another location, taking with them the audience for storytellers. In safeguarding Jemaa el-Fna, Marrakechi authorities succeed, at long last, in bringing order to Jemaa el-Fna. That begs the question: is this the alternative to the shopping center? Are we faced with a choice between eliminating difference for the sake of homogeneity—for good parking, the Body Shop, and Benetton—or choreographing difference under the sign of heritage, in a neatly ordered performance of pleasant diversity?

Refusing to stop at the success story's happily-ever-after casts a different light on all that goes before it. It is no less important, however, to refuse to begin only at "Once upon a time." The beginning represents an arbitrary cutoff point, concealing what came before. Reaching back prior to that point may radically alter our understanding of what comes after. The provenance of "El Condor Pasa" and its cosmopolitan circulation in the twentieth century offer a very different vantage point on the story often told in UNESCO about Simon and Garfunkel's alleged appropriation of an indigenous Andean melody and how it motivated the Bolivian government to write a letter in 1973 soliciting UNESCO's support to protect intangible culture. "Knowledge is not made for understanding; it is made for cutting," Michel Foucault once remarked (1984, 88). Disrupting the general understanding of how intangible heritage became a UNESCO priority, cutting into the linear origin story opens alternative perspectives on safeguarding. Knowing that the 1973 letter was sent by a fascist serving as foreign minister in one of the most brutal military regimes in Latin American history, a dictatorship that oppressed and dispossessed indigenous peoples in Bolivia, is surely an invitation to consider anew the opening question: if intangible heritage is the solution, what is the problem?

Narrative is a critical device. That is how I deploy it in this book. This approach refuses closure; it seeks instead to open up policies and practices to scrutiny and imagination. A powerful genre, the origin story demonstrates the critical capacities of narrative. Going back to the beginning, revising genesis—taking a different starting point, amplifying suppressed voices, undoing erasures—brings back into view long buried hatchets and disagreements; along with them, it exhumes roads not taken, missed opportunities, and options dispensed with. As Pierre Bourdieu remarks, in recounting genesis differently we retrieve "the possibility that things could have been (and still could be) otherwise" (1994, 4).

This is one task for the field of folklore in the domain of heritage. As modernity's storyteller (Köstlin 1997, 1999), folklore studies can add critical edge to intangible heritage. But there are other tasks. Those of the archivist, for example, who inventories cultural practices; the curator who interprets them; the teacher who educates people about them; and the culture broker who builds bridges and brings people together across their differences.

Perhaps the most encouraging upshot of the creation of intangible heritage—the concept and the convention—is that it brings together diverse practices and various people who before inhabited different cultural categories. There is no finer demonstration of the performative power of concepts and their creative possibility. The concept invites us to imagine what unites diverse customs, cultural practices, and traditional expressions: what singing has in common with knitting; what building has in common with dancing; what cooking has in common with carving, or acupuncture with playing the accordion. Here lie opportunities to explore and meetings to broker. We can reach out, foster collaboration, and promote alliances.

What unites them is the aesthetic capacity to make beauty, form, and meaning out of innumerable particular circumstances; the capability to relate to previous generations through expressions and practices that rehearse their words, sounds, gestures; and the social ability to share these with others. This is the creative dynamic at the heart of intangible heritage. The Intangible Heritage Convention, flawed as it is, imperfect and inadequate, is about enabling this dynamic. To stand a chance of sometimes succeeding, it needs the critical eye, the caring hand, and the crosscutting perspective of folklore studies.

Acknowledgments

LIKE AN INTERNATIONAL convention, this book was a long time in the making but took shape in a short period. Many people helped me write it, colleagues and friends for whose support I am more grateful than I can say. Parts of the book have appeared in journals and edited volumes over the past ten years and I am indebted to the editors and anonymous reviewers, as well as to my friends and colleagues who have read parts of this book in manuscript, then or now, and whose criticism I have endured with poise: Natsuko Akagawa, Regina Bendix, Chiara Bortolotto, Michael Dylan Foster, Laurent-Sébastien Fournier, Lisa Gilman, Sigurjón B. Hafsteinsson, Galit Hasan-Rokem, Dorothee Hemme, Deborah Kapchan, Áki G. Karlsson, Barbara Kirshenblatt-Gimblett, John Lindow, Fabio Mugnaini, Jón Þór Pétursson, Ólafur Rastrick, Marteinn Helgi Sigurðsson, Martin Skrydstrup, Laurajane Smith, Markus Tauschek, Tok Thompson, and Francisco Vaz da Silva. The book is better by far thanks to their comments, suggestions, and encouragement.

A mighty roar of thanks goes out to my teachers, dead or alive, at the University of Iceland, the University of California, Berkeley, the University of Pennsylvania, and New York University: in order of appearance, Jón Hnefill Aðalsteinsson, Gísli Sigurðsson, Terry Gunnell, Rannveig Traustadóttir, Alan Dundes, John Lindow, Regina Bendix, Roger D. Abrahams, and Barbara Kirshenblatt-Gimblett.

My sincere gratitude to colleagues in the Department of Conservation at the University of Gothenburg, where I spent a sabbatical year that allowed me to organize my thoughts for this book: first to Bosse Lagerqvist, my host and friend who invited me, and then to my friends in conservation, Gunnar Almevik, Ingrid Martins-Holmberg, Eva Löfgren, Anneli Palmsköld, Katarina Saltzman, and Ola Wetterberg, as well as to Christer Ahlberger, Henric Benesch, Kerstin Gunnemark, Christine Hansen, Kristian Kristiansen, Mikela Lundahl, and Fredrik Skott, who work in different parts of the university.

For his invitation to the Meertens Institute in Amsterdam, his friendship and inspiration, I thank Peter Jan Margry, and I also thank our ethnological Amsterdam colleagues, especially Hester Dibbits and Sophie Elpers. Furthermore, I tip my hat to my co-conspirators on the executive board of SIEF, the International Society for Ethnology and Folklore, from 2013 to 2017: in addition to Peter Jan and Sophie, they are Pertti Anttonen, Jasna Čapo, Tine Damsholt, Laurent-Sébastien Fournier, Arzu Öztürkmen, Clara Saraiva, Monique Scheer, and Nevena Škrbić Alempijević, propped up by Rohan Jackson and Triinu Mets. Our cooperation held up the publication of this book for years.

Other colleagues and friends who have inspired the thinking in this book in conversation and in writing include, apart from those already mentioned, Pertti Anttonen, Robert Baron, Tony Bennett, Charles Briggs, JoAnn Conrad, Kristín Einarsdóttir, Lizette Gradén, Gunnar Ól. Hansson, Ellen Hertz, Cornelius Holtorf, Jason Baird Jackson, Marc Jacobs, Jón Jónsson, Barbro Klein, Richard Kurin, Kristin Kuutma, Hanne Pico Larsen, Leah Lowthorp, Stephen Mitchell, Dorothy Noyes, Elliott Oring, Cristina Sánchez-Carretero, Kristinn Schram, Gísli Sigurðsson, Wend Wendland, Guðrún Whitehead and Rósa Þorsteinsdóttir.

A very special thank you to Rieks Smeets, who directed UNESCO's Intangible Cultural Heritage Section when I did my fieldwork in Paris. He gave me unique access to documents and staff and was incredibly generous with his time and knowledge.

Lisa Gilman, Deborah Kapchan, Leah Lowthorp, and Markus Tauschek all generously shared with me photographs from their fieldwork to use as illustrations in this book in contexts where I engage with their research. For those acts of collegial generosity—and for their research—I am grateful to them.

For all his encouragement, for his warm and cheerful support, and for his gentle but well-positioned kicks, I thank my friend, my colleague, and lifelong conference roommate, Tok Thompson. For never failing to inquire what kind of progress I was making with the book, I am indebted to my friend Elliott Oring.

Filmmaker and anthropologist, Áslaug Einarsdóttir, and I produced a thirty-minute narrative documentary film together on the story of "El Condor Pasa," as told in the second chapter of this book, available online in Open Access (just look it up!). I have learned a lot from her.

Finally, I have good reason to be very grateful to fellow folklorist/ethnologist, Auður Viðarsdóttir, who helped me pull this manuscript together in the last weeks before it went to press. Without her help, the book's date of publication would have been a year later and its contents far less coherent.

As always, I am grateful to the University of Iceland for letting me get away with this. I also recognize that a grant from Rannís—the Icelandic Centre for Research and from HERA (Humanities in the European Research Area) helped me move the research forward (and for the latter, a big nod of appreciation to my partners in the HERA-funded project, Copyrighting Creativity—Creative

Values, Cultural Heritage Institutions and Systems of Intellectual Property: Helle Porsdam, Lucky Belder, Eva Hemmungs Wirtén, and Fiona Macmillan).

As for other sources of inspiration, well, the list of works cited that follows this section is really an extension of the acknowledgments section. Not listed there, however, are my wife, Brynhildur, and our children, Hannes and Ragnheiður. Without them, there might still be a book, but everything else would suck.

A good part of this book, roughly one-half, appeared in earlier versions in journals and edited volumes. These appear here heavily revised. In writing the book, I have shuffled contents between chapters, distributing arguments, themes, and texts that once belonged together into different sections of the book. I have eliminated the outdated and I have updated what remains important. I have expanded and diverted arguments and kept spinning those threads that seem more interesting now than they did in earlier sittings. I have taken into account some of the more recent scholarship in a burgeoning field with a proliferating critical literature, of which I now only have partial command, a welcome change from the dearth of critical interest in these topics when I began my research on cultural heritage, traditional knowledge, and international organizations. I have also added many new examples drawn from the implementation of the Intangible Heritage Convention over the past decade. I have devised (what seems to me) a logical division of labor between chapters while maintaining (what seems to me) a solid storyline throughout. The postlude wraps it up with (what I like to think of as) a ribbon and a bow.

The previously published work I have drawn on and revised in this book appeared in the following publications:

"Intangible Heritage as Diagnosis, Safeguarding as Treatment." *Journal of Folklore Research* 52 (2–3), 281–298. Bloomington: Indiana University Press, 2015. (Comment/critical discussion for a special issue titled "UNESCO on the Ground. Local Perspectives on Intangible Cultural Heritage," edited by Michael Dylan Foster and Lisa Gilman).

"Protection as Dispossession: Government in the Vernacular." In *Cultural Heritage in Transit: Intangible Rights as Human Rights*, edited by Deborah Kapchan, 25–57. Philadelphia: University of Pennsylvania Press, 2014. (Book chapter).

"Cultural Heritage." In *A Companion to Folklore*, edited by Regina Bendix and Galit Hasan-Rokem, 500–519. London: Blackwell, 2012. (Book chapter).

"Intangible Heritage as a List: From Masterpieces to Representation." In *Intangible Heritage*, edited by Laurajane Smith and Natsuko Akagawa, 93–111. London: Routledge, 2009. (Book chapter).

Works Cited

Abélès, Marc. 1992. *La vie quotidienne au Parlement européen*. Paris: Hachette.

———. 1995. "Pour une anthropologie des institutions." *L'Homme* 35 (135): 65–85.

———. 1996. "La Communauté européenne: une perspective anthropologique." *Social Anthropology* 4 (1): 33–45.

———. 2000. *Un ethnologue à l'Assemblée*. Paris: Odile Jacob.

Abercrombie, Thomas. 1992. "La fiesta del carnaval postcolonial en Oruro: Clase, etnicidad y nacionalismo en la danza folklórica." *Revista Andina* 10 (2): 279–352.

———. 2001. "To Be Indian, to Be Bolivian. 'Ethnic' and 'National' Discourses of Difference." In *Nation-States and Indians in Latin America*, edited by Greg Urban and Joel Sherzer, 95–30. 2nd ed. Tucson: Hats Off Books.

Abeyta, Loring. 2005. "Resistance at Cerro de Pasco. Indigenous Moral Economy and the Structure of Social Movements in Peru." PhD dissertation, University of Denver.

Abrahams, Roger D. 1982. "The Language of Festivals: Celebrating the Economy." In *Celebration: Studies in Festivity and Ritual*, edited by Victor W. Turner, 161–177. Washington, DC: Smithsonian.

———.1993. "Phantoms of Romantic Nationalism in Folkloristics." *Journal of American Folklore* 106 (419): 3–37.

Adell, Nicolas, Regina Bendix, Chiara Bortolotto, and Markus Tauschek, eds. 2015. *Between Imagined Communities and Communities of Practice. Participation, Territory, and the Making of Heritage*. Göttingen: Universitätsverlag Göttingen.

Agrawal, Arun. 2005. "Environmentality. Community, Intimate Government, and the Making of Environmental Subjects in Kumaon, India." *Current Anthropology* 46 (2): 161–190.

Agrawal, Arun, and Clark C. Gibson. 2001. The Role of Community in Natural Resource Conservation. In *Communities and the Environment. Ethnicity, Gender, and the State in Community-Based Conservation*, edited by Arun Agrawal and Clark C. Gibson, 1–31. New Brunswick: Rutgers University Press.

Akagawa, Natsuko. 2015. *Heritage Conservation and Japan's Cultural Diplomacy: Heritage, National Identity and National Interest*. London: Routledge.

Al Jazeera. 2012. "Ansar Dine Destroy More Shrines in Mali." July 10, 2012. http://www.aljazeera .com/news/africa/2012/07/201271012301347496.html.

Albro, Robert. 2005. "The Challenges of Asserting, Promoting, and Performing Cultural Heritage." *Theorizing Cultural Heritage* 1 (1): 2–8.

Alivizatou, Marilena. 2016. *Intangible Heritage and the Museum: New Perspectives on Cultural Preservation*. New York: Routledge.

Allias, L. 2012. "The Design of the Nubian Desert: Monuments, Mobility, and the Space of Global Culture." In *Governing by Design: Architecture, Economy, and Politics in the Twentieth Century*, edited by Aggregate, 179–215. Pittsburgh: University of Pittsburgh Press.

Almevik, Gunnar. 2016. "From Archive to Living Heritage. Participatory Documentation Methods in Craft." In *Crafting Cultural Heritage*, edited by Anneli Palmsköld, Johanna Rosenqvist, and Gunnar Almevik, 77–99. Gothenburg: University of Gothenburg.

Anderson, Benedict. 1991. *Imagined Communities. Reflections on the Origin and Spread of Nationalism*. 2nd ed. London: Verso.

Andina. 2009. "INC: Danza la diablada debe ser entendida como un bien común del pueblo del altiplano." August 6, 2009. http://www.andina.com.pe/agencia/noticia-inc-danza-diablada-debe-ser-entendida-como-un-bien-comun-del-pueblo-del-altiplano-247025.aspx.

Anttonen, Pertti J. 2005. *Tradition through Modernity. Postmodernism and the Nation-State in Folklore Scholarship*. Studia Fennica Folkloristica, 15. Helsinki: Finnish Literature Society.

———. 2012. "Oral Traditions and the Making of the Finnish Nation." In *Folklore and Nationalism in Europe during the Long Nineteenth Century*, edited by Timothy Baycroft and David Hopkin, 325–350. Leiden: Brill.

Apotsos, Michelle Moore. 2017. "Timbuktu in Terror: Architecture and Iconoclasm in Contemporary Africa." *International Journal of Islamic Architecture* 6 (1): 97–120.

Appadurai, Arjun. 1996. *Modernity at Large: Cultural Dimensions of Globalization*. Minneapolis: University of Minnesota Press.

Arizpe, Lourdes, and Cristina Amescua, eds. 2013. *Anthropological Perspectives on Intangible Cultural Heritage*. New York: Springer.

Árnason, Arnar, and Sigurjón Baldur Hafsteinsson. 2018. *Death and Governmentality in Iceland. Neo-Liberalism, Grief and the Nation-Form*. Reykjavík: University of Iceland Press.

Arnold, Matthew. 1998 [1869]. "Culture and Anarchy." In *Cultural Theory & Popular Culture. A Reader*, edited by John Storey. 2nd ed. Athens: University of Georgia Press.

Ashworth, Gregory J., Brian Graham, and John E. Tunbridge. 2007. *Pluralising Pasts. Heritage, Identity and Place in Multicultural Societies*. London: Pluto Press.

Australian Department of Environment and Heritage. n.d. "Implications of World Heritage Listing." Accessed October 14, 2017. http://www.environment.gov.au/heritage/about /world-heritage/implications-world-heritage-listing.

Aykan, Bahar. 2013. "How Participatory Is Participatory Heritage Management? The Politics of Safeguarding the Alevi Semah Ritual as Intangible Heritage." *International Journal of Cultural Property* 20 (4): 381–405.

———. 2015. "'Patenting' Karagöz: UNESCO, Nationalism and Multinational Intangible Heritage." *International Journal of Heritage Studies* 21 (10): 949–961.

———. 2016. "The Politics of Intangible Heritage and Food Fights in Western Asia." *International Journal of Heritage Studies* 22 (10): 799–810.

Baird, Melissa. 2015. "Natural Heritage. Heritage Ecologies and the Rhetoric of Nature." In *Heritage Keywords. Rhetoric and Redescription in Cultural Heritage*, edited by Kathryn Lafrenz Samuels and Trinidad Rico, 207–220. Boulder: University Press of Colorado.

Baptista Gumucio, Mariano. 1978. *Cultural Policy in Bolivia*. Paris: UNESCO.

Baron, Robert. 2016. "Public Folklore Dialogism and Critical Heritage Studies." *International Journal of Heritage Studies* 22 (8): 588–606.

Baron, Robert, and Nicholas R. Spitzer, eds. 2010. *Public Folklore*. 2nd ed. Washington, DC: Smithsonian Institution Press.

Bauman, Richard. 1986. "Performance and Honor in 13th-Century Iceland." *Journal of American Folklore* 99 (392): 131–150.

Bauman, Richard, and Charles L. Briggs. 2003. *Voices of Modernity. Language Ideologies and the Politics of Inequality*. Cambridge: Cambridge University Press.

Bausinger, Hermann. 1986. "Toward a Critique of Folklorism Criticism." In *German Volkskunde: A Decade of Theoretical Confrontation, Debate, and Reorientation (1967–1977)*, edited by James Dow and Hannjost Lixfeld, 113–123. Bloomington: Indiana University Press.

Baycroft, Timothy, and David Hopkin, eds. 2012. *Folklore and Nationalism in Europe during the Long Nineteenth Century*. Leiden: Brill.

Beardslee, Thomas. 2014. "Questioning Safeguarding: Heritage and Capabilities at the Jemaa el Fnaa." PhD dissertation, Ohio State University.

———. 2016. "Whom Does Heritage Empower, and Whom Does It Silence? Intangible Cultural Heritage at the Jemaa el Fnaa, Marrakech." *International Journal of Heritage Studies* 22 (2): 89–101.

Beck, Ulrich. 1992. *Risk Society: Towards a New Modernity*. London: Sage.

Beck, Ulrich, Anthony Giddens, and Scott Lash. 1994. *Reflexive Modernization: Politics, Tradition and Aesthetics in the Modern Social Order*. Cambridge: Polity Press.

Bedjaoui, Mohammed. 2004. "The Convention for the Safeguarding of the Intangible Cultural Heritage: The Legal Framework and Universally Recognized Principles." *Museum International* 56 (1–2): 150–155.

Bedoya Garland, Eduardo. 1997. "Bonded Labor, Coercion and Capitalist Development in Peru." *Quaderns de l'Institut Català d'Antropologia* 10: 9–38.

Bellier, Irène. 2013. "'We Indigenous Peoples . . .' Global Activism and the Emergence of a New Collective Subject at the United Nations." In *The Gloss of Harmony: The Politics of Policy-Making in Multilateral Organizations*, edited by Birgit Müller, 177–201. London: Pluto Press.

———. 2015. "L'avenir que veulent les peuples autochtones. Stratégies institutionnelles, mobilisations collectives et force de négociation, à Rio +20." In *Regards croisés sur Rio+20. La modernisation écologique à l'épreuve*, edited by Jean Foyer, 259–279. Paris: CNRS.

Bendix, Regina. 1997. *In Search of Authenticity. The Formation of Folklore Studies*. Madison: University of Wisconsin Press.

———. 2000. "Heredity, Hybridity and Heritage from One Fin-de-Siècle to the Next." In *Folklore, Heritage Politics and Ethnic Diversity*, edited by Pertti J. Anttonen, 37–54. Botkyrka: Multicultural Centre.

———. 2009. "Heritage between Economy and Politics. An Assessment from the Perspective of Cultural Anthropology." In *Intangible Heritage*, edited by Laurajane Smith and Natsuko Akagawa, 253–269. London: Routledge.

———. 2013. "The Power of Perseverance. Exploring Negotiation Dynamics at the World Intellectual Property Organization." In *The Gloss of Harmony: The Politics of Policy-Making in Multilateral Organisations*, edited by Birgit Müller, 23–49. London: Pluto Press.

Bendix, Regina, Aditya Eggert, and Arnika Peselmann, eds. 2013. *Heritage Regimes and the State*. 2nd ed. Göttingen: Universitätsverlag Göttingen.

Bendix, Regina, and Valdimar Tr. Hafstein. 2009. "Culture and Property. An Introduction." *Ethnologia Europaea: Journal of European Ethnology* 39 (2): 5–10.

Benjamin, Walter. 1968. *Illuminations*. New York: Schocken Books.

Bennett, Tony. 1995. *The Birth of the Museum: History, Theory, Politics*. London: Routledge.

———. 1998. *Culture: A Reformer's Science*. London: Sage.

———. 2000. "Acting on the Social: Art, Culture and Government." *American Behavioral Scientist* 43 (9): 1412–1428.

———. 2001a. "Cultural Policy: Issues of Culture and Governance." In *Culture, Society, Market*, edited by Folke Snickars, 13–28. Stockholm: Bank of Sweden Tercentenary Fund/Swedish National Council for Cultural Affairs.

———. 2001b. *Differing Diversities: Cultural Policy and Cultural Diversity*. Strasbourg: Council of Europe.

———. 2003. "Culture and Governmentality." In *Foucault, Cultural Studies, and Governmentality*, edited by Jack Z. Bratich, Jeremy Packer, and Cameron McCarthy, 47–63. Albany: State University of New York Press.

Berg, Lennart. 1978. "The Salvage of the Abu Simbel Temples." *Monumentum* 17: 25–56.

Berliner, David. 2010. "Perdre l'esprit du lieu: Les politiques de l'Unesco à Luang Prabang (RDP Lao)." *Terrain* 55: 90–105.

Bernard, Rosemarie. 2000. "The Image World of Jingu: Media Representation and the Performance of Rites of Renewal at the Grand Shrines of Ise, 1869–1993." PhD dissertation, Harvard University.

Bessmann, Sandra, and Mathias Rota. 2008. "Espace public de la medina. La place 'Jemaa el Fna.'" In *Etude de terrain. La Gentrification dans la Median de Marrakech*, 113–126. Neuchâtel: Université de Neuchâtel, Institut de géographie.

Betts, Paul. 2015. "The Warden of World Heritage: UNESCO and the Rescue of the Nubian Monuments." *Past & Present* 226 (suppl_10): 100–125.

Bharne, Vinayak, and Iku Shimomura. 2003. "Wood and Transience." *Asianart.com: The Online Journal for the Study and Exhibition of the Arts of Asia*, February 6, 2003. http://www.asianart.com/articles/wood/.

Bigenho, Michelle. 2006. "Embodied Matters: Bolivian Fantasy and Indigenismo." *Journal of Latin American Anthropology* 11 (2): 267–293.

Bigenho, Michelle, Juan Carlos Cordero, Richard Mújica, Bernardo Rozo, and Henry Stobart. 2015. "La propiedad intelectual y las ambigüedades del dominio público: Casos de la producción musical y la patrimonialización." In *Lo público en la pluralidad. Ensayos desde Bolivia y América Latina*, edited by Gonzalo Rojas Ortuste, 131–161. La Paz: Plural editores.

Bigenho, Michelle, and Henry Stobart. 2016. "Grasping Cacophony in Bolivian Heritage Otherwise." Pre-publication version (accepted for publication in *Anthropological Quarterly*). https://pure.royalholloway.ac.uk/portal/files/26545063/BigenhoStobart_Grasping_Cacophony_AQ_pre_pub_submitted_28_May_16.pdf.

Bille, Mikkel. 2012. "Assembling Heritage: Investigating the UNESCO Proclamation of Bedouin Intangible Heritage in Jordan." *International Journal of Heritage Studies* 18 (2): 107–123.

Bismarck, Otto. 1895. *Fürst Bismarck: Neue Tischgespräche und Interviews*, edited by Heinrich Ritter von Poschinger. Vol. 1. Stuttgart: Deutsche Verlags-Anstalt.

Blake, Janet. 2001. *Developing a New Standard-setting Instrument for the Safeguarding of Intangible Cultural Heritage. Elements for Consideration*. CLT-2001/WS/8. Paris: UNESCO.

———. 2006. *Commentary on the UNESCO 2003 Convention on the Safeguarding of the Intangible Cultural Heritage*. Crickadarn: Institute of Art and Law.

———. 2009. "UNESCO's 2003 Convention on Intangible Cultural Heritage: The Implications of Community Involvement in 'Safeguarding.'" In *Intangible Heritage*, edited by Laurajane Smith and Natsuko Akagawa, 45–73. London: Routledge.

Bognar, Botond. 1997. "What Goes Up, Must Come Down: Recent Urban Architecture in Japan." *Harvard Design Magazine* 3 (Fall): 1–8.

Boissevain, Jeremy, ed. 1992. *Revitalizing European Rituals*. London: Routledge.

Bondaz, Julien, Florence Graezer Bideau, Cyril Isnart, and Anais Leblon, eds. 2017. *Les vocabulaires locaux du "patrimoine." Traductions, negociations et transformations*. Münster: LIT.

Bondy, Juan Carlos. 2008. "El cine, los libros, la muerte" (Interview with Armando Robles Godoy). *La Primera (Semana-Lima)*, July 6, 2008.

Bonet, Lluís, and Emmanuel Négrier. 2011. "The End(s) of National Cultures? Cultural Policy in the Face of Diversity." *International Journal of Cultural Property* 17 (5): 574–589.

Boorstin, D. J. 1992. *The Image: A Guide to Pseudo-Events in America*. New York: Vintage.

Bortolotto, Chiara. 2008. "Il processo di definizione del concetto di 'patrimonio culturale immateriale': Elementi per una riflessione." In *Il patrimonio immateriale secondo l'Unesco. Analisi e prospettive*, edited by Chiara Bortolotto, 7–48. Rome: Istituto Poligrafico e Zecca dello Stato.

———. 2009. "The Giant Cola Cola in Gravina. Intangible Cultural Heritage, Property, and Territory between Unesco Discourse and Local Heritage Practice." *Ethnologia Europaea: Journal of European Ethnology* 39 (2): 81–94.

———. 2010. "Globalising Intangible Cultural Heritage? Between International Arenas and Local Appropriations." In *Heritage and Globalisation*, edited by Colin Long and Sophie Labadi, 95–112. London: Routledge.

———, ed. 2011. *Le patrimoine culturel immatériel: Enjeux d'une nouvelle catégorie*. Paris: Maison des sciences de l'homme.

———. 2013. "Authenticity: A Non-Criterion for Inscription on the Lists of UNESCO's Intangible Cultural Heritage Convention." In *2013 IRCI Meeting on ICH—Evaluating the Inscription Criteria for the Two Lists of UNESCO's Intangible Cultural Heritage Convention. The 10th Anniversary of the 2003 Convention. Final Report*, 73–79. Osaka: International Research Centre for Intangible Cultural Heritage in the Asia-Pacific Region (IRCI).

———. 2015. "UNESCO and Heritage Self-Determination: Negotiating Meaning in the Intergovernmental Committee for the Safeguarding of the ICH." In *Between Imagined Communities and Communities of Practice*, edited by Nicolas Adell, Regina Bendix, Chiara Bortolotto, and Markus Tauschek, 249–272. Göttingen: Universitätsverlag Göttingen.

Bourdieu, Pierre. 1984. *Distinction: A Social Critique of the Judgement of Taste*. Cambridge, MA: Harvard University Press.

———. 1994. "Rethinking the State. Genesis and Structure of the Bureaucratic Field." *Sociological Theory* 12 (1): 1–18.

Brown, Dwayne, Laurie Cantillo, Elizabeth Landau, and Jia-Rui Cook. 2017. "NASA's Voyager Spacecraft Still Reaching for the Stars after 40 Years." *NASA Jet Propulsion Laboratory, California Institute of Technology*, July 31, 2017. https://www.jpl.nasa.gov/voyager/news/details.php?article_id=48.

Brown, Michael. 1998. "Can Culture Be Copyrighted?" *Current Anthropology* 39 (2): 193–222.

Brumann, Christoph. 2013. "Comment le patrimoine mondial de l'Unesco devient immatériel." *Gradhiva* 18: 22–49.

———. 2014. "Shifting Tides of World-Making in the UNESCO World Heritage Convention: Cosmopolitanisms Colliding." *Ethnic and Racial Studies* 37 (12): 2176–2192

———. 2016. "Conclusion. Imagining the Ground from Afar. Why the Sites Are So Remote in World Heritage Committee Sessions." In *World Heritage on the Ground. Ethnographic Perspectives*, edited by Christoph Brumann and David Berliner, 294–317. New York: Berghahn.

Brumann, Christoph, and David Berliner. 2016. "Introduction. UNESCO World Heritage—Grounded?" In *World Heritage on the Ground: Ethnographic Perspectives*, edited by Christoph Brumann and David Berliner, 1–34. New York: Berghahn.

Camal, Jerome. 2016. "Putting the Drum in Conundrum: Guadeloupean Gwoka, Intangible Cultural Heritage and Postnationalism." *International Journal of Heritage Studies* 22 (5): 395–410.

Canclini, Néstor García. 2001. "The Dynamics of Global Cultural Industries." In *Recognising Culture: A Series of Briefing Papers on Culture and Development,* edited by François Matarasso, 11–19. London: Comedia, the Department of Canadian Heritage and UNESCO.

Carruthers, William. 2016. "Multilateral Possibilities: Decolonization, Preservation and the Case of Egypt." *Future Anterior* 13 (1): 37–48

Casas Ballón, Leo. 2017. "José María Arguedas y la música andina." *La Mula.* January 22, 2017. https://redaccion.lamula.pe/2017/01/22/jose-maria-arguedas-y-la-musica-andina/redaccionmulera/.

Caust, Josephine, and Marilena Vecco. 2017. "Is UNESCO World Heritage Recognition a Blessing or Burden? Evidence from Developing Asian Countries." *Journal of Cultural Heritage* 27 (October): 1–9. http://www.sciencedirect.com/science/article/pii/S1296207416302394.

Cerrón Fetta, Mario. 2017. "Las grabaciones musicales de Jose Maria Arguedas." *Hawansuyo. Poeticas indigenas y originarias,* February 2, 2017. https://hawansuyo.com/2017/02/02/las-grabaciones-musicales-de-jose-maria-arguedas-mario-cerron-fetta/.

Choay, Françoise. 1995. "Sept propositions sur le concept d'authenticité et son usage dans les pratiques du patrimoine historique." In *Nara Conference on Authenticity, Japan 1994, Proceedings,* edited by Knut Einar Larsen, 101–120. Tokyo: Agency for Cultural Affairs/UNESCO World Heritage Centre/ICCROM/ICOMOS.

Choplin, Marie-Astrid, and Vincent Gatin. 2010. "L'espace public comme vitrine de la ville marocaine: Conceptions et appropriations des places Jemaa El Fna à Marrakech, Boujloud à Fès et Al Mouahidine à Ouarzazate. *Norois. Environnement, aménagement, société* 214 (1): 23–40. http://norois.revues.org/3095.

Christiansen, Palle Ove. 2005. "Den folkelige kultur. Almuens nye betydning som dansk og national." In *Veje til danskheden. Bidrag til den moderne nationale selvforståelse,* edited by Palle Ove Christiansen, 124–153. Copenhagen: C. A. Reitzels.

———. 2007. "Folket – både fundet og opfundet. Folkets og folkekulturens rolle i dansk og europæisk nationalitet 1770–1900." In *Det ombejlede folk. Nation, følelse og social bevægelse,* edited by Palle Ove Christiansen and Jens Henrik Koudal, 18–45. Copenhagen: C.A. Reitzels.

Claessen, Henri J. M. 2002. Comment on "Masterpieces of Oral and Intangible Culture: Reflections on the UNESCO World Heritage List" by Peter J. M. Nas. *Current Anthropology* 43 (1): 144.

Clarin Notícias. 2009. "La 'danza de la Diablada,' el nuevo conflicto entre Perú y Bolivia." August 20, 2009. http://www.clarin.com/ediciones-anteriores/danza-diablada-nuevo-conflicto-peru-bolivia_0_ryxmpgKAaYx.html.

Clayton, Lawrence A. 1999. *Peru and the United States: The Condor and the Eagle.* Athens: University of Georgia Press.

Clayton, Peter A., and Martin J. Price. 2013. *The Seven Wonders of the Ancient World.* London: Routledge.

Cleere, Henry. 1995. "Discussion: Session Report." In *Nara Conference on Authenticity, Japan 1994, Proceedings,* edited by Knut Einar Larsen, 251–254. Tokyo: Agency for Cultural Affairs/UNESCO World Heritage Centre/ICCROM/ICOMOS.

———. 1998. "The Uneasy Bedfellows: Universality and Cultural Heritage." Paper presented at the World Archaeological Congress: The Destruction and Preservation of Cultural Property, Island of Brac, Croatia, May 3–7.

CNN. 2001. "World Appeals to Taleban to Stop Destroying Statues." March 3, 2001. https://web
.archive.org/web/20071224155700/http://archives.cnn.com/2001/WORLD/asiapcf/central
/03/03/afghan.buddhas.03/index.html.

———. 2009. "Bolivia, Peru Fight over 'National Costume.'" August 26, 2009. http://edition.cnn
.com/2009/WORLD/americas/08/25/bolivia.peru/index.html?_s=PM:WORLD.

Collins, Henry. 2011. "Culture, Content, and the Enclosure of Human Being. UNESCO's 'Intangible' Heritage in the New Millenium." *Radical History Review* (109):121–135.

Community Heritage Partners. n.d. "Building New Life for Old Places." http://www.chpartners
.net.

Cook, Lorne. 2017. "ICC Orders Mali Extremist to Pay $3.2 Million in Reparations." AP News,
August 17, 2017. https://apnews.com/a826cb5b0bc64d7891ca2dc14f703b2c.

Coombe, Rosemary J., and Lindsay M. Weiss. 2015. "Neoliberalism, Heritage Regimes, and
Cultural Rights." In *Global Heritage. A Reader*, edited by Lynn Meskell, 43–69. Hoboken:
Wiley-Blackwell.

Cordova, Ximena. 2012. "Carnival in Oruro (Bolivia). The Festive and the 'Eclipse' of the Indian
in the Transmission of National Memory." PhD dissertation, Newcastle University.
https://theses.ncl.ac.uk/dspace/handle/10443/1496.

Coronado, Jose. 2009. *The Andes Imagined: Indigenismo, Society, and Modernity.* Pittsburgh:
University of Pittsburgh Press.

Correo. 2009a. "Ahora Bolivia reclama El cóndor pasa." September 20, 2009. http://diariocorreo
.pe/politica-y-economia/ahora-bolivia-reclama-el-condor-pasa-339442/.

———. 2009b. "Bolivia difunde 'El Cóndor Pasa' como suyo." September 21, 2009. http://diariocorreo
.pe/ciudad/bolivia-difunde-el-condor-pasa-como-suyo-356689/.

Crehan, Kate. 2016. *Gramsci's Common Sense: Inequality and Its Narratives.* Durham, NC: Duke
University Press.

d'Harcourt, Raoul, and Marguerite d'Harcourt. 1925. *La musique des Incas et ses survivances.*
Paris: Paul Geuthner.

DaCosta Holton, Kimberly. 2005. *Performing Folklore: Ranchos Folcloricos from Lisbon to Newark.*
Bloomington: Indiana University Press.

de Certeau, Michel. 1986. *Heterologies: Discourse on the Other.* Minneapolis: University of
Minnesota Press.

De Cesari, Chiara. 2015. "Post-Colonial Ruins: Archaeologies of political violence and IS."
Anthropology Today 31 (6): 22–26.

de Jong, Ferdinand. 2013. "Le secret exposé. Révélation et reconnaissance d'un patrimoine
immatériel au Sénégal." *Gradhiva* 18: 98–123.

———. 2016. "A Masterpiece of Masquerading: Contradictions of Conservation in Intangible
Heritage." In *Reclaiming Heritage: Alternative Imaginaries of Memory in West Africa*, edited
by Ferdinand de Jong and Michael Rowlands, 161–184. London: Routledge.

Deustua, José. 2000. *The Bewitchment of Silver: The Social Economy of Mining in Nineteenth-Cen-
tury Peru.* Columbus: Ohio University Press.

Dewind, Adrian. 1975. "From Peasants to Miners: The Background to Strikes in the Mines of Peru."
Science & Society 39 (1): 44–72.

Di Giovine, Michael A. 2009. *The Heritage-Scape. UNESCO, World Heritage, and Tourism.* Lanham, MD: Lexington Books.

———. 2015. "UNESCO's World Heritage Program. The Challenges and Ethics of Community Participation." In *Between Imagined Communities and Communities of Practice. Participation,
Territory, and the Making of Heritage*, edited by Nicolas Adell, Regina Bendix, Chiara Bortolotto, and Markus Tauschek, 83–108. Göttingen: Universitätsverlag Göttingen.

Dorian, Nancy C. 1987. "The Value of Language-Maintenance Efforts Which Are Unlikely to Succeed." *International Journal of the Sociology of Language* 68: 57–67.

Dorr, Kirstie A. 2007. "Mapping 'El Condor Pasa.' Sonic Translocations in the Global Era. *Journal of Latin American Cultural Studies* 16 (1): 11–25.

Droste, Bernd von, and Ulf Bertilsson. 1995. "Authenticity and World Heritage." In *Nara Conference on Authenticity, Japan 1994, Proceedings*, edited by Knut Einar Larsen, 3–15. Tokyo: Agency for Cultural Affairs/UNESCO World Heritage Centre/ICCROM/ICOMOS.

Dundes, Alan, ed. 1965. *The Study of Folklore*. Englewood Cliffs, NJ: Prentice-Hall.

———. 1969. "The Devolutionary Premise in Folklore Theory." *Journal of the Folklore Institute* 6: 5–19.

———. 1977. "Who Are the Folk?" In *Frontiers of Folklore*, edited by William Bascom, 17–35. Boulder, CO: Westview Press.

———. 1985. "Nationalistic Inferiority Complexes and the Fabrication of Fakelore: A Reconsideration of Ossian, the *Kinder- und Hausmärchen*, the *Kalevala*, and Paul Bunyan." *Journal of Folklore Research* 22 (1): 5–18.

———, ed. 1988. *The Flood Myth*. Berkeley: University of California Press.

———. 1989. *Folklore Matters*. Knoxville: University of Tennessee Press.

Early, James, and Peter Seitel. 2002. "UNESCO Meeting in Rio: Steps toward a Convention." *Talk Story* 21:13–14.

Eastwood, Lauren E. 2013. *The Social Organization of Policy: An Institutional Ethnography of UN Forest Deliberations*. London: Routledge.

EcoDiario. 2009. "Denuncian en Perú la difusión de 'El cóndor pasa' como una canción boliviana." September 19, 2009. http://ecodiario.eleconomista.es/flash/noticias/1552777/09/09 /Denuncian-en-Peru-la-difusion-de-El-condor-pasa-como-una-cancion-boliviana.html.

El Comercio. 2009. "Evo Morales invita a Miss Perú a ver baile de 'La Diablada' en Bolivia." October 8, 2009. http://archivo.elcomercio.pe/tvmas/television/evo-morales-invita-miss -peru-ver-baile-diablada-bolivia-noticia-352391.

El Rhazoui, Zineb. 2011. "Ilham's Story: Torture to the Beat of Jamaa al Fna Drums." *Kasama Project*, July 29, 2011. https://web.archive.org/web/20150105035300/http://kasamaproject.org /repression/3409-41ilham-039-s-story-torture-to-the-beat-of-jamaa-al-fna-drums.

Elias, Jamal J. 2007. "(Un)Making Idolatry. From Mecca to Bamiyan." *Future Anterior* 4 (2): 13–29.

———. 2013. "The Taliban, Bamiyan, and Revisionist Iconoclasm." In *Striking Images, Iconoclasms Past and Present*, edited by Stacy Boldrick, Leslie Brubaker, and Richard Clay, 145–164. London: Routledge.

Emol.Mundo. 2009a. "Bolivia rechaza que representant peruana en Miss Universo use traje de la 'Diablada,'" August 1, 2009. http://www.emol.com/noticias/internacional/2009 /08/01/369781/bolivia-rechaza-que-representante-peruana-en-miss-universo-use-traje-de -la-diablada.html.

———. 2009b. "Perú y Bolivia incluyen a Chile en disputa por traje de Diablada." August 14, 2009. http://www.emol.com/noticias/internacional/detalle/detallenoticias.asp?idnoticia=371622.

———. 2009c. "Bolivia propondrá a la CAN crear mapa del patrimonio cultural de la región andina." September 13, 2009. http://www.emol.com/noticias/internacional /2009/09/13/375905/bolivia-propondra-a-la-can-crear-mapa-del-patrimonio-cultural-de-la -region-andina.html.

Eriksen, Anne. 2014. *From Antiquities to Heritage: Transformations of Cultural Memory*. New York: Berghahn Books.

Escribano, Pedro. 2004. "'El Condor Pasa' Patrimonio cultural de la nación." *La República*, April 13, 2004.

EU National Commissions for UNESCO. 2002. "Echanges de vues sur la sauvegarde du pci—Réunion des Commissions nationales pour l'UNESCO de l'Union européenne, 9 et 10 juillet 2002." Unpublished document.

Feldman, Heidi. 2006. *Black Rhythms of Peru: Reviving African Musical Heritage in the Black Pacific*. Middletown, CT: Wesleyan University Press.

Fernandez, James, and Mary Taylor Huber, eds. 2001. *Irony in Action. Anthropology, Practice, and the Moral Imagination*. Chicago: University of Chicago Press.

Flood, Finbarr Barry. 2016. "Idol-Breaking as Image-Making in the 'Islamic State.'" *Religion and Society: Advances in Research* 7: 116–138.

Flores Galindo, Alberto. 2010. *In Search of an Inca: Identity and Utopia in the Andes*. New York: Cambridge University Press.

Foster, Michael Dylan. 2011. "The UNESCO Effect: Confidence, Defamiliarization, and a New Element in the Discourse on a Japanese Island." *Journal of Folklore Research* 48 (1): 63–107.

———. 2015. "Imagined UNESCOs: Interpreting Intangible Cultural Heritage on a Japanese Island." *Journal of Folklore Research* 52 (2): 217–232.

Foster, Michael Dylan, and Lisa Gilman, eds. 2015. *UNESCO on the Ground: Local Perspectives on Intangible Cultural Heritage*. Bloomington: Indiana University Press.

Foucault, Michel. 1984. "Nietzsche, Genealogy, History." In *The Foucault Reader*, edited by Paul Rabinow, 76–100. New York: Pantheon.

Foucault, Michel. 1991 [1978]. "Governmentality." In *The Foucault Effect: Studies in Governmentality*, edited by Graham Burchell, Colin Gordon, and Peter Miller, 87–104. London: Harvester Wheatsheaf.

Fournier, Laurent Sébastien. 2011. "La Tarasque métamorphosée." In *Le patrimoine culturel immatériel. Enjeux d'une nouvelle catégorie*, edited by Chiara Bortolotto, 149–166. Paris: Maison des sciences de l'homme.

———. 2012. "The Impacts of the Intangible Cultural Heritage UNESCO Policies in France." *Traditiones* 41 (2): 193–206.

———. 2016. "Un terrain à histoire." *Espaces Temps. Revue indisciplinaire de sciences sociales*. Accessed March 18, 2017. https://www.espacestemps.net/articles/un-terrain-a-histoire/.

FCVB (Fukuoka Convention & Visitors Bureau). 2016. "Hakata Gion Yamakasa Festival Registered as UNESCO Intangible Cultural Heritage!" December 2, 2016. https://www.welcome-fukuoka.or.jp/english/2291.html.

Galla, Amareswar. 1995. "Authenticity: Rethinking Heritage Diversity in a Pluralistic Framework." In *Nara Conference on Authenticity, Japan 1994, Proceedings*, edited by Knut Einar Larsen, 315–322. Tokyo: Agency for Cultural Affairs/UNESCO World Heritage Centre/ICCROM/ICOMOS.

Gamboni, Dario. 1997. *The Destruction of Art: Iconoclasm and Vandalism since the French Revolution*. London: Reaktion Books

———. 2001. "World Heritage: Shield or Target?" *Conservation: The Getty Institute Conservation Newsletter* 16 (2): 5–11.

Gauthier, Lionel. 2009. "Jemaa El-Fna ou l'exotisme durable." *Géographie et cultures* (72): 117–136. http://gc.revues.org/2258.

Gencarella, Stephen Olbrys. 2010. "Gramsci, Good Sense, and Critical Folklore Studies." *Journal of Folklore Research* 47 (3): 221–252.

Gfeller, Aurélie Élisa. 2015. "Anthropologizing and Indigenizing Heritage: The Origins of the UNESCO Global Strategy for a Representative, Balanced and Credible World Heritage List." *Journal of Social Archaeology* 15 (3): 366–386.

———. 2017. "The Authenticity of Heritage: Global Norm-Making at the Crossroads of Cultures." *American Historical Review* 122 (3): 758–791.

Gfeller, Aurélie Élisa, and Jaci Eisenberg. 2016. "UNESCO and the Shaping of Global Heritage." In *A History of UNESCO: Global Actions and Impacts*, edited by Poul Duedahl, 279–299. New York: Springer.

Gilman, Lisa. 2015. "Demonic or Cultural Treasure? Local Perspectives on Vimbuza, Intangible Cultural Heritage, and UNESCO in Malawi." *Journal of Folklore Research* 52 (2–3): 199–216.

Goody, Jack. 1977. *The Domestication of the Savage Mind.* Cambridge: Cambridge University Press.

Goytisolo, Juan. 2002. "Entrevista de Arcadi Espada a Juan Goytisolo." *La Espia del Sur.* Accessed October 15, 2017. https://web.archive.org/web/20021020065811/http://www.geocities.com /laespia/goytisolo2.htm.

Graezer Bideau, Florence. 2012. Inventorier les "traditions vivantes." Approches du patrimoine culturel immatériel dans le système fédéral suisse. *ethnographiques.org* 24 (July). http://www.ethnographiques.org/2012/Graezer-Bideau.

Gramsci, Antonio. 1999. *Selections from the Prison Notebooks of Antonio Gramsci.* Edited by Quintin Hoare and Geoffrey Nowell Smith. London: Electric Book.

Grossberg, Lawrence, Toby Miller, and Jeremy Packer. 2003. "Mapping the Intersection of Foucault and Cultural Studies. An Interview with Lawrence Grossberg and Toby Miller, October 2000." In *Foucault, Cultural Studies, and Governmentality*, edited by Jack Z. Bratich, Jeremy Packer, and Cameron McCarthy, 23–46. Albany: State University of New York Press.

Groth, Stefan. 2011. "Perspectives on Differentiation: Negotiating Traditional Knowledge on the International Level." *Journal of Ethnology and Folkloristics* 4 (1): 7–24.

———. 2016. *Negotiating Tradition: The Pragmatics of International Deliberations on Cultural Property.* Göttingen: Universitätsverlag Göttingen.

Gunnell, Terry. 2010. "Daisies Rise to Become Oaks. The Politics of Early Folktale Collection in Northern Europe." *Folklore* 121 (1): 12–37.

———. 2012. "National Folklore, National Drama and the Creation of Visual National Identity: The Case of Jón Árnason, Sigurður Guðmundsson and Indriði Einarsson in Iceland." In *Folklore and Nationalism in Europe during the Long Nineteenth Century*, edited by Timothy Baycroft and David Hopkin, 301–324. Leiden: Brill.

Guss, David M. 2000. *The Festive State. Race, Ethnicity, and Nationalism as Cultural Performance.* Berkeley: University of California Press.

———. 2006. "The Gran Poder and the Reconquest of La Paz." *Journal of Latin American Anthropology* 11 (2): 294–328.

Habinc, Mateja. 2012. "Folklorization as Diversification or Molding: Comparing Two 'Traditional' Holidays." *Traditiones* 41 (1): 185–196.

Hafstein, Valdimar Tr. 2012. "Cultural Heritage." In *A Companion to Folklore*, edited by Regina Bendix and Galit Hasan-Rokem, 500–519. Hoboken, NJ: Wiley-Blackwell.

Hafstein, Valdimar Tr., and Peter Jan Margry. 2014. "What's in a Discipline?" *Cultural Analysis* 13: 1–10.

Hagedorn, Katherine. 2001. *Divine Utterances: The Performance of Afro-Cuban Santeria.* Washington, DC: Smithsonian Institution.

Hall, Stuart. 2005. "Whose Heritage? Un-settling 'the Heritage,' Re-Imagining the Post-Nation." In *The Politics of Heritage. The Legacies of "Race,"* edited by Jo Littler and Roshi Naidoo, 23–35. London: Routledge.

Hansen, Gregory. 1999. "Theorizing Public Folklore: Folklore Work as Systemic Cultural Intervention." *Folklore Forum* 30 (1–2): 35–44.

Hansen, Christine, and Ingrid Martins Holmberg. 2016. "Motion and Flow in Heritage Institutions: Two Cases of Challenges from Within." *Nordisk Museologi* 1: 40–51.

Harlow, Ilana, ed. 1998. "Folklore: What's in a Name?" Special issue of the *Journal of American Folklore* 111 (441).

Harmanşah, Ömür. 2015. "ISIS, Heritage, and the Spectacles of Destruction in the Global Media." *Near Eastern Archaeology* 78 (3): 170–177.

Harrison, Rodney. 2010. "Multicultural and Minority Heritage." In *Understanding Heritage and Memory*, edited by Tim Benton, 164–201. Manchester: Manchester University Press.

Hassan, Fekri A. 2007. "The Aswan High Dam and the International Rescue Nubia Campaign." *African Archaeological Review* 24 (3–4): 73–94.

Hertz, Ellen. 2010. *Excessively Up at the International Labour Organisation: Notes on "Note on the Proceedings TMITI/2007/10."* Working Paper no. 9. Neuchâtel: Université de Neuchâtel.

———. 2014. "On Bureaucracy: Excessively Up at the International Labour Organisation." In *Up, Down, and Sideways: Anthropologists Trace the Pathways of Power*, edited by Rachael Stryker and Roberto González, 63–84. New York: Berghahn Books.

Herzfeld, Michael. 1982. *Ours Once More: Folklore, Ideology, and the Making of Modern Greece*. Austin: University of Texas Press.

Hobsbawm, Eric. 1989. *The Age of Empire 1875–1914*. New York: Vintage Books.

Hobsbawm, Eric, and Terence Ranger, eds. 1983. *The Invention of Tradition*. Cambridge: Cambridge University Press.

Holtorf, Cornelius. 2006. "Can Less Be More? Heritage in the Age of Terrorism." *Public Archeology* 5 (2): 101–109.

———. 2012. "The Heritage of Heritage." *Heritage & Society* 5 (2): 153–174.

Holtorf, Cornelius, and Troels Myrup Kristensen. 2015. "Heritage Erasure: Rethinking 'Protection' and 'Preservation.'" *International Journal of Heritage Studies* 21 (4): 313–317.

Honko, Lauri. 2001. "Copyright and Folklore." Paper presented at the National Seminar on Copyright Law and Matters, Mangalore University, Mangalore, Karnataka, India, on February 9, 2001. *FF Network* 21: 8–10.

Hopkin, David. 2012. "Folklore beyond Nationalism: Identity Politics and Scientific Cultures in a New Discipline." In *Folklore and Nationalism in Europe during the Long Nineteenth Century*, edited by Timothy Baycroft and David Hopkin, 371–402. Leiden: Brill.

Hylton, Forrest, and Sinclair Thomson. 2007. *Revolutionary Horizons: Popular Struggle in Bolivia*. New York: Verso.

Hymes, Dell. 1975. "Folklore's Nature and the Sun's Myth." *Journal of American Folklore* 88 (350): 345–369.

ICOMOS (International Council on Monuments and Sites). 1994. "The Nara Document on Authenticity." http://www.icomos.org/charters/nara-e.pdf.

Imber, Mark F. 1989. *The USA, ILO, UNESCO and IAEA: Politicization and Withdrawal in the Specialized Agencies*. New York: Palgrave Macmillan.

Inaba, Nobuko. 1995. "What Is the Test of Authenticity for Intangible Properties?" In *Nara Conference on Authenticity, Japan 1994, Proceedings*, edited by Knut Einar Larsen, 329–332. Tokyo: Agency for Cultural Affairs/UNESCO World Heritage Centre/ICCROM/ICOMOS.

———. 2001. "Authenticity and Value Judgement: Cultural Diversity and Global Standards in Conservation Practice." Paper presented at the International Meeting on Preservation of Modern Architecture, Helsinki, February 2001.

Istanbul Declaration—Final Communiqué. 2002. UNESCO. Third Round Table Meeting of Ministers of Culture. September 17, 2002. http://portal.unesco.org/en/ev.php-URL _ID=6209&URL_DO=DO_TOPIC&URL_SECTION=201.html.

Istasse, Manon. 2016. "Affects and Senses in a World Heritage Site: People–House Relations in the Medina of Fez." In *World Heritage on the Ground: Ethnographic Perspectives*, edited by Christoph Brumann and David Berliner, 37–59. New York: Berghahn Books, 2016.

Ito, Nobuo. 1995. "'Authenticity' Inherent in Cultural Heritage in Asia and Japan." In *Nara Conference on Authenticity, Japan 1994, Proceedings*, edited by Knut Einar Larsen, 35–45. Tokyo: Agency for Cultural Affairs/UNESCO World Heritage Centre/ICCROM/ICOMOS.

Jacobs, Marc. 2013. "Criteria, Apertures and Envelopes. ICH Directives and Organs in Operation." In *2013 IRCI Meeting on ICH. Evaluating the Inscription Criteria for the Two Lists of UNESCO's Intangible Cultural Heritage Convention. The 10th anniversary of the 2003 Convention. Final report*, edited by Misako Ohnuki, 129–137. Osaka: International Research Centre for Intangible Cultural Heritage in the Asia-Pacific Region (IRCI).

———. 2014. "Bruegel and Burke Were Here! Examining the Criteria Implicit in the UNESCO Paradigm of Safeguarding ICH. The First Decade." *International Journal of Intangible Heritage* 9: 99–117.

James, Luke, and Tim Winter. 2017. "Expertise and the Making of World Heritage Policy." *International Journal of Cultural Policy* 23 (1): 361–351.

Ise Jingu. 2015a. "About Ise Jingu: History." Accessed October 14, 2017. http://www.isejingu.or.jp /en/about/index.html.

———. 2015b. "Rituals and Ceremonies: Shikinen Sengu." Accessed October 14, 2017. http://www .isejingu.or.jp/en/ritual/index.html.

Jokilehto, Jukka, and Joseph King. 2001. "Authenticity and Conservation: Reflections on the Current State of Understanding." In *Authenticity and Integrity in an African Context: Expert Meeting—Great Zimbabwe, Zimbabwe, 26–29 May 2000*, edited by Galia Saouma-Forero, 33–39. Paris: UNESCO.

Jokilehto, Jukka. 1995a. "Authenticity: A General Framework for the Concept." In *Nara Conference on Authenticity, Japan 1994, Proceedings*, edited by Knut Einar Larsen, 17–34. Tokyo: Agency for Cultural Affairs/UNESCO World Heritage Centre/ICCROM/ICOMOS.

———. 1995b. "Changing Concepts of Authenticity: Session Report." In *Nara Conference on Authenticity, Japan 1994, Proceedings*, edited by Knut Einar Larsen, 69–75. Tokyo: Agency for Cultural Affairs/UNESCO World Heritage Centre/ICCROM/ICOMOS.

Jones, Siân. 2010. "Negotiating Authentic Objects and Authentic Selves: Beyond the Deconstruction of Authenticity." *Journal of Material Culture* 15 (2): 181–203.

Jones, Siân, and Thomas Yarrow. 2013. "Crafting Authenticity: An Ethnography of Conservation Practice." *Journal of Material Culture* 18 (1): 3–26.

Joy, Charlotte. 2016. "UNESCO Is What? World Heritage, Militant Islam and the Search for a Common Humanity in Mali." In *World Heritage on the Ground: Ethnographic Perspectives*, edited by Christoph Brumann and David Berliner, 60–77. New York: Berghahn.

Kaneff, Deema. 2004. *Who Owns the Past? The Politics of Time in a "Model" Bulgarian Village*. New York: Berghahn Books.

Kapchan, Deborah. 1996. *Gender on the Market: Moroccan Women and the Revoicing of Tradition*. Philadelphia: University of Pennsylvania Press.

———. 2014. "Intangible Heritage in Transit. Goytisolo's Rescue and Moroccan Cultural Rights." In *Cultural Heritage in Transit: Intangible Rights as Human Rights Rights*, edited by Deborah Kapchan, 177–194. Philadelphia: University of Pennsylvania Press.

Khan, Naseem. 2005. Taking Root in Britain. The Process of Shaping Heritage. In *The Politics of Heritage. The Legacies of "Race,"* edited by Jo Littler and Roshi Naidoo, 133–143. London: Routledge.

Kharmawphlang, Desmond, Arupjyoti Saikia , Laltluangiana Khiangte, and Chandan Kumar Sharma. 2004. "Conversation 2: Folklore and Identity." *Indian Folklife: A Quarterly Newsletter from National Folklore Support Centre* 3 (2):18–20. http://www.indianfolklore .org/publications_news.htm.

Kingston, Victoria. 1997. *Simon and Garfunkel: The Definitive Biography*. London: Pan Books.

Kirshenblatt-Gimblett, Barbara. 1988. "Mistaken Dichotomies." *Journal of American Folklore* 101 (400): 140–155.

———. 1996. "Topic Drift: Negotiating the Gap between Our Field and Our Name." *Journal of Folklore Research* 33 (3): 245–254.

———. 1998. *Destination Culture: Tourism, Museums, and Heritage*. Berkeley: University of California Press.

———. 2006. "World Heritage and Cultural Economics." In *Museum Frictions: Public Cultures/ Global Transformations*, edited by Ivan Karp and Corinne Kratz, 161–202. Durham, NC: Duke University Press.

Klein, Barbro. 1997. "Tillhörighet och utanförskap: Om kulturarvspolitik och folklivsforskning i en multietnisk värld." *Rig - Kulturhistorisk tidskrift*, 80 (1–2): 15–32.

———. 2001. "More Swedish than in Sweden, More Iranian than in Iran: Folk Culture and World Migrations." In *Upholders of Culture: Past and Present*, edited by Bo Sundin, 67–80. Stockholm: Royal Swedish Academy of Engineering Sciences.

———. 2006. "Cultural Heritage, the Swedish Folklife Sphere, and the Others." *Cultural Analysis* 5: 57–80.

Klekot, Ewa. 2010. "The Seventh Life of Polish Folk Art and Craft." *Etnološka tribina* 40 (33): 71–85.

Köstlin, Konrad. 1997. "The Passion for the Whole: Interpreted Modernity or Modernity as Interpretation." *Journal of American Folklore* 110 (437): 260–276.

———. 1999. On the Brink of the Next Century: The Necessary Invention of the Present. *Journal of Folklore Research* 36 (2–3): 289–298.

Kurin, Richard. 2002. "Comments on Peter J. M. Nas' Masterpieces of Oral and Intangible Culture: Reflections on the UNESCO World Heritage List." *Current Anthropology* 43 (1): 144–145.

———. 2004. "Safeguarding Intangible Cultural Heritage in the 2003 UNESCO Convention: A Critical Appraisal." *Museum International* 56 (221–222): 66–76.

Kuutma, Kristin. 2007. "The Politics of Contested Representation: UNESCO and the Masterpieces of Intangible Cultural Heritage." In *Prädikat "Heritage": Perspektiven auf Wertschöpfungen aus Kultur*, edited by Dorothee Hemme, Markus Tauschek, and Regina Bendix, 177–195. Berlin: Lit.

———. 2009. "Who Owns Songs? Authority of Heritage and Resources for Restitution." *Ethnologia Europaea: Journal of European Ethnology* 39 (2): 26–40.

———. 2012. "Between Arbitration and Engineering: Concepts and Contingencies in the Shaping of Heritage Regimes." In *Heritage Regimes and the State*, edited by Regina Bendix, Aditya Eggert, and Arnika Peselmann, 21–36. 2nd ed. Göttingen: Universitätsverlag Göttingen.

Kwon, Hyeokhui. 2017. "Villagers' Agency in the Intangible Cultural Heritage Designation of a Korean Village Ritual." *International Journal of Heritage Studies* 23 (3): 200–214.

La Razón. 2011. "La diablada ya es Patrimonio Cultural," July 12, 2011. http://www.la-razon.com /index.php?_url=/la_revista/diablada-Patrimonio-Cultural_0_1429657077.html.

Labadi, Sophie. 2013. *UNESCO, Cultural Heritage, and Outstanding Universal Value: Value-based Analyses of the World Heritage and Intangible Cultural Heritage Conventions*. Lanham, MD: Rowman and Littlefield.

Lafranz-Samuels, Kathryn. 2015. "Introduction: Heritage as Persuasion." In *Heritage Keywords: Rhetoric and Redescription in Cultural Heritage*, edited by Kathryn Lafrenz Samuels and Trinidad Rico, 3–28. Boulder: University Press of Colorado.

Larsen, Knut Einar, ed. 1995a. *Nara Conference on Authenticity, Japan 1994, Proceedings*. Tokyo: Agency for Cultural Affairs/UNESCO World Heritage Centre/ICCROM/ICOMOS.

———. 1995b. "Preface." In *Nara Conference on Authenticity, Japan 1994, Proceedings*, edited by Knut Einar Larsen, xi–xiii. Tokyo: Agency for Cultural Affairs/UNESCO World Heritage Centre/ICCROM/ICOMOS.

———. 1995c. "'The Test of Authenticity' and National Heritage Legislation." In *Nara Conference on Authenticity, Japan 1994, Proceedings*, edited by Knut Einar Larsen, 363–364. Tokyo: Agency for Cultural Affairs/UNESCO World Heritage Centre/ICCROM/ICOMOS.

Latino Perspectives Magazine. 2009. "The Devil Has Its Home in Bolivia." October 1, 2009. Accessed August 5, 2017. https://latinopm.com/opinion/lp-journal/the-devil-has-its-home -in-bolivia-2926#.WYXUd9PyhE4.

Laville, Yann. 2014. "Festivalisation? Esquisse d'un phénomène et bilan critique." *Cahiers d'ethnomusicologie* 27:11–25.

Leal, João. 2016. "Festivals, Group Making, Remaking and Unmaking." *Ethnos: Journal of Anthropology* 81 (4): 584–599.

Leersen, Joep. 2007. *National Thought in Europe: A Cultural History.* Amsterdam: Amsterdam University Press.

———. 2012. "Oral Epic: The Nation Finds a Voice." In *Folklore and Nationalism in Europe during the Long Nineteenth Century*, edited by Timothy Baycroft and David Hopkin, 11–26. Leiden: Brill.

Lévi-Strauss, Laurent. 2001. "The African Cultural Heritage and the Application of the Concept of Authenticity in the 1972 Convention." In *Authenticity and Integrity in an African Context: Expert Meeting—Great Zimbabwe, Zimbabwe, 26–29 May 2000*, edited by Galia Saouma-Forero, 70–73. Paris: UNESCO.

Li, Tania Murray. 2001. "Boundary Work: Community, Market, and State Reconsidered." In *Communities and the Environment: Ethnicity, Gender, and the State in Community-Based Conservation*, edited by Arun Agrawal and Clark C. Gibson, 157–179. New Brunswick, NJ: Rutgers University Press.

Library of Congress Copyright Office. 1933. *Catalogue of Copyright Entries. Published by the Authority of the Acts of Congress of March 3, 1891, of June 30, 1906, and of March 4, 1909. Part 3: Musical Compositions.* New Series 28 (5). Washington, DC: Government Printing Office.

Littler, Jo, and Roshi Naidoo, eds. 2005. *The Politics of Heritage. The Legacies of "Race."* London: Routledge.

Llórens Amico, José Antonio. 1983. *Música popular en Lima: Criollos y andinos.* Lima: Instituto de Estudios Peruanos.

Löfgren, Eva. 2011. *Hantverkslaboratorium.* Gothenburg: University of Gothenburg.

Löfgren, Orvar. 1989. "Nationalization of Culture." *Ethnologia Europaea: Journal of European Ethnology* 19: 5–25.

Logan, William. 2012. "Cultural Diversity, Cultural Heritage and Human Rights: Towards Heritage Management as Human Rights-Based Cultural Practice." *International Journal of Heritage Studies* 18 (3): 231–244.

Los Andes. 2009. "Gobierno de Bolivia reconoce que 'El Cóndor Pasa' es peruano." September 22, 2009. http://www.losandes.com.pe/Nacional/20090922/27482.html.

Lowenthal, David. 1998. *The Heritage Crusade and the Spoils of History.* Cambridge: Cambridge University Press.

Lowthorp, Leah. 2007. "The Cultural Politics of UNESCO's Intangible Cultural Heritage in India: Kutiyattam Sanskrit Theatre." Paper presented at the Annual Meeting of the American Folklore Society and the Folklore Studies Association of Canada in Quebec City, Canada, October 17–21.

———. 2013. "Scenarios of Endangered Culture, Shifting Cosmopolitanisms: Kutiyattam and UNESCO Intangible Cultural Heritage in Kerala, India." PhD dissertation, University of Pennsylvania.

———. 2015. "Voices on the Ground: Kutiyattam, UNESCO, and the Heritage of Humanity." *Journal of Folklore Research* 52 (2–3): 157–180.

Luftig, Stacey, ed. 1997. *The Paul Simon Companion: Four Decades of Commentary*. London: Omnibus.

Luxen, Jean-Louis. 1995. "Approches de l'authenticité: modestie et pluralisme." In *Nara Conference on Authenticity, Japan 1994, Proceedings*, edited by Knut Einar Larsen, 371–374. Tokyo: Agency for Cultural Affairs/UNESCO World Heritage Centre/ICCROM/ICOMOS.

Margry, Peter Jan. 2014. "UNESCO en de paradox van bescherming: Immaterieel erfgoed in Nederland." *Ons Erfdeel* 1, 56–66.

Mathisen, Stein R. 2009. "Narrated Sámi Siedis: Heritage and Ownership in Ambiguous Border Zones." *Ethnologia Europaea: Journal of European Ethnology* 39 (2): 11–25.

Mayor Zaragoza, Federico. 2010. "Patrimonio cultural inmaterial en el siglo XXI: Entrevista con Federico Mayor Zaragoza, ex director general de la Unesco." *Quaderns de la Mediterrània* 13: 231–234.

Mazzarella, William. 2012. "Affect: What Is It Good For?" In *Enchantments of Modernity: Empire, Nation, Globalization*, edited by Saurabh Dube, 291–309. London: Routledge.

McArver, Charles. 1977. "Mining and Diplomacy: United States Interests at Cerro de Pasco, Peru, 1876–1930." PhD dissertation, University of North Carolina.

McDermott, Melanie Hughes. 2001. "Invoking Community: Indigenous People and Ancestral Domain in Palawan, the Philippines." In *Communities and the Environment: Ethnicity, Gender, and the State in Community-Based Conservation*, edited by Arun Agrawal and Clark C. Gibson, 32–62. New Brunswick, NJ: Rutgers University Press.

McDowell, John H. 2010. "Rethinking Folklorization in Ecuador: Multivocality in the Expressive Contact Zone." *Western Folklore* 69 (2): 181–209.

McKernan, Bethan. 2016a. "Isis 'Destroys Thousands of Years of Culture Almost Overnight' as It Flees Iraqi Army Near Mosul." *Independent*, November 15, 2016. http://www.independent .co.uk/news/world/middle-east/isis-mosul-iraq-army-terrorists-destroy-demolish-nimrud -temples-artefacts-a7418136.html.

———. 2016b. "Mosul: Isis Destruction of Ancient Iraqi City Revealed for First Time with New Photos." *Independent*, November 16, 2016. http://www.independent.co.uk/news/world /middle-east/mosul-offensive-latest-isis-destruction-ancient-city-of-mesopotamia -nimrud-a7421036.html.

McLaughlin, Donald H. 1945. "Origin and Development of the Cerro de Pasco Copper Corpora-tion." *Mining and Metallurgy* 26 (November): 509–511.

McSherry, J. Patrice. 2005. *Predatory States: Operation Condor and Covert War in Latin America*. Lanham, MD: Rowman and Littlefield.

Mendoza, Zoila S. 1998. "Defining Folklore. Mestizo and Indigenous Identities on the Move." *Bulletin of Latin American Research* 17 (2): 165–183.

Merry, Sally Engle. 2006. *Human Rights and Gender Violence: Translating International Law into Local Justice*. Chicago: University of Chicago Press.

Meskell, Lynn. 2002. "Negative Heritage and Past Mastering in Archaeology." *Anthropological Quarterly* 75 (3): 557–574.

———. 2011. "From Paris to Pontdrift: UNESCO Meetings, Mapungubwe and Mining." *South African Archaeological Bulletin* 66 (194): 149–156.

——. 2012. "The Rush to Inscribe: Reflections on the 35th Session of the World Heritage Committee, UNESCO Paris, 2011." *Journal of Field Archaeology* 37 (2): 145–151.

——. 2013. "UNESCO and the Fate of the World Heritage Indigenous Peoples Council of Experts (WHIPCOE)." *International Journal of Cultural Property* 20 (2): 155–174.

——. 2014. "States of Conservation: Protection, Politics, and Pacting within UNESCO's World Heritage Committee." *Anthropological Quarterly* 87 (1): 217–244.

Meskell, Lynn, Claudia Liuzza, Enrico Bertacchini, and Donatella Saccone. 2015. "Multilateralism and UNESCO World Heritage: Decision-Making, States Parties and Political Processes." *International Journal of Heritage Studies* 21 (5): 423–440.

Mitchell, Timothy. 1998. "Fixing the Economy." *Cultural Studies* 12 (1): 82–101.

——. 2002. *Rule of Experts: Egypt, Techno-politics, Modernity*. Berkeley University of California Press.

Morgan, Andy. 2013. *Music, Culture and Conflict in Mali*. Raleigh: Freemuse.

Moser, Hans. 1962. "Vom Folklorismus in unserer Zeit." *Zeitschrift für Volkskunde* 58 (2): 177–209.

——. 1964. "Der Folklorismus als Forschungsproblem der Volkskunde." *Hessische Blätter für Volkskunde* 55: 9–57.

Mugnaini, Fabio. 2016. "The Haunted Discipline: On the Political Nature of Folklore and the Political Destiny of Its Study." *Narodna Umjetnost* 53 (1): 15–41.

Müller, Birgit. 2011. "The Elephant in the Room: Multistakeholder Dialogue on Agricultural Biotechnology in the Food and Agriculture Organization." In *Policy Worlds: Anthropology and the Analysis of Contemporary Power*, edited by Cris Shore and Susan Wright, 281–299. New York: Berghahn Books.

Munjeri, Dawson. 2001. "The Notions of Integrity and Authenticity: The Emerging Patterns in Africa." In *Authenticity and Integrity in an African Context: Expert Meeting—Great Zimbabwe, Zimbabwe, 26–29 May 2000*, edited by Galia Saouma-Forero, 17–19. Paris: UNESCO.

Muños-Vinas, Salvador. 2005. *Contemporary Theory of Conservation*. Oxford: Elsevier.

Murphy, Colin. 2001. "Immaterial Civilization." *Atlantic Monthly* 288, no. 2 (September): 20–22.

Nader, Laura. 1969. "Up the Anthropologist: Perspectives Gained from Studying Up." In *Reinventing Anthropology*, edited by Dell Hymes, 284–311. New York: Vintage Books.

Nas, Peter J. M. 2002. "Masterpieces of Oral and Immaterial Culture: Reflections on the UNESCO World Heritage List." *Current Anthropology* 43 (1): 139–143.

Négrier, Emmanuel. 2015. "Festivalisation: Patterns and Limits." In *Focus on Festivals: Contemporary European Case Studies and Perspectives*, edited by Chris Newbold, Jennie Jordan, Franco Bianchini, and Christopher Maughan, 18–27. Oxford: Goodfellow.

Nora, Pierre. 1989. "Between Memory and History: Les Lieux de Mémoire." *Representations* 26 (Spring): 7–24.

Nordenstreng, Kaarle. 2012. "The History of NWICO and Its Lessons." In *From NWICO to WSIS: 30 Years of Communication Geopolitics. Actors and Flows, Structures and Divides*, edited by Divina Frau-Meigs, Julia Pohle, and Patricio Tupper, 29–40. Bristol: Intellect Books.

Noyes, Dorothy. 2003. "Group." In *Eight Words for the Study of Expressive Culture*, edited by Burt Feintuch, 7–41. Urbana: University of Illinois Press.

——. 2006. "The Judgment of Solomon: Global Protections for Tradition and the Problem of Community Ownership." *Cultural Analysis* 5: 25–76.

Ó Giolláin, Diarmuid. 2000. *Locating Irish Folklore. Tradition, Modernity, Identity*. Cork: Cork University Press.

Ong, Aihwa. 2006. *Neoliberalism as Exception: Mutations in Citizenship and Sovereignty*. Durham, NC: Duke University Press.

Ortiz, Carmen. 1999. "The Uses of Folklore by the Franco Regime." *Journal of American Folklore* 112 (446): 479–496.

Ortner, Sherry. 1974. "Is Female to Male as Nature Is to Culture?" In *Woman, Culture, and Society*, edited by Michelle Rosaldo and Louise Lamphere, 67–88. Stanford, CA: Stanford University Press.

Palmsköld, Anneli. 2011. "Hantverkskunskap som immateriellt kulturarv." In *Hantverkslaboratorium*, edited by Eva Löfgren, 96–105. Gothenburg: University of Gothenburg.

Palonen, Ville. 2013. "Winds of Change over Morocco." *Blue Wings Gift Issue*, December 2013. Published online September 30, 2016: https://issuu.com/finnair_bluewings/docs/blue _wings_10_2013_pieni/19.

Palumbo, Berardino. 2003. *L'UNESCO e il Campanile. Antropologia, politica e beni culturali in Siciliaorientale.* ROMA: Meltemi.

———. 2011. "Politics, Heritage, and Globalization: South Eastern Sicily in the 'Patrimonialization' Process (1996–2011)." *Il nostro tempo e la speranza* 7:7–15.

Patterson, Thomas C. 2016. "Too Much Common Sense, Not Enough Critical Thinking." *Dialectical Anthropology* 40 (3): 251–258.

"Periodic Reporting on the Convention for the Safeguarding of the Intangible Cultural Heritage: Belgium." 2012. Report submitted on December 15, 2012, and examined by the Committee in 2013. *UNESCO: Intangible Cultural Heritage*, accessed May 29, 2017: https://ich.unesco.org /en/state/belgium-BE?info=periodic-reporting#pr-2013-2013.

"Periodic Reporting on the Convention for the Safeguarding of the Intangible Cultural Heritage: Madagascar." 2012. Report submitted on December 15, 2012, and examined by the Committee in 2013. *UNESCO: Intangible Cultural Heritage*, accessed May 29, 2017. https:// ich.unesco.org/en/state/madagascar-MG?info=periodic-reporting#pr-2013-2013.

"Periodic Reporting on the Convention for the Safeguarding of the Intangible Cultural Heritage: Morocco." 2013. Report submitted on December 15, 2012, and examined by the Committee in 2014. *UNESCO: Intangible Cultural Heritage*, accessed May 29, 2017: https://ich.unesco .org/en/state/morocco-MA?info=periodic-reporting.

"Periodic Reporting on the Convention for the Safeguarding of the Intangible Cultural Heritage: Vietnam." 2013. Report submitted on December 15, 2012, and examined by the Committee in 2014. *UNESCO: Intangible Cultural Heritage*, accessed May 29, 2017. https://ich.unesco .org/en/state/viet-nam-VN?info=periodic-reporting#pr-2012-2012.

Picard, David, and Mike Robinson, eds. 2006. *Festivals, Tourism and Social Change: Remaking Worlds.* Bristol: Channel View.

Poulot, Dominique. 1997. *Musée, nation, patrimoine.* Paris: Gallimard-Jeunesse.

———. 2006. *Une histoire du patrimoine en Occident.* Paris: Presses Universitaires De France.

Pressouyre, Léon. 1997. "Cultural Heritage and the 1972 Convention: Definition and Evolution of a Concept." In *African Cultural Heritage and the World Heritage Convention. Second Global Strategy Meeting*, edited by Bertrand Hirsch, Laurent Lévi-Strauss, and Galia Saouma-Forero, 56–64. Paris: UNESCO.

Proef de Cultuur Djemaa el Fna Rotterdam. 2017. Accessed March 18, 2017. http://djemaaelfnarotterdam .stichtingdeloodsen.nl/.

Rana, Jasmijn, Marlous Willemsen, and Hester Dibbits. 2017. "Moved by the Tears of Others. Emotion Networking in the Heritage Sphere." *International Journal of Heritage Studies* 23 (10): 977–988.

Rastrick, Ólafur. 2007. "Menningararfur í fjölmenningarsamfélagi: Einsleitni, fjölhyggja, tvíbendni." In *Þriðja íslenska söguþingið 18.–21. maí 2006: Ráðstefnurit*, edited by Benedikt Eyþórsson and Hrafnkell Lárusson, 333–341. Reykjavík: Sagnfræðingafélag Íslands.

Redacción La Industria. 2013. "El Cóndor pasa levanta vuelo a complir un siglo de vida." December 22, 2013. Accessed October 15, 2017. https://issuu.com/alobso/docs/la_industria _regional_22_dic_2013/5.

Rico, Trinidad. 2017. "Heritage Studies and Islam: A Crisis of Representation." *Review of Middle East Studies,* 1–5. doi:10.1017/rms.2017.96.

Rios, Fernando. 2005. "Music in Urban La Paz, Bolivian Nationalism, and the Early History of Cosmopolitan Andean Music: 1936–1970." PhD dissertation, University of Illinois at Urbana-Champaign.

———. 2006. "Andean Music, the Left, and Pan-Latin Americanism: The Early History." *Diagonal: Journal of the Center for Iberian and Latin American Music* 2: 1–13. http://www.cilam.ucr .edu/diagonal/issues/2006/Rios.pdf.

———. 2008. "La Flûte Indienne: The Early History of Andean Folkloric-Popular Music in France and Its Impact on Nueva Canción." *Latin American Music Review* 29 (2): 145–189.

———. 2010. "Bolero Trios, Mestizo Panpipe Ensembles, and Bolivia's 1952 Revolution: Urban La Paz Musicians and the Nationalist Revolutionary Movement." *Ethnomusicology* 54 (2): 281–317.

———. 2014. "'They're Stealing Our Music': The Argentinísima Controversy, National Culture Boundaries, and the Rise of a Bolivian Nationalist Discourse." *Latin American Music Review* 35 (2): 197–228.

Rodenberg, Jeroen, and Pieter Wagenaar. 2016. "Essentializing 'Black Pete': Competing Narratives Surrounding the Sinterklaas Tradition in the Netherlands." *International Journal of Heritage Studies* 22 (9): 716–728.

Ronström, Owe 2008. *Kulturarvspolitik: Visby från sliten småstad till medeltidsikon.* Stockholm: Carlsson.

———. 2016. "Four Facets of Festivalisation." *Puls: Musik- och dansetnologisk tidskrift/Journal for Ethnomusicology and Ethnochoreology* 1: 67–83.

Rose, Nikolas. 1999. *Powers of Freedom. Reframing Political Thought.* Cambridge: Cambridge University Press.

RPP Notícias. 2009a. "Bolivianos irán a Miss Universo para protestar por traje de 'La Diablada.'" August 11, 2009. http://rpp.pe/famosos/celebridades/bolivianos-iran-a-miss-universo-para -protestar-por-traje-de-la-diablada-noticia-200587.

———. 2009b. "Miss Perú defiende traje típico de 'La Diablada' ante prensa boliviana." August 12, 2009. http://rpp.pe/lima/actualidad/miss-peru-defiende-traje-tipico-de-la-diablada -ante-prensa-boliviana-noticia-200881.

———. 2009c. "Diablada peruana es más antigua que la de Bolivia asegura directora del INC." August 14, 2009. http://rpp.pe/cultura/literatura/diablada-peruana-es-mas-antigua-que-la -de-bolivia-asegura-directora-del-inc-noticia-201626

———. 2009d. "Piden que Perú se pronuncie por difundir 'El Cóndor Pasa' como boliviano." September 21, 2009. http://rpp.pe/peru/actualidad/piden-que-peru-se-pronuncie-por -difundir-el-condor-pasa-como-boliviano-noticia-210214.

———. 2009e. "Bolivia reconoce que 'El Cóndor Pasa' es una canción peruana." September 22, 2009. http://rpp.pe/mundo/actualidad/bolivia-reconoce-que-el-condor-pasa-es-una -cancion-peruana-noticia-210605.

RTBF. 2014. "Les friteries font désormais partie de l'héritage culturel immatériel flamand." January 10, 2014. https://www.rtbf.be/info/belgique/detail_les-friteries-font-desormais-partie -de-l-heritage-culturel-immateriel-flamand?id=8173201.

———. 2016. "Le 'fritkot' devient patrimoine oral et immatériel de la Fédération Wallonie-Bruxelles." November 24, 2016. https://www.rtbf.be/info/societe/detail_le

-fritkot-devient-patrimoine-oral-et-immateriel-de-la-federation-wallonie-bruxelles?
id=9462253.

Sáenz Vargas, Virginia. 2014. "Semblanza de una boliviana: Julia Elena Fortún." In *Otras Miradas Presencias femeninas en una historia de larga duración*, edited by Walter Sánchez Canedo and Claudia Rivera Casanovas, 35–70. Cochabamba: Instituto de Investigaciones Antropológicas y Museo Arqueológico de la Universidad Mayor de San Simón (INIAM-UMSS).

Sagan, Carl, E. D. Drake, Ann Dryuan, Timothy Ferris, Jon Lomberg, Linda Salzman Sagan. 1978. *Murmurs of Earth: The Voyager Interstellar Record*. New York: Random House.

Saikawa, Takashi. 2016. "Returning to the International Community: UNESCO and Post-war Japan, 1945–1951." In *A History of UNESCO: Global Actions and Impacts*, edited by Poul Duedahl, 116–130. New York: Springer.

Salazar Mejía, Luis. 2014. "El Cóndor Pasa . . . y sus misterios." Revista de Crítica Literaria Latinoamericana 40 (80): 11–37.

Sánchez Carretero, Cristina. 2015. "Heritagization of the Camino to Finisterre." In *Heritage, Pilgrimage and the Camino to Finisterre*, edited by Cristina Sánchez Carretero, 95–120. Cham: Springer.

Saouma-Forero, Galia. 2001. "Synthesis Report of the Expert Meeting on Authenticity and Integrity in the African Context." In *Authenticity and Integrity in the African Context: Expert Meeting—Great Zimbabwe, Zimbabwe 26–29 May 2000*, edited by Galia Saouma-Forero, 144–164. Paris: UNESCO.

Schmitt, Thomas. 2005. "Jemaa el Fna Square in Marrakech: Changes to a Social Space and to a UNESCO Masterpiece of the Oral and Intangible Heritage of Humanity as a Result of Global Influences." *Arab World Geographer* 8 (4): 173–195.

———. 2008. "The UNESCO Concept of Safeguarding Intangible Cultural Heritage: Its Background and Marrakchi Roots." *International Journal of Heritage Studies* 14 (2): 95–111.

———. 2009. "Global Cultural Governance: Decision-Making Concerning World Heritage between Politics and Science." *Erdkunde* 63 (2): 103–121.

Schuster, J. Mark. 2002. "Making a List and Checking It Twice: The List as a Tool of Historic Preservation." Working paper no. 14. The Cultural Policy Center at the University of Chicago. https://culturalpolicy.uchicago.edu/sites/culturalpolicy.uchicago.edu/files/Schuster14.pdf.

Semaine de la frite. 2016. Accessed March 18, 2017. http://www.semainedelafrite.be/.

Sherkin, Samantha. 2001. "A Historical Study on the Preparation of the 1989 Recommendation on the Safeguarding of Traditional Culture and Folklore." In *Safeguarding Traditional Cultures. A Global Assessment*, edited by Peter Seitel, 42–56. Washington, DC: Center for Folklife and Cultural Heritage, Smithsonian Institution.

Silverman, Carol. 2015. "Macedonia, UNESCO, and Intangible Cultural Heritage: The Challenging Fate of Teškoto." *Journal of Folklore Research* 52 (2–3): 233–251.

Skrydstrup, Martin. 2009. "Theorizing Repatriation." *Ethnologia Europaea: Journal of European Ethnology* 39 (2): 54–66.

———. 2012. "Cultural Property." *A Companion to Folklore*, edited by Regina Bendix and Galit Hasan-Rokem, 520–536. Hoboken, NJ: Blackwell.

Smeets, Rieks, and Harriet Deacon. 2017. "The Examination of Nomination Files under the UNESCO Convention for the Safeguarding of the Intangible Cultural Heritage." In *The Routledge Companion to Intangible Cultural Heritage*, edited by Michelle L. Stefano and Peter Davis, 22–39. London: Routledge.

Smith, Claire, Heather Burke, Cherrie de Leiuen, and Gary Jackson. 2016. "The Islamic State's Symbolic War: Da'esh's Socially Mediated Terrorism as a Threat to Cultural Heritage." *Journal of Social Archeology* 16 (2): 164–188.

Smith, Laurajane. 2006. *Uses of Heritage.* London: Routledge.

Smith, Laurajane, and Natsuko Akagawa, eds. 2009. *Intangible Heritage.* London: Routledge.

Soko, Boston. 2014. *Vimbuza The Healing Dance of Northern Malawi.* Lilongwe: Mzuni Press.

Statistics Lithuania. 2013. "2011 Census." https://osp.stat.gov.lt/en_GB/pradinis.

Stefano, Michelle L. and Peter Davis, eds. 2017. *The Routledge Companion to Intangible Cultural Heritage.* London: Routledge.

Stefano, Michelle L., Peter Davis, and Gerard Corsane, eds. 2014. *Safeguarding Intangible Cultural Heritage.* Suffolk: Boydell & Brewer.

Stenou, Katérina. 2003. *UNESCO and the Issue of Cultural Diversity. Review and Strategy, 1946–2003: A Study Based on Official Documents.* Revised version. Paris: UNESCO Division of Cultural Policies and Intercultural Dialogue.

Stovel, Herb. 1995. "Foreword: Working Towards the Nara Document." In *Nara Conference on Authenticity, Japan 1994, Proceedings,* edited by Knut Einar Larsen, xxxiii–xxxvi. Tokyo: Agency for Cultural Affairs/UNESCO World Heritage Centre/ICCROM/ICOMOS.

Ströbele-Gregor, Juliana. 1996. "Culture and Political Practice of the Aymara and Quechua in Bolivia: Autonomous Forms of Modernity in the Andes." *Latin American Perspectives* 23 (2): 72–90.

Swenson, Astrid. 2007. "'Heritage,' 'Patromoine' und 'Kulturerbe': Eine vergleichende historische Semantik." In *Prädikat Heritage: Wertschöpfungen aus kulturellen Ressourcen,* edited by Dorothee Hemme, Markus Tauschek, and Regina Bendix, 53–74. Berlin: Lit.

———. 2013. *The Rise of Heritage: Preserving the Past in France, Germany and England, 1789–1914.* Cambridge: Cambridge University Press.

Tauschek, Markus. 2009. "Cultural Property as Strategy: The Carnival of Binche, the Creation of Cultural Heritage and Cultural Property." *Ethnologia Europaea: Journal of European Ethnology* 39 (2): 67–80.

———. 2010. *Wertschöpfung aus Tradition: der Karneval von Binche und die Konstituierung kulturellen Erbes.* Münster: LIT.

Tebbaa, Ouidad. 2010. "Le patrimoine de la place Jemaa El Fna de Marrakech: Entre le matériel et l'immatériel." *Quaderns de la Mediterrània* 13: 51–58.

Tebbaa, Ouidad and Ahmed Skounti. 2011. "Patrimoine mondial et patrimoine culturel immatériel, le problème de la double reconnaissance de l'UNESCO. Cas de Marrakech." In *De l'immatérialité du patrimoine culturel,* edited by Ouidad Tebbaa and Ahmed Skounti, 44–64. Marrakech: Marrakech Culture Patrimoine et Tourisme / Faculté des Lettres et des Sciences Humaines, Université Cadi Ayyad.

Telegraph. 2012. "Timbuktu Shrine Destruction 'a War Crime.'" July 2, 2012. http://www.telegraph.co.uk/news/worldnews/africaandindianocean/mali/9369271/Timbuktu-shrine-destruction-a-war-crime.html.

Telemetro. 2009. "Miss Perú rechaza invitación de Evo Morales para bailar." October 9, 2009. http://www.telemetro.com/entretenimiento/espectaculo/Miss-Peru-invitacion-Evo-Morales_0_194080599.html

Thompson, Tok. 2006. "Heritage versus the Past." In *The Past in the Present: A Multidisciplinary Approach,* edited by Fabio Mugnaini, Pádraig Ó Hélaí, and Tok Thompson, 197–208. Catania: Edit Press.

Titchen, Sarah M. 1995. "On the Construction of Outstanding Universal Value: UNESCO's World Heritage Convention (Convention Concerning the Protection of the World Cultural and Natural Heritage, 1972) and the Identification and Assessment of Cultural Places for Inclusion in the World Heritage List." PhD Dissertation, Australian National University.

Toledo Brückmann, Ernesto. 2011. *El cóndor pasa: Mandato y obediencia; Análisis político y social de una zarzuela*. Lima: Editorial San Marco

Tolia-Kelly, Divya P., Emma Waterton, and Steve Watson. 2017. *Heritage, Affect and Emotion: Politics, Practices and Infrastructures*. Oxford: Routledge.

Tornatore, Jean-Louis. 2007. "Qu'est ce qu'un ethnologue politisé? Expertise et engagement en socio-anthropologie de l'activité patrimoniale." *ethnographiques.org* 12 (February). http://www.ethnographiques.org/2007/Tornatore.

———. 2011. "Du patrimoine ethnologique au patrimoine immatériel. Suivre la voie politique de l'immatérialité culturelle." In *Le patrimoine culturel immatériel: Enjeux d'une nouvelle catégorie*, edited by Chiara Bortolotto, 213–232. Paris: Maison des sciences de l'homme.

———. 2012. "Retour d'anthropologie: 'Le Repas gastronomique des Français.' Éléments d'ethnographie d'une distinction patrimoniale." *ethnographiques.org* 24 (July). http://www.ethnographiques.org/2012/Tornatore.

TripAdvisor User Review. 2013. "Aminated." April 9, 2013. https://www.tripadvisor.co.uk/Show UserReviews-g293734-d318047-r157242126-Jemaa_el_Fnaa-Marrakech_Marrakech_Tensift _El_Haouz_Region.html#.

Trujillo, Oscar Ramírez. 2012. "El Cóndor Pasa es Patrimonio Cultural de nuestra Nación." *El Cóndor Pasa*, November 18, 2012. http://www.elcondorpasa.org/gort/2012/11/18/el-condor -pasa-es-patrimonio-cultural-de-nuestra-nacion-el-peru/.

Tschofen, Bernhard. 2007. "Antreten, ablehnen, verwalten? Was der Heritage-Boom der Kulturwissenschaften aufträgt." In *Prädikat "Heritage": Perspektiven auf Wertschöpfungen aus Kultur*, edited by Dorothee Hemme, Markus Tauschek, and Regina Bendix, 19–32. Berlin: Lit.

Tucker, Joshua. 2013. *Gentleman Troubadours and Andean Pop Stars: Huayno Music, Media Work, and Ethnic Imaginaries in Urban Peru*. Chicago: University of Chicago Press.

Turino, Thomas. 1988. "The Music of Andean Migrants in Lima, Peru: Demographics, Social Power, and Style." *Latin American Music Review* 9 (2): 127–150.

———. 2003. "Nationalism and Latin American Music: Selected Case Studies and Theoretical Considerations." *Latin American Music Review / Revista De Música Latinoamericana* 24 (2): 169–209.

Turtinen, Jan. 2000. *Globalising Heritage: On UNESCO and the Transnational Construction of World Heritage*. SCORE Rapportserie 2000: 12. Stockholm: Stockholm Center for Organizational Research.

———. 2006. *Världsarvets villkor. Intressen, förhandlingar och bruk i internationell politik*. Acta universitatis stockholmiensis, Stockholm Studies in Ethnology, 1. Stockholm: Stockholms Universitet.

UN News Centre. 2008. "UN's Intangible Cultural Heritage List Comes into Being with 90 Entries." November 4, 2008. http://www.un.org/apps/news/story.asp?NewsID=28812#.WeNt AluoPIU.

———. 2012. "Ban Voices Concern by Worsening Humanitarian Situation in Mali." July 1, 2012. http://www.un.org/apps/news/story.asp?NewsID=42368#.WZS6wdPyhE4.

UNESCO. 1971. "Possibility of Establishing an International Instrument for the Protection of Folklore." Document B/EC/IX/11-IGC/XR.1/15.

———. 1977. "Letter from the Ministry of Foreign Affairs and Religion, Republic of Bolivia, 24 April 1973." Document FOLK/I/3, Annex. Paris.

———.1982. *Nubia. A Triumph of International Solidarity. Official Inauguration of the Temples of Philae and the Twentieth Anniversary of the International Campaign to Save the Monuments of Nubia*. Paris: UNESCO.

———. 1993. "Establishment of a System of 'Living Cultural Properties' (Living Human Treasures) at UNESCO." Executive Board, 142nd session, August 10, 1993. Document 142 EX/18, Paris: UNESCO.

———. 2001a. *Proclamation of Masterpieces of the Oral and Intangible Heritage of Humanity. Guide for the Presentation of Candidature Files.* Paris: Intangible Heritage Section, Division of Cultural Heritage, UNESCO.

———. 2001b. *Première Proclamation des chefs-d'œuvre du patrimoine oral et immatériel de l'humanité.* Paris: Intangible Heritage Section, Division of Cultural Heritage, UNESCO.

———. 2002a. *Guidelines for the Establishment of Living Human Treasures Systems.* Paris: UNESCO Section of Intangible Cultural Heritage and Korean National Commission for UNESCO.

———. 2002b. "Intangible Cultural Heritage: Priority Domains for an International Convention. Impacts of the First Proclamation on the Nineteen Masterpieces Proclaimed Oral and Intangible Heritage of Humanity." Expert Meeting, Rio de Janeiro, 2002. Document RIO/ITH/2002/INF.

———. 2002c. "Study with a View to the Establishment of Consolidated Administrative and Financial Procedures for the Implementation of the Project Concerning the 'Proclamation of Masterpieces of the Oral and Intangible Heritage of Humanity.'" Executive Board, 164th session, May 6, 2002. Document 164 EX/18, Paris: UNESCO.

———. 2003a. "Intersessional Working Group of Government Experts on the Preliminary Draft Convention for the Safeguarding of the Intangible Cultural Heritage." Report, April 22–30, 2003. Document CLT-2003/CONF.206/3, Paris: UNESCO.

———. 2003b. "Preliminary Draft International Convention for the Safeguarding of the Intangible Cultural Heritage and Report by the Director-General on the Situation Calling for Standard-Setting and on the Possible Scope of such Standard-Setting." General Conference, 32nd session, July 18, 2003. Document 32 C/26, Paris: UNESCO.

———. 2004a. *Deuxième Proclamation des chefs-d'œuvre du patrimoine oral et immatériel de l'humanité.* Paris: Intangible Heritage Section, Division of Cultural Heritage, UNESCO.

———. 2004b. "Address by Mr Koïchiro Matsuura, Director-General of UNESCO, on the Convention for the Safeguarding of the Intangible Cultural Heritage." Copenhagen, Denmark, June 1, 2004. Document DG/2004/079, Paris: UNESCO.

UNESCO Intangible Cultural Heritage. 2014. "Decision of the Intergovernmental Committee: 9.COM 10.34." Accessed October 13, 2017. https://ich.unesco.org/en/decisions/9.COM/10.34.

UNESCO Intangible Cultural Heritage Lists. 2008a. "Carnival of Barranquilla." Accessed May 29, 2017. https://ich.unesco.org/en/RL/carnival-of-barranquilla-00051.

———. 2008b. "Vimbuza Healing Dance." Accessed September 6, 2017. https://ich.unesco.org/en/RL/vimbuza-healing-dance-00158.

———. 2013. "Kimjang, Making and Sharing Kimchi in the Republic of Korea." Accessed October 30, 2017. https://ich.unesco.org/en/RL/kimjang-making-and-sharing-kimchi-in-the-republic-of-korea-00881.

———. 2016. "Yama, Hoko, Yatai, Float Festivals in Japan." Accessed September 6, 2017. https://ich.unesco.org/en/RL/yama-hoko-yatai-float-festivals-in-japan-01059.

UNESCO World Heritage Centre. n.d. "Historic Centre of Warsaw." Accessed October 13, 2017. http://whc.unesco.org/en/list/30.

———. n.d. "The World Heritage Convention: Brief History." Accessed October 13, 2017. http://whc.unesco.org/en/convention/

———. 2009. "50th Anniversary of Nubia Campaign." March 31, 2009. http://whc.unesco.org/en/news/497/.

———. 2015. "UNESCO Director General Condemns Destruction of Nimrud in Iraq." March 6, 2015.

United Nations General Assembly. 2015. "Saving the Cultural Heritage of Iraq. Sixty-ninth session, Agenda item 14, Culture of Peace." May 21, 2015. Document A/69/L.71. http://www.un.org/ga/search/view_doc.asp?symbol=A/69/L.71.

Varallanos, José. 1988. *El Cóndor Pasa. Vida y obra de Daniel Alomía Robles*. Lima: Talleres Gráficos P. L. Villanueva.

Vargas Luza, Jorge Enrique. 1998. *La diablada de Oruro: sus máscaras y caretas*. La Paz: Plural Editores/Centro de Información para el Desarrollo.

Velure, Magne. 1972. "Levande dansetradisjon eller stagnasjon og kopiering: Folkedans som folklorisme-fenomen." *Tradisjon* 2: 3–9.

Viejo-Rose, Dacia, and Marie Louise Stig Sørensen. 2015. "Cultural Heritage and Armed Conflict. New Questions for an Old Relationship." In *The Palgrave Handbook of Contemporary Heritage Research*, edited by Emma Waterton and Steve Watson, 281–296. Hampshire: Palgrave Macmillan.

Whisnant, David E. 1983. *All that Is Native and Fine: The Politics of Culture in an American Region*. Chapel Hill: University of North Carolina Press.

———. 1988. "Public Sector Folklore as Intervention: Lessons from the Past, Prospects for the Future." In *The Conservation of Culture: Folklorists and the Public Sector*, edited by Burt Feintuch, 233–47. Lexington: University Press of Kentucky.

Williams, Gareth. 2002. *The Other Side of the Popular: Neoliberalism and Subalternity in Latin America*. Durham, NC: Duke University Press.

Winter, Tim. 2010. "Heritage Tourism: The Dawn of a New Era?" In *Heritage and Globalisation*, edited by Sophia Labadi and Colin Long, 117–129. Abingdon: Taylor & Francis.

———. 2014. "Beyond Eurocentrism? Heritage Conservation and the Politics of Difference." *International Journal of Heritage* 20 (2): 123–137.

———. 2015. "Heritage Diplomacy." *International Journal of Heritage Studies* 21 (10): 997–1015.

———. 2016. "Heritage Diplomacy: Entangled Materialities of International Relations." *Future Anterior* 13 (1): 16–34.

WIPO Lex. 2010. "Lithuania: Law on the Principles of State Protection of Ethnic Culture VIII-1328 of September 21, 1999 (as amended on January 9, 2006). WIPO Lex No. LT042. http://www.wipo.int/wipolex/en/details.jsp?id=5572.

———. 2011. Ley No. 149. Bolivia. http://www.wipo.int/edocs/lexdocs/laws/es/bo/bo062es.pdf.

World Heritage Newsletter. 2001. "AFRICA 2009: Interview with Joseph King of ICCROM." No. 32 (October–November): 2.

You, Ziying. 2015. "Shifting Actors and Power Relations: Contentious Local Responses to the Safeguarding of Intangible Cultural Heritage in Contemporary China." *Journal of Folklore Research* 52 (2–3): 253–268.

Yúdice, George. 2004. *The Expediency of Culture: Uses of Culture in the Global Era*. Durham, NC: Duke University Press.

Yun, Kyoim. 2015. "The Economic Imperative of UNESCO Recognition: A South Korean Shamanic Ritual." *Journal of Folklore Research* 52 (2–3): 181–198.

Zaeef, Abdul Salam. 2010. *My Life with the Taliban*. New York: Columbia University Press.

Zapata-Barrero, Ricard. 2016. "Diversity and Cultural Policy: Cultural Citizenship as a Tool for Inclusion." *International Journal of Cultural Policy* 22 (4): 534–552.

Index

Page numbers in italics refer to illustrations.

VALDIMAR TR. HAFSTEIN

is Professor of Folklore, Ethnology,
and Museum Studies at the
University of Iceland. Former Chair
of Iceland's National Commission
for UNESCO and ex-president of the
International Society for Ethnology
and Folklore (SIEF), he is author of
a number of articles and books on
intangible heritage, cultural property,
international heritage politics, folklore,
and copyright in traditional knowledge.

www.ingramcontent.com/pod-product-compliance
Lightning Source LLC
Chambersburg PA
CBHW070327270326
41926CB00017B/3797